New Forms of Environmental Writing

Environmental Cultures Series

Series Editors:
Greg Garrard, University of British Columbia, Canada
Richard Kerridge, Bath Spa University

Editorial Board:
Frances Bellarsi, Université Libre de Bruxelles, Belgium
Mandy Bloomfield, Plymouth University, UK
Lily Chen, Shanghai Normal University, China
Christa Grewe-Volpp, University of Mannheim, Germany
Stephanie LeMenager, University of Oregon, USA
Timothy Morton, Rice University, USA
Pablo Mukherjee, University of Warwick, UK

Bloomsbury's *Environmental Cultures* series makes available to students and scholars at all levels the latest cutting-edge research on the diverse ways in which culture has responded to the age of environmental crisis. Publishing ambitious and innovative literary ecocriticism that crosses disciplines, national boundaries, and media, books in the series explore and test the challenges of ecocriticism to conventional forms of cultural study.

Titles Available:
Bodies of Water, Astrida Neimanis
Cities and Wetlands, Rod Giblett
Civil Rights and the Environment in African-American Literature, 1895–1941, John Claborn
Climate Change Scepticism, Greg Garrard, George Handley, Axel Goodbody, Stephanie Posthumus
Climate Crisis and the 21st-Century British Novel, Astrid Bracke
Colonialism, Culture, Whales, Graham Huggan
Ecocriticism and Italy, Serenella Iovino
Fuel, Heidi C. M. Scott
Literature as Cultural Ecology, Hubert Zapf
Nerd Ecology, Anthony Lioi
The New Nature Writing, Jos Smith
The New Poetics of Climate Change, Matthew Griffiths
This Contentious Storm, Jennifer Mae Hamilton
Climate Change Scepticism, Greg Garrard, Axel Goodbody, George B. Handley and Stephanie Posthumus
Ecospectrality, Laura A. White
Teaching Environmental Writing, Isabel Galleymore
Radical Animism, Jemma Deer
Cognitive Ecopoetics, Sharon Lattig
Digital Vision and Ecological Aesthetic, Lisa FitzGerald
Weathering Shakespeare, Evelyn O'Malley
Imagining the Plains of Latin America, Axel Pérez Trujillo Diniz
The Living World, Samantha Walton
Reclaiming Romanticism, Kate Rigby
Ecocollapse Fiction and Cultures of Human Extinction, Sarah E. McFarland
Environmental Cultures in Soviet East Europe, Anna Barcz
Contemporary Fiction and Climate Uncertainty, Marco Caracciolo

Forthcoming Titles:
Ecocriticism and Turkey, Meliz Ergin
Reading Underwater Wreckage, Killian Quigley
Climate Fiction, John Thieme

New Forms of Environmental Writing

Gleaning and Fragmentation

Timothy C. Baker

BLOOMSBURY ACADEMIC
LONDON • NEW YORK • OXFORD • NEW DELHI • SYDNEY

BLOOMSBURY ACADEMIC
Bloomsbury Publishing Plc
50 Bedford Square, London, WC1B 3DP, UK
1385 Broadway, New York, NY 10018, USA
29 Earlsfort Terrace, Dublin 2, Ireland

BLOOMSBURY, BLOOMSBURY ACADEMIC and the Diana logo
are trademarks of Bloomsbury Publishing Plc

First published in Great Britain 2022

Cover design: Burge Agency
Cover image: Aberdeen Beach © Ian Rennie / Alamy Stock Photo

A catalogue record for this book is available from the British Library.

A catalog record for this book is available from the Library of Congress.

ISBN: HB: 978-1-3502-7131-9
        ePDF: 978-1-3502-7132-6
       eBook: 978-1-3502-7133-3

Series: Environmental Cultures

Typeset by Integra Software Services Pvt. Ltd.

To find out more about our authors and books visit www.bloomsbury.com
and sign up for our newsletters.

Contents

Acknowledgements

Although much of the first draft of this book was written in isolation, I benefitted immensely from two scholarly communities. In summer 2020 I participated in an online, interdisciplinary reading group on ecofeminism. Reading Val Plumwood, Karen Barad and other thinkers with scholars such as Linda Hess, Anna Lawrence, Anna Stenning and Eline Tabak gave me insights I could never have found on my own. At Aberdeen I benefitted enormously from discussions with colleagues in the School of Language, Literature, Music and Visual Culture who read drafts, suggested new ways of thinking and kept me in good cheer. I am immensely grateful to Elizabeth Anderson, Tara Beaney, Silvia Casini, Elizabeth Elliott, Andrew Gordon, Helena Ifill, Julia Kotzur, Alan Macpherson, Clémence O'Connor, Patience Schell and Sarah Sharp. I have also benefitted from the advice and support of Caitlin Beveridge, Alex Calder, Lisa Collinson, Jennifer Cooke, Katherine Groo, Noémi Keresztes, Caroline Magennis, Darryl Peers, Kristian Shaw, Linda Tym, Sara Upstone and many others. I am especially grateful to my fourth-year students in Vulnerable Bodies, Precarious Lives in 2021, who taught me more about the value of care than I could ever have expected. More than anything I've written, working on this book reminded me that writing is itself an act of entanglement, formed in relation.

Ben Doyle at Bloomsbury has been a supporter of this project from the beginning; I am also very grateful for helpful and incisive comments from the peer reviewers.

This book has been written not only in a time of global precarity, but also in a time when academic research in the humanities is increasingly devalued, and far too many young scholars remain precarious. This book is dedicated to the PhD students I have had the pleasure of supervising over the period I wrote it: Pimpawan Chaipanit, Christina Connors, Hyginus Eze, Ines Kirschner, Heather Milligan, Sarinah O'Donoghue, Chomploen Pimphakorn, Graham Stephen and Marlene Simoes. May we all work to build a more inclusive and less hierarchical world, and university structure, in which new voices can thrive.

Prologue: Aberdonian gleanings – MacGillivray, Jamie and the natural fragment

I received the e-mail late in the day, from Lisa Collinson, at the University of Aberdeen's Museums and Special Collections department. 'I've just remembered, you like birds. Would you like to see some?' It was an unusual invitation, and although I had other plans, an hour later I trundled over to the Sir Duncan Rice Library for the opening of a new exhibition on the relation between William MacGillivray, a son of Old Aberdeen, and later the Regius Professor of Natural History at Marischal College, and James Audubon, the great American ornithologist. I knew Audubon's *Birds of America*, of course; it is hard to imagine any American child who likes wild things growing up and doesn't have some of those plates etched on their memory. But I had never seen the book itself, had not been aware of quite how large a double elephant folio was, the volume standing in the centre of the room like an altar. But before the volume, there was sound and sight, and there was Aberdeen.

The path from the library entrance to the exhibition room was covered with decals of footprints, both human shoes and bird claws. The footprints were roughly the same size as each other, and roughly the same size as my own feet. I was immediately struck by the way the human footprint was defined by its lack of detail: two blunt shapes, heel and toe, against the nine segments of the bird print, showing joints and nails. The large print, if it were taken from a living animal, would surely be from a dinosaur, and yet in its detail it felt more immediate, more present, than the human one; my own feet, looked down on, seem similarly unanchored. To see birds as they are, the exhibition suggested, you have to understand who you are, and that requires first understanding your distance from the designation of 'natural'. You and the birds stand on the same ground, but you are separate from it. And yet in the exhibition itself taxidermied birds were placed in glass chambers and on platforms close to the ceiling, having left the ground behind. My colleague Andrew Gordon has recently claimed, in work on Renaissance literature, that the 'foot is the human body's primary printing instrument. Its impressions constitute a fundamental effect of human presence on earth.'[1] Seeing the prints of shoes and claws side by side, equal in size, made me consider how many creatures, human and non-human, have impressed themselves upon the earth, and how many have taken flight, or left the world behind. The footprint is a form of knowledge and of memory, a way of seeing how we have inhabited the earth, and calling to mind what we have stamped out.

The first case in the exhibition presents the manuscript of MacGillivray's record of his walk to London in 1819, when he was twenty-three years old. Born in Old Aberdeen, MacGillivray spent much of his youth in Harris, and would walk home at the end of each academic year, so he was no stranger to long journeys, but this trip was something else: taking a circuitous route, he ended up walking 828 miles. The bulk of his journey, the first 501 miles, was spent in Scotland, and he records the bird and plant life he saw on his way. The trip was for the simple purpose of visiting the British Museum, to see the collection of birds there, or as he describes it, 'a great collection of Beast and Fishes, of Birds and other flying things, of Reptiles and Insects – in short of all the creatures which have been found upon the face of the earth. I hither therefore shall direct my steps – because I am desirous of furthering my cognition of these things.'[2] The non-human world can be collected and known, but it must also be approached from the perspective of a body; the trip implies that MacGillivray will appreciate the collection more, will know it better, because he has walked there.

Birds are everywhere in MacGillivray's account, and entering the Aberdeen exhibition, I could hear the sounds of the birds he would have encountered, recorded in the places he visited on his walk. Yet listening to the birds, recorded in the present, is somewhat misleading for, like other ornithologists of his day, MacGillivray observed through his gun more than his binoculars. In his previous journal, covering the years 1817–18, he frequently describes birds as material for his knowledge, not as creatures in their own right:

> On Monday I went round the farm by the shore. Yesterday I scampered through Moll with my gun, and killed three Oyster-catchers, but they fell into the sea and drifted away. The birds which I saw on these two days were the Golden Plover, Oystercatcher, Great Black-backed Gull, Black-tailed Godwit, Turnstone, Lapwing, Shag, Skylark, Meadow Pipit, Stock Dove, Starling, Song Thrush, Raven, Hooded Crow, Curlew, Linnet, and Wren. Today I did not stir from home, but skinned the head and feet of the Eagle – I also dissected it in part. The whole body was thickly set with fine long down, which appeared without being mixed with feathers on the parts usually bare, viz a line on either side of the neck, one on each side of the wings, one along the centre of the sternum.[3]

Knowing birds requires knowing their corpses, preserving, cataloguing, analysing. The individual and the collective are interchangeable. Throughout his journals there are almost no accounts of avian behaviour, and there is no scope for interaction save at the end of a gun. Birds are there to be recorded, listed, preserved on the page.

I see oystercatchers almost every day from my office, and find their peeps cheering. I cannot imagine needing to kill three just to see how they work.

MacGillivray's cataloguing is pervasive. In the journal of his walk to London he spends many pages listing the plants he has seen, arguing that this 'is the proper way of studying botany', and that the academic who looks at a garden, book in hand, 'is just like a parrot chattering over the jargon of scientific nomenclature, without knowing anything more of the matter'.[4] He lists poems he has loved and women he has loved; he provides his favourite recipe for a hot toddy and many comments on class and national culture. The world, for MacGillivray, is knowable. More than that, it exists to be known. The world can be rendered as a list. He ends his journal with his arrival at the British Museum, and he is pleased by what he sees, and by the fact that it is he who sees it:

> Today I went to the British Museum. The rooms were open at eleven, and I was among the first there. I was not surprised. I had formed high ideas of the museum of the greatest nation in the world, nor was I disappointed. It is richest in minerals and shells, but I paid most attention to the birds, particularly to the collection of British Birds which occupies a separate apartment. The system of Linnaeus has been superseded by that of Cuvier, and justly in my estimation. I was glad to find that most of my opinions regarding the genera of birds were deemed correct, for the improvements upon the Linnaean system which had occurred to me on my journey through the Western Isles last year were here realised, and I felt proud that I had been able to think for myself on such a subject, and think correctly too. However I do not altogether agree with modern ornithologists, and possibly I may become some day the author of a new system, at least I have the assurance to think so.[5]

MacGillivray reflects that the museum increases his love for natural history, even as it confirms to him that he prefers to encounter specimens in the wild. Curiously, however, he only mentions two particular genuses of birds, ducks and gannets, and only to congratulate himself for having arrived at similar categorical divisions as the museum curators. There is no mention of the way the birds are preserved or displayed, of their beauty or other physical attributes. Instead, the museum only confirms that he is right to continue on his decision to think of birds in terms of systems and divisions. The birds themselves are almost extraneous.[6]

The final panel in the Aberdeen exhibition reflects both this ambition and its cost, noting that Audubon's fortune was made through slavery and that the University's collection of Native American artefacts, including human remains, was sent by Audubon to MacGillivray, and must be repatriated. The conservators note, in the final lines, that Audubon and MacGillivray would kill up to one hundred birds to create a single illustration, and that, in the exhibition's final words, 'Environmental destruction and climate change are a much greater threat than could have been imagined in the worst nightmares of the nineteenth century'.

Cataloguing is not enough. It is thrilling, perhaps, to see the skins and taxidermied remains that Audubon and MacGillivray shared and drew from, and yet impossible to remain ignorant of the cost. One of my students, a month after the exhibition opened, said how much she had disliked it, because it was so sad: she had just wanted to see the birds and not be reminded of the environmental devastation that surrounds us. The introduction of human concerns, and atrocities, in the exhibition made it impossible for her to see the natural world as both remote and whole in itself. And yet the exhibition is framed between self and other: the world that is opened to you, as a body, as an individual, is one that has been made by others, and organized and presented. There is no escape from complicity.

The artefact that struck me that first evening was not Audubon's book of birds, or MacGillivray's journals, or the birds themselves or the historical contextualization, but another notebook, opened to a page on which the word 'blackbird' was written nineteen times, in a variety of styles. Sometimes the word is capitalized, sometimes it resembles various typefaces; in its final appearance it is a childish scrawl. Twice it is misspelled, once missing the 'c', which has been inserted above, and once, curiously, as 'Birdbird'. 'I know, too', writes Wallace Stevens, 'That the blackbird is involved / In what I know'.[7] Are these blackbirds involved? The page suggests a penmanship exercise. Numbers appearing to the right of the list suggest that it might be a catalogue of sightings.

I do not know what this list means. I do not know if it refers to blackbirds at all. And yet this, too, is a form of knowledge, nineteen ways of looking, of transcribing, the blackbirdness of the blackbird, neither right nor wrong. For all MacGillivray's care, for all his observational slaughter, for all the beauty of his own illustrations, which to my unpractised eye are every bit as striking as Audubon's more famous ones, there is still the capacity for surprise.

Several worlds away from MacGillivray you might find the work of Agnès Varda, whose 2000 film *The Gleaners and I* I watched only a few weeks after visiting the MacGillivray exhibition. The film is about, in part, agricultural gleaning, figures in urban and rural landscapes who survive off agricultural waste; it is just as much about Varda's own cinematic gleaning. In a director's note included with the American press release, she writes that the film is 'woven from various strands: from emotions I felt when confronted with precariousness', from the possibilities of digital cinematography, from her desire to film her ageing body, from her love for painting.[8] The work cannot be a simple whole, but is about the tension between waste and collection – what is included in our world, in our art, and what we leave behind.

The film opens with paintings by Jules Breton and Jean-François Millet, old film clips, dictionaries: an attempt to glean the meaning of gleaning. Varda says that she is struck, seeing urban gleaners, by the way 'each gleans on his own, whereas in paintings they were always in clusters, rarely alone'.[9] She shows a clip of visitors to the Musée d'Orsay, posing in front of a Millet painting, sped up, a community of viewers. In Arras she looks at Breton's painting of a woman gleaning alone, from 1877. The woman is barefoot, clothed in blue, a giant bundle of wheat on her left shoulder. She keeps it balanced with a single finger on her right hand, which also points to another gleaner in the background, stooped, without a clear face. The gleaner looks miserable, or angry, but the viewer's attention, or mine, is drawn to her feet.

As a child I would harvest hay with my father: he would throw sheaves into the back of our old pickup truck, and I would stamp about on the hay, compressing it so we could get a bigger load. I'd finish those days covered with tiny bumps from where individual stalks had bruised my skin, nauseated by the smell of the hay, normally so sweet. How much more, I wonder, must this woman's feet hurt, trampling on the remnants underfoot?

Varda poses beneath the painting with her own sheaf, carried loosely on her right shoulder. She looks bemused, and since the sheaf is tied more loosely than the one in Breton's painting, Varda needs to stabilize it with the whole of her left hand. Her expression, and the placement of the sheaf, echoes not the 1877 painting she is mimicking so much as an earlier version, from 1875, that I doubt that Varda had ever seen. The same woman is portrayed, in the same outfit, although the ground on which she treads is greener, more lush. The figure looks at the painter – she knows she is being painted – and yet her feet point towards the side of the painting, as if she is simply pausing on her way. If the 1877 version is static and confrontational, the 1875 seems simply an arrested moment. Unlike the later painting, there are no haystacks in the field, no other woman in the background. She is alone, and the sun catches on the stalks.

The earlier painting is, as it happens, in Aberdeen. This version was commissioned by one Alexander Macdonald, and purchased, for £160, on

20 April 1875; Macdonald bequeathed it to the Aberdeen Art Gallery in 1901. Macdonald was a granite merchant and the proprietor of Aberdeen Granite Works in Aberdeen and commissioned the painting from Breton for his house at Kepplestone. His conduit, Leon Durand, writes on 20 October 1871 that Breton is very busy, but when he has some free time, 'he will be happy to execute the wishes of the Scottish gentleman who wishes a painting of a young girl on canvas of 50 or 60cm'.[10] Durand writes again on 8 November 1871, and Breton finally responds on 1 January 1872. Nine months later, Breton writes that he cannot guarantee the subject, only that it will be a young girl in the country. He writes again two years later, promising he has not forgotten the commission. On 30 December 1874, he promises that the painting is done, but needs to dry; on 2 March 1875, he admits he has not completed it. Twenty-six days later the painting has a name, 'The Gleaner', and it arrives in Aberdeen within the month.

The arrival of Audubon's birds in Aberdeen, displayed next to the notebook with which I am so taken, is almost as torturous. Robert Ralph writes, in the introduction to his book on MacGillivray – itself a catalogue – that he came across 'a small collection of very old bird specimens' in 1988, which were labelled on the back 'presented by Mr. Audubon'.[11] As Jenny Downes, the exhibition curator, explained on the opening night tour, the specimens were found at the back of a drawer, having been neglected for over a century; it was only from this moment of finding something material, unarchived but preserved, that MacGillivray's connection with Audubon was brought back to the present.

That this painting and these birds found their way to Aberdeen is a matter of chance, and the perseverance of a few individuals. That they struck me as meaningful and connected, however, was because I already knew both MacGillivray and Jenny Downes, the curator, through the writings of Kathleen Jamie. The afternoon before I attended the exhibition I had been reading Jamie's just-published volume of essays *Surfacing*. The collection begins with two fragments before launching into a much longer essay, 'In Quinhagak', which takes up almost half the volume. At the start of that essay Jamie describes her interest in Inuit articles found in museums on the east coast of the UK:

> In Aberdeen there are actual sealskin kayaks, slender and responsive. So much wit and knowing in the materials, and all the materials are natural, of course. I like them because they suggest a powerful relationship with the non-human world.
>
> In Aberdeen University's museum I met a young curator called Jenny Downes and she went one step further.[12]

Downes introduces Jamie to an Aberdeen-based archaeologist, Rick Knecht, who works on a Yup'ik site in Alaska, and becomes Jamie's own initial conduit to Indigenous communities, a story that takes up the following sixty pages. It is happenstance that this story begins in Aberdeen, and yet it does.

Jamie's discussion of MacGillivray is not set in Aberdeen, but in Edinburgh, in an essay on the collection at the Royal College of Surgeons, where she finds one of his paintings next to a jar filled with conjoined human twins:

> A wren, and a branch full of linnets, and the warbler that bears his name – facing the twins in their jars are the bird paintings of William MacGillivray, the naturalist who was conservator of this museum in the 1830s. His pictures of the birds he shot, then painted so exquisitely in their natural colours, enable us to see the birds clearly; they are fixed in the moment before they fly. By these pictures, we know the birds. By the specimens, we know our bodies, our conditions. In this place of silence and slow time, it's as though the conjoined twins hug each other and look happily forever upon the bright linnets and wrens. Which, I remind myself through tears, is ridiculous. But in the bodily business of weeping, I'm reminded that I'm hungry, and suddenly time begins again, and the Playfair Hall looses its sense of stilled catastrophe, and it is proper to leave.[13]

Context is all. We experience the world as a body, and as an emplaced body. I see these links between MacGillivray and Varda and Jamie, and Breton and Downes, because I am in Aberdeen. I see them because I am someone who likes birds. I have paused in the writing of this piece to leave my office and look for robins, for oystercatchers. And what I see is not what Jamie sees, nor MacGillivray. A month later, when I go to Surgeons' Hall myself, I am taken in not by the twins, but by the jars with scraps of tattooed skin, shorn from the rest of the body, clumsy and delicate and beautiful. I imagine my limbs, my organs, my flesh and skin preserved like this: I am not sure if it makes me happy or not, if my own body will be seen as beautiful, if it will survive me. But I want to see what Jamie sees, the fleck of beauty in the periphery, the wren and linnet looking on.

I am uncomfortable beginning an academic book in this way. Privileging myself at the opening of a work dedicated to other writers seems potentially narcissistic, and at least misleading. Yet, as Sonja Boon asks in the introduction to *Autoethnography and Feminist Theory at the Water's Edge: Unsettled Islands*, co-written with Lesley Butler and Daze Jeffries, 'What does it mean to make theory through self and place? What might an embodied approach to theory-making look like?'[14] My understanding of gleaning and fragmentation, of archives and catalogues, of self and environment, is not born in the ether as some abstract intellectual pursuit, but arises from being an embodied self in a real place. I cannot understand the works discussed below without admitting that I am reading them in Aberdeen, and that I am the one reading them. And because my training is in Scottish Literature, I cannot approach these questions without thinking of Jamie.

Two essays after the one on Surgeons' Hall in *Findings*, Jamie includes an essay called 'Sabbath'. At the start of the Covid-19 pandemic, in March 2020, I recorded brief excerpts from books I liked, and had in my flat, on my phone, and uploaded them to Twitter, as a way of trying to feel connected in lockdown, and this is the piece of Jamie I chose: it spoke to me, that day, of enmeshment in the world, when the world itself seemed impossible and terrifying. At the start of the essay Jamie describes taking 'earnest' notes of the skyline and the gannets she sees, but immediately pulls back:

> I made notes, but the reason I'd come to the end of the road to walk along the cliffs is because language fails me there. If we work always in words, sometimes we need to recuperate in a place where language doesn't join up, where we're thrown back on a few elementary nouns. Sea. Bird. Sky.[15]

Camille Manfredi reads this passage, in relation to the work of Robert Macfarlane, as combining walking and writing in 'a process of self-inspection' that resolves a disjunction between language and 'elemental nature [...] through the spatialisation of the mind'.[16] As much as this passage could be read simply in terms of recuperation and what might be called a nature cure, however, the collection of elementary nouns is equally important. Language may not join up, but it does not disappear: what remains are words as index, and the individual writer, or watcher, as respondent. As will be discussed further in the Introduction, Jamie's work frequently emphasizes the encounter that cannot wholly be explained. The disjunction here is not between language and the natural environment, but rather between the self and world: what is needed is not introspection, but a letting go of self. Jamie writes in the essay not only of her need 'to clear my head' but to 'relinquish', and this letting go is both personal and communal, tied to the land and the language.[17] She makes the relation clear a few pages later, at the site of an archive:

> Everything will fall into the sea, so far as I could tell, looking at the archaeologists' reports in Stornoway Library. Does this matter? A team of archaeologists had walked and mapped all the features on that part of the coast and, with their expert eye, and by dint of asking local people, had measured and defined and assessed every human intervention in that landscape: illicit stills, sheep fanks,

standing stones. Their anxiety was coastal erosion, things were in danger of slipping away forever. The report itself had been poorly bound, pages slithered out and fell on the library floor.[18]

Finding, in Jamie's essays, is also a process of recognizing loss; archives only preserve temporarily; human impressions are fleeting. The human record is itself subject to erosion, and yet it is seen, and interpreted, and responded to. We archive precisely because we know that the archive will not survive.

This tension between archiving and relinquishing is what, following Varda, I am calling gleaning.[19] Gleaning is a process of collecting what has been abandoned, repurposing it, as a way of turning attention to the momentary encounter between self and world. Domietta Torlasco reads Varda's film alongside the late writings of Maurice Merleau-Ponty to argue that the work 'crosses the boundaries between the personal and collective, the human body and the landscape, and the ephemeral and the long-lasting'. This, Torlasco says, can be seen as a notion of impression, defined as 'a folding of the visible onto itself, a turning inside-out or rolling back that occurs within the texture of perception'.[20] Gleaning, she concludes, is the archiving of perception.

Torlasco's discussion of archives inevitably invokes Jacques Derrida, who links the archive to a Freudian drive towards death and destruction. The archive, he writes, 'will never be either memory or anamnesis as spontaneous, alive and internal experience. On the contrary: the archive takes place at the place of originary and structural breakdown of the said memory.'[21] The archive requires destruction; it requires externalization. Carolyn Steedman clarifies that for Derrida the archive is a figure of state power: it is a rupturing of history, of experience, that commemorates and destroys.[22] Derrida's work is not, in the end, about archives themselves, so much as questions of origin and narrative; Steedman's text embeds the idea of narrative back in the discussion of archives themselves in order to look at the work of history. She points to the tension between ideas of history, which recounts a story that has no end, and personal narrative, which does. A story becomes narrative, she claims, when the teller and the audience have the same sense of meaning, and when they have found and agreed on the necessary conclusion. 'That end', she writes, 'the finished place, is the human being, a body in time and space, telling a story'.[23] History is temporary and incomplete; narrative ends with the teller, and with their body.

It is these bodies that fascinate me, the bodies of the tellers and the bodies they encounter. I am fascinated by Varda's focus on her hands, but also her focus on heart-shaped potatoes, and by the potatoes that fans send her after the film, which she shows in her short follow-up film. I am fascinated by the skins of birds displayed next to taxidermied bodies and illustrations. I am fascinated by the meeting of page and landscape. And I am fascinated by the way I encounter these elements in a place, familiar and remote.

It would be crude to propose a simple binary between archive and gleaning: one can interpret Varda's films, or Jamie's essays, as archives in themselves, selective and personal, but fixed the moment they are shared. And yet, in their precarity, their fragility, they gesture towards a way to understand the world, to perceive it, outside traditional rubrics of power and knowledge, of catalogues and genealogies. They suggest that to understand the world requires a focus on the fragmentary and the fleeting.

The Romantics saw this as well, of course, and Walter Benjamin too. And yet this idea of the fragment is more necessary than ever before, because it is our best hope of understanding the rapid changes to the natural environment that are occurring around and through us. As different as the writers discussed below are, they share a belief in the importance of the immediate encounter, in the fragmentary and the unfinished, in the recovered and the preserved, as well as in what fades away. For the problem they all must wrestle with is simply that of totality. The problem is that we think of stories as having conclusions, and the only conclusions we can imagine to our current crises are apocalyptic. The problem is that the world is, still, 'crazier and more of it than we think, / Incorrigibly plural'.[24] The problem is scale, the problem is concern, the problem is our desire to catalogue and understand. The problem is that claiming to know the world positions ourselves as outside it, looking in.

These problems have been spoken about often, from critics from a variety of perspectives. And they reach similar conclusions. We 'need new myths and new stories', writes Roy Scranton.[25] We need to 'resituate [ourselves] in the space-time-matter of the planet', writes Mary Louise Pratt.[26] We need the arts to 'refract this encounter with ecological crisis into plural visions and questions', write Robert S. Emmett and David E. Nye.[27] The message is repeated again and again. But academic calls to create new stories do not yield new stories, and perhaps Amitav Ghosh is right when he discusses the 'many ways in which the age of global warming defies both literary fiction and contemporary common sense'.[28] The problem with stories, it seems to me, is that they have ends. Whatever we term the age in which we live, whether we talk about climate change or environmental crisis or the Anthropocene, it is not a time that has an end. As Kathryn Yusoff argues, alongside thinkers as diverse as Edouard Glissant, Dionne Brand and N.K. Jemisin, it is also a time that is only beginning to reconcile itself with a long history of ends, enacted through imperialism, colonialism and racial subjugation.[29]

So how can we tell a story of a time that has no end and is filled with ends? How can we catalogue or archive our present? Jane Bennett returns to the fragment itself, and its Romantic lineage, arguing that '[t]he literary fragment is a synecdoche of the self in a disenchanted world', and is consequently, in its failure to complete, a way to think about finitude.[30] And yet gleaning, I want to suggest, is more than an archive of fragments. Rather, gleaning allows fragments to exist in constellation. Gleaning is a way of moving through the world from the body first. It is a way of speaking not of the environment as an abstract other, but of a place that is known to us, and through our bodies. It is a form, in a very different sense than Sarah Kofman's, of community without community. It is a way of approaching the cosmos, in Zach Horton's words, as 'a fragmented whole, always incomplete but by the same token always open to differentiation'.[31] Gleaning is a form of conversation that stretches the borders between self and other, human and non-human, matter and spirit. It is a dialogue predicated on precarity. It is the way we can talk about our navigation of the world.

Notes

1   Andrew Gordon, 'The Renaissance Footprint: The Material Trace in Print Culture from Dürer to Spenser', *Renaissance Quarterly* 71 (2018): 479.

2   William MacGillivray, *A Walk to London*, ed. Robert Ralph (Stornoway: Acair, 1998), 10.

3   William MacGillivray, *A Hebridean Naturalist's Journal 1817–1818*, ed. Robert Ralph (Stornoway: Acair, 2017), 127.

4   MacGillivray, *Walk*, 29.

5   MacGillivray, *Walk*, 133.

6   In the following decades habitat or life groups became increasingly popular, grouping taxidermied animals so that they might be viewed 'less as an anatomical specimen than as an artist's creation'. Alison Griffiths, *Wondrous Difference: Cinema, Anthropology, and Turn-of-the-Century Visual Culture* (New York: Columbia University Press, 2002), 31.

7   Wallace Stevens, *The Palm at the End of the Mind: Selected Poems and a Play*, ed. Holly Stevens (New York: Vintage, 1990), 21.

8   Agnès Varda, 'Director's Note', *The Gleaners and I*, press release. https://zeitgeistfilms.com/media/films/44/presskit.pdf [Accessed 26 December 2019].

9   Agnès Varda, *The Gleaners and I* (Ciné-tamaris, 2000), *The Agnès Varda Collection Volume 1* (Artificial Eye, 2009).

10 Summary of Letter to Alexander Macdonald of Kepplestone from Leon Durand, 20 October 1871, Papers of Alexander Macdonald of Kepplestone and his trustees, *c.* 1852–1903. DD391/13/10/1. https://www.aberdeencity.gov.uk/sites/default/files/Alexander_Macdonald_of_Kepplestone_o.pdf [Accessed 26 December 2019].

11 Robert Ralph, *William MacGillivray: Creatures of Air, Land and Sea* (London: Merrell Holberton and The Natural History Museum, 1999), 7.

12 Kathleen Jamie, *Surfacing* (London: Sort Of, 2019), 17.

13 Kathleen Jamie, *Findings* (London: Sort Of, 2005), 142.

14 Sonja Boon, Lesley Butler and Daze Jeffries, *Autoethnography and Feminist Theory at the Water's Edge: Unsettled Islands* (Cham: Palgrave Macmillan, 2018), 5.

15 Jamie, *Findings*, 164.

16 Camille Manfredi, *Nature and Space in Contemporary Scottish Writing and Art* (Cham: Palgrave Macmillan, 2019), 33.

17 Jamie, *Findings*, 173.

18 Jamie, *Findings*, 178–9.

19 Jamie uses the same term in her essay on Surgeons' Hall, quoting Dr John Barclay, the Edinburgh anatomist whose collections form part of the basis of the museum, and who compares the work of the anatomist to gleaners in the field. Jamie, *Findings*, 135.

20 Domietta Torlasco, 'Digital Impressions: Writing Memory after Agnès Varda', *Discourse* 33.3 (2011): 393.

21 Jacques Derrida, *Archive Fever: A Freudian Impression*, trans. Eric Prenowitz (Chicago and London: University of Chicago Press, 1996), 11.

22 Carolyn Steedman, *Dust* (Manchester: Manchester University Press, 2001), 1.

23 Steedman, *Dust*, 147.

24 Louis MacNeice, *Collected Poems* (London: Faber, 1979), 30.

25 Roy Scranton, *Learning to Die in the Anthropocene: Reflections on the End of a Civilization* (San Francisco: City Lights, 2015), 19.

26 Mary Louise Pratt, 'Coda: Concept and Chronotope', in *Arts of Living on a Damaged Planet*, ed. Anna Tsing et al. (Minneapolis and London: University of Minnesota Press, 2017), G170.

27 Robert S. Emmett and David E. Nye, *The Environmental Humanities: A Critical Introduction* (Cambridge, MA: MIT Press, 2017), 107.

28 Amitav Ghosh, *The Great Derangement: Climate Change and the Unthinkable* (Chicago and London: University of Chicago Press, 2016), 26.

29 Kathryn Yusoff, *A Billion Black Anthropocenes or None* (Minneapolis: University of Minnesota Press, 2018), 8.

30 Jane Bennett, *The Enchantment of Modern Life: Attachments, Crossings, and Ethics* (Princeton and Oxford: Princeton University Press, 2001), 77.

31 Zach Horton, 'Composing a Cosmic View: Three Alternatives for Thinking Scale in the Anthropocene', in *Scale in Literature and Culture*, ed. Michael Tavel Clarke and David Wittenberg (Cham: Palgrave Macmillan, 2017), 56–7.

Introduction: Gleaning, storytelling and constellations – The uses of fragmentation

Introductory constellation

I want to begin not with theories or definitions, nor with an explanatory framework, but with a series of textual encounters that highlight the importance of ideas of gleaning and fragmentation in contemporary environmental writing. Kathleen Jamie's 2012 collection *The Overhaul* is bookended by two poems depicting humans collecting storm-thrown detritus at the water's edge. 'The Beach', at the collection's start, is optimistic and anthropocentric: 'What a species', Jamie exclaims in praise of the 'few brave souls' collecting driftwood and plastic rope, 'hoping for the marvellous' and the prospect of a 'changed life'.[1] The combined activities of scavenging and cleansing, where humans encounter both material that might be considered natural, or suited to the place, and what Alexandra Campbell calls 'the global networks of pollution and commodity production that position the Atlantic as both a resource and medium of exploitation', are a recurrent concern in Jamie's writing.[2] In the essay 'Findings', with which this poem is frequently paired in scholarship on Jamie's work, Jamie finds herself on an unpopulated Hebridean island where the dunes and beaches are covered with '[b]rushes, masking tape, training shoes, orange polypropylene net, [...] seals' vertebrae and whalebones, driftwood and plastic garbage'.[3] The 'surprise of connection', in David Farrier's words, allows Jamie and her critics to consider the challenges of the Anthropocene and note the constancy of human intervention.[4] Farrier notes how Jamie's work calls attention to 'sacrifice zones' or 'shadow places', referring to the work of Naomi Klein and Val Plumwood, respectively: places that are overlooked or considered expendable, smoothed over as 'landscape' when they are viewed at all. In this reading Jamie's work highlights human entanglement in the natural environment, along with the concomitant waste and abuse generated by capitalist production. Campbell more forcefully writes that Jamie depicts 'a weird plastic wilderness that reflects the uncanny futurity and ubiquity of waste'.[5] *The Overhaul*'s closing poem, 'Materials', supports such a reading: the opening invocation, '[s]ee when it all unravels', refers not only to the scraps of nylon fishing net found along the beach but the entire human project.[6] All humans are complicit in the production of this waste material, and responsiveness to the world necessitates responsibility.

Other critics have found a more optimistic note in the poems. Rachel Falconer, for instance, in framing *The Overhaul* as a midlife collection, argues that 'The Beach' echoes Dante's *Purgatorio*, inviting the reader or listener in to its story of the middle of a journey, or a life, while the depiction of gannets using plastic rope to make their nests in 'Materials' permits a comparison of human and non-human creativity.[7] Jamie's poems and essays move so swiftly between the personal and the collective that both readings are plausible: the work can be considered simultaneously as a depiction of late-stage capitalism and an account of individual creative development. The combination of these two points of focus suggests a perspective that is central to the argument of this book: there can be no account of environmental crisis, or environmental entanglement, that does not begin with individual experience. In these pieces of Jamie's, that experience is known and clarified through material objects, themselves presented as fragments. At the end of 'Materials' Jamie offers a brief catalogue followed by a collective promise: 'Bird-bones, rope-scraps, a cursory sketch – but a bit o' bruck's / all we need to get us started, all we'll leave behind us when we're gone.'[8] The fragments are carefully selected, combining the non-human and the human, seen both in terms of mass production and artistic creativity, while the use of the Scots word 'bruck' in a poem, and a collection, that has largely been presented in Standard English represents a different form of fragmentation. While 'bruck', also written as 'brock', is most simply defined as 'scraps of food, left-overs, refuse, broken pieces', it is also part of the phrase 'stock and brock', or 'the whole concern'; it is closely related to 'brak', or a break or breach, and 'brouk', or soil, as well as 'breuk', 'to have or enjoy the use or possession of'.[9] The refuse and scraps are already part of a larger framework, a starting point and an endpoint at once. The fragment, in Jamie's writing, is not a simple metonym for planetary environmental concerns, nor is it simply seen as refuse: it is complete in itself and at the same time is knowable only in relation.

Jamie's embrace of the fragmentary object is also found in 'Findings', one of the clearest textual examples of what I am calling 'gleaning'. The essay begins with a visceral scene of encounter combining preservation with destruction: 'I hacked off the gannet's head with my penknife.'[10] Preserving the head as an object of aesthetic beauty requires separating it from both the creature of which it is a part and the environment in which it is placed. This act of reclamation is not limited to non-human remains. As Jamie summarizes her findings: 'This is what we chose to take away from Ceann Iar: a bleached whale's scapula, not the door of a plane; an orb of quartz, not a doll's head. As for Tim he'd picked up a two-foot-long plastic duck, which he carried under his arm.'[11] While the man-made detritus washed up on the beach may not immediately lend itself to aesthetic contemplation or home decoration, the options are more varied, and Jamie refuses to develop a hierarchy between the human and non-human fragment. The closing paragraph of the essay is particularly revealing:

> On the table made of the washed-up pier-stanchion are two pale sticks, like eels, or the first man and the first woman. There's the gannet's shank, its tiny orchid-shaped bone, and the whale's vertebra. These are in my study. Tim had celebrated his birthday on the yacht, and as a present I'd given him the orb of quartz. The bits of aeroplane, traffic cone and whale will still be on the shores of the Monach Islands. The penknife, the one I'd used to cut off the original gannet's head, is presently in my handbag. I'd found it – did I mention this? – one spring day on a beach in Fife. The gannet's beak is beside me here. Holding it up to the window light, I've just noticed a tiny bit of feather still clinging to the bone. I wish now I'd brought home the doll's head too. I'd have put her on a corner of my desk like a paperweight, with her mad tufts of hair and those sea-blue blinking eyes.[12]

The objects on the table, and the table itself, blur any boundary between human and non-human, natural and constructed. Objects find new uses in their new environments, and lose their own boundaries: bone becomes flower, wood becomes animal and remembered plastic evokes the sea.[13] These objects function as souvenirs in Susan Stewart's sense: they are framed as traces of a former life and recontextualized in their present surroundings, so that 'nature is removed from the domain of struggle into a domestic sphere of the individual and the interior'.[14] The act of identification and recontextualization highlights the way objects gain new meaning when they are brought into the sphere of individual human space and temporality.

At the same time, however, Jamie's emphasis on the randomness of the selection suggests that these objects have a life outside of the human collector. The return to the opening scene of the essay offers a sense of closure, but the very late discussion of the penknife, with its offset address to the presumed reader, indicates that the act of finding and reclamation is ongoing. There will be other beaches, other gannets, other bits of bruck. Jamie delights in the found object not simply as a memento, or a catalyst for artistic creation or a way to make use of what has been abandoned, but for its own sake: our understanding of the world, she implies, is known through the fragments we have gathered around us. This act of gathering is a choice, but also arbitrary, the doll's head as good as a bone.

Jamie's scenes of gleaning and gathering, of fragments and found objects, thus work in three directions. The objects are symbols of the world as it is revealed to us, or as we encounter it. There is no pristine environment waiting to be found: the world is always known in relation to the human, either through the pieces of human waste or through the simple presence of a human observer. The objects likewise gain meaning as they are used, in a way that reveals something of the person writing. The objects are also known in and of themselves: the significance they gain is fleeting, but they themselves outlast the observer or the user. This 'fleeting touch' is well characterized by Sarah Ensor in a discussion of Agnès Varda's documentary *The Gleaners and I*, discussed in the Prologue. As Ensor writes:

> rather than memorializing the figures that her camera provisionally captures, [Varda's] cinematography privileges relinquishment over retention, rhythm over reification, and chance over premeditation, ultimately using playfulness as a mode of social critique. Her account and performance of gleaning, which suspend an emphasis on the objects (or images) gleaned in favor of the rhythmic relations that they inaugurate, encourage us to exchange our transitive practices of stewardship for the intransitive verbs and paratactic habits of association that the film subtly emphasizes.[15]

Ensor clarifies that gleaning is not a process simply of reclamation or retention, nor is it fundamentally elegiac. Gleaning is not a form of environmental encounter that privileges ideas of preservation; rather, it foregrounds the accidental and the arbitrary, and ideas of decay as well as growth. These ideas of relinquishment, rhythm and chance are central to Jamie's writing as well: as the following discussion will show, they are equally important to many of the other writers discussed in this book. Varda's and Jamie's works suggest an approach to environmental or ecopoetic encounter that resists familiar narratives of climate change and environmental collapse not in order to deny their importance, but to emphasize the value of individual responsiveness.

Nicole M. Merola articulates the value of such an approach in a discussion of the poet Juliana Spahr, arguing that literary forms 'can also trap the more embodied and personal forms that scientific technologies sieve; they engage affective registers not conventionally appropriate to scientific forms'.[16] Spahr uses a selection of avant-garde literary forms including, in her own words, 'fragmentation, quotation, disruption, disjunction, agrammatical syntax, and so on', in order to challenge familiar narratives of temporal and spatial experience.[17] This catalogue of forms is repeated dozens of times in her 2007 text *The Transformation*, sometimes several times in one sentence, working both as an accurate description of Spahr's poetics and self-parody. In *The Transformation* Spahr recounts the 'barely truthful' story of a three-person relationship, which she is careful not to designate as polyamorous or queer, on an island in the Pacific, which she is careful not to designate as Hawai'i, at the end of the twentieth and dawn of the twenty-first centuries.[18] The text, which is not straightforwardly a memoir, a novel or a poem, but somewhere between all three, is narrated in a series of fragments centring on an undifferentiated 'they' who contemplate their role as colonizers, ongoing environmental devastation and the rise of the American military complex after 9/11. The three figures are known by the objects they keep on their desks: 'One had papers and books strewn about in piles, abandoned birds nests, and several lamps. One had ashtrays and matches and voodoo dolls and candles. One had shells and weird materials found on the ground and math books.'[19] The reader has no way to know which of these figures stands for Spahr: gleaning and collection can only reveal the individual as part of a constellation of other individuals. The three are torn between nostalgia and responsibility: to think about place requires thinking 'about the responsibilities of writing to place', and memory requires engagement with 'the devastation of the ocean that had happened in the last twenty years'.[20]

The trio's concerns include questions of gender and sexual identity, and while they have a particular focus on the construction of American military power, their environmental concerns often echo those found in Jamie's writing:

> They talked about these things and they talked about other things that filled them with the patheticness of their inaction amongst themselves at the breakfast table in the morning or on the lanai at night. They talked about how it was announced on the television news that one of the poles of the earth that had been frozen for many years was now a giant melting puddle. They talked about how the ocean was huge and it was filled with 'o'opu and 'ala'ihi and 'ū'ū and limu and plastic. [...] They talked about how it was both beautiful and horrible. They wondered together if there could be a word for this fearful symmetry in any language. A word for this emotion that combined intense, awful loss with a recognition of continuing and endless beauty despite, perhaps even caused by, the loss. [...] This recognition of human-induced horrible beauty caused talk also about what it meant to be part of the place that uses the most energy.[21]

This litany, which extends for two pages, represents one of Spahr's central concerns in the text: the conversations appear to engage with environmental change, but the repetition also becomes a way of avoiding individual agency. As Meliz Ergin argues, over the course of the text Spahr is 'transform[ed] through an acknowledgement of her own complicity'; the shift from 'we' to 'they' likewise marks a form of '[s]elf-estrangement [that] shatters their views about who they are and what they identify with'.[22] Spahr can only write in what she repeatedly calls 'the expansionist language', and repeatedly reflects on how this language use becomes a way to disengage from the world, such that 'the beauty of the plants and animals was lost in the fragmented mistranslations'.[23] While Spahr's work is more formally disruptive than that of Jamie and Varda, perhaps, all three artists focus on the fragmentary and the surprising in order to contest the metanarratives and forms of knowing that explain our current predicament. Whether framed in terms of climate change, Anthropocene anxiety or even late-stage capitalism, the world is not a story that can be told, but can only be revealed in part: a set of fragments gains its own significance.

Jamie, Spahr and Varda's focus on ideas of waste material highlights global perspectives on consumption, but also allows for ideas of both individual and collective reclamation. In a study of Latin American *editoriales cartoneras* – 'small, independent publishers that make their books by hand out of recycled cardboard' and sell them at low prices – Lucy Bell discusses how while urban scavenger might initially be associated 'with the waste he or she collects, and suffering from the same rejection, exclusion, and invisibility', the activities of waste pickers, and the way in which waste is transformed into literary production, valorize both the waste and the person who works with it.[24] While Jamie, Spahr and Varda work from more economically and socially privileged positions, this idea of transformation is similarly key to their work. Focusing on fragmentation and gleaning highlights the way literature (and film) can be seen not as passive reflections of social and scientific discourses, but as active, if qualified, responses and interventions.

For all three artists, focusing on ideas and forms of fragmentation and gleaning provides an ability to rethink the politics and affective experiences of environmental encounter. Just as importantly, it becomes an opportunity to rethink the relation between individual and collective experience. As well as the 'they' of *The Transformation*, Spahr's poetry frequently uses a first-person plural that refers to North American or Western identities, where a collective 'we' is 'Just dealing with. Together.'[25] Varda focuses more locally. In *The Gleaners and I* she comments that while in nineteenth-century paintings gleaners 'were always in clusters, rarely alone', when she sees gleaners in the fields now, each works on their own. This observation becomes, in the same passage of voiceover narration, a directive to herself: 'There is another woman gleaning in this film, that's me. I'm happy to drop the ears of wheat and pick up my camera.'[26] As Cole Swensen writes in an essay-poem on Varda's work, itself presented as a series of fragments, *The Gleaners and I* reveals that it is 'left-over light, that not absorbed by things, which makes us aware that the same principle determines all that we are and are not able to see'.[27] Gleaning the light reveals not simply a commonality of experience, but the way sensory experience creates a shared environment. Swensen describes an image in Varda's late film *Visages, Villages* as: 'Landscape as seeing // the hand as landscape'.[28] Gleaning changes our sense of scale, and what it means to observe, and be observed; it reveals the environment as actively constituted by human relationship.

Varda's film, like Spahr and Jamie's poetry, demands audience responsiveness: her follow-up film, *The Gleaners and I: Two Years Later* contains not only interviews with the original subjects of her documentary, but images of the photographs, letters, paintings and potatoes that viewers have sent her.[29] There is a community within the film, of assorted urban and rural gleaners, and a community surrounding the film, of audience members and critics, but these are both enabled solely by Varda's own gleaning process. Both films, like Varda's other work, are filled with images of Varda's hands, offering a reflection on her own ageing and the importance of film as a tactile medium.[30] The 'we' of the film is one that centres around one individual. At the time, the focus on bodily precarity and contingency allows the audience to consider their own relation both to the film they are watching and to their own practices of gleaning and observation.

The combination of multiple genres and forms is central to the project of each of these artists: in discussing the fragmentation of both human experience and environmental encounter, no single narrative or explanatory strategy is sufficient. The use of multiple media to expand the horizons of what might be considered an environmental or ecopoetic project can also be seen in the work of the Marshallese poet Kathy Jetñil-Kijiner, whose work thematically parallels Spahr's work from the perspective of the Indigenous Pacific islanders whose lives have been destroyed by American power. Jetñil-Kijiner's status as a 'climate change poet' has been cemented by her appearance at the opening ceremony of the UN Climate Change Summit in 2014, as well as her performance poetry, film and other digital art which, as Michelle Keown notes, has not only reached 'millions of international viewers', but is particularly a way of reaching 'a globally dispersed audience of Pacific Islanders as well as non-Oceanians'.[31] Like Jamie's

The Overhaul, Jetñil-Kijiner's debut collection *Iep Jāltok* is bookended with two poems, both titled 'Basket', that combine gleaning and fragmentation. Each poem occupies a two-page spread, the brief lines arranged to mimic the shape of a basket. The shape of the poem becomes its meaning, and grants a momentary wholeness to a series of disconnected words. In the first poem, the 'receptacle / littered / with scraps / tossed by / others' is both the basket the central woman of the poem is weaving or holding and her own womb, while in the latter the scope has expanded to 'a seabed / to scrape / a receptacle / to dump with scraps // your / body / is a country / we conquer / and devour'.[32] There is no firm separation between self and community, between domestic space and landscape, between the abuse done to individuals and that done to an entire culture. The image of the basket, however, allows these fragments to be woven into a form of protest and reclamation.[33]

This dual motion is best exemplified in the poem 'Anointed', which was published on Jetñil-Kijiner's website in 2018 with an accompanying film co-directed by Dan Lin. The poem surveys the history of nuclear testing in the Marshall Islands, transforming them from 'a whole island' to a 'concrete shell'; in a line that stands entirely on its own, Jetñil-Kijiner writes: 'I am looking for more stories. I look and I look.'[34] Only the silence of the blank page, or the screen, responds. While the poet continues to look for stories, the poem ends with despair: 'Who anointed them with the power to burn?' The accompanying film provides more initial contextualization, with several sentences describing the United States' nuclear testing in the Marshall Islands and the collection of contaminated waste in a crater on Runit Island in Enewetak Atoll. The film depicts Jetñil-Kijiner as she travels to the island, incorporating images of the beaches and concrete shells, and not only the poet herself but also a number of islanders. The performance's soundtrack includes a simple orchestral plaint and the crashing of the waves. At the end of the poem, intertitles appear on the screen, showing children playing fifteen miles from the radioactive waste dump and rows of houses in an area deemed 'uninhabitable'. Over the film's end-credits, the orchestral soundtrack is replaced by 'A Song for Runit', written and performed by Helina Kaiko, and untranslated. The perseverance of island culture is not attested to in the poem so much as it is manifested aurally and visually. While Jetñil-Kijiner, in both written and performed versions of the poem, functions as a gleaner, selecting fragments of experience, the film as a whole gestures towards a recuperation that the text itself cannot hold. Jetñil-Kijiner's poetry simultaneously functions as a document of atrocities and an indication that artistic form can provide moments of unification.

The importance of the relation between individual and community is central to all of these artists. As the quotations from Jamie above illustrate, in relatively few of her essays and poems on gleaning or scavenging is she alone: she is surrounded by scientists, family and neighbours, each working together but separately. The idea of collective response is central to Jamie's work, often framed in terms of political and social consciousness. In '23/9/14' she ends her reflection on the failed Scottish Independence Referendum with the lines 'It's Tuesday. On wir feet. / Today we begin again'.[35] The 'we' is specifically a national, Scottish collective, but the impulse to begin again is one that echoes 'The Beach' in her previous collection. Both poems depict storms, and suggest the importance of collective response. In her earlier poem 'Lucky Bag' she characterizes Scottish identity as 'an orderly rabble', with the two final words separated by a large space, to allow for new formulations and perspectives.[36] Yet this collectivity is more challenging when she writes of climate change. *Surfacing* begins and ends with short pieces in the second person, where Jamie voices her own experience as an address to the reader. 'The Reindeer Cave' begins with a specific 'you': 'You're sheltering in a cave, thinking about the Ice Age'.[37] By the end of the essay, however, that 'you' has given way to an undefined 'we':

> At your cave-mouth, you wonder if the ice will ever return, a natural cycle, or if we've gone too far with our Anthropocene. But who can answer that? We just can't grasp the scale of our species' effects. But the single falling stone which could smash our brains out – that we understand.
>
> Now the rain's easing, and a small scruffy terrier appears at the cave-mouth. Following the dog come children. Their voices carry from down the slope: Daddy! Look! The caves![38]

The final sentences point to a sense of continuance, and reproductive futurity, which might seem to counteract the Anthropocene anxiety of the previous paragraph: even if there is no way for the individual to conceive of the scale of environmental devastation surrounding us, Jamie seems to imply, there will still be children and dogs and caves, and the sound of joy. Jamie's turn to the collective is not, however, a turn away from responsibility, but a claim to the importance of collective experience. If 'you', or 'we', or the elided narrative 'I' cannot conceive of climate change in the abstract, our experiences with the world can still reveal something important to us. In the collection's final essay, 'Voice of the Wood', the 'you' repeats their struggle: 'No, not to think about it exactly but consider what to do with the weight of it all, the knowing... how to cope with it scroll down flick the page unplug the telly send a few quid. Really?'[39] This unpunctuated, frantic list presents response as itself fragmented: these activities are placebos, ways for the individual to feel they have contributed to the world without asking anything further of them. Wandering in the woods instead is, as Jamie admits, a privileged position, and yet it is the only one available to her.

The piece ends with another litany of natural fragments, moments of encounter that are not meaningful in themselves, but represent a form of engagement:

> Green ferns in the groin of an oak. Green moss cloaking a stone. Voice of a crow. Voice of a chiding wren. A smirr of rain too soft to possess a voice. Voice of the shrew, the black slug. Voice of the forest... Did you hear something move out of the corner of your eye? The same moth come back? Or another leaf falling? You are not lost, just melodramatic. The path is at your feet, see? Now carry on.[40]

The passage is as simple as it appears, with its familiar allusion to Robert Frost and its insistence that the world is knowable because it is observable. It is also more complex. In both lists, that of technological response and the sounds of the woods, the presence of an ellipsis points to objects or experiences that Jamie cannot name or summarize, and which are still important. The world is organized by the gleaner, but that organization is not definitive or permanent. There is only this moment, now, these particular voices. The shift between hearing and seeing, and the repeated questions, points to a self that is not fully at home in the world, and yet has no choice but to inhabit it. What is important, as in Ensor's account of Varda, is the rhythm generated by this litany of voices and this set of questions. The world must be relinquished at the same time it must be preserved, and so must the human self. As Spahr writes, 'This ability to recognize one's self as lost and belonging with the others in the lostness, this is what made the place matter.'[41] Whether the peripheral flicker in Jamie's text is a leaf or a moth is not as important as that something is encountered, and seen, and exists, and can be shared. The fragment is what permits momentum.

Jamie, Varda, Jetñil-Kijiner and Spahr are very different artists. Their shared concern with gleaning and fragmentation, with the experiences of loss and recovery, and with the relation between individual and collective experience, however, represents a prominent direction in twenty-first-century writing and art. Each of them poses moments of encounter, integration and relinquishment not as ways of explaining the world, but of drawing attention to the chance encounter as an approach to contemporary concerns. The world is that which resists totalizing narrative, but these moments of collection and finding provide a way to reconsider questions of spatial and temporal scale. All four, like the writers discussed throughout this book, posit attention to the momentary encounter – whether with other people, material objects or the non-human and more-than-human world – as a way of thinking and perceiving the omnipresent crises of modern life.

In opening the Introduction with this discussion of individual artworks – a model followed by the subsequent chapters – I also want to highlight the way these principles of gleaning and fragmentation are also central to this book. Rather than analysing creative texts with reference to extant theoretical models, and in so doing offering a voice of apparent authority, I wish to show that thinkers in a variety of fields, both poetic and philosophical, are grappling with similar problems, and can best be understood in relation to each other. The echoes between different texts, implicit and explicit, allow the writers discussed here to be seen in constellation, in similarity and difference. In this I follow Ursula K. Le Guin's turn, in the frequently cited essay 'The Carrier Bag Theory of Fiction', from the 'killer story' – the text which highlights a single hero and his (always his) linear actions – to a model of narrative that can be compared to a sack or bag. A novel, claims Le Guin – and I would add here a poem, a film, a song, or a theoretical treatise – is 'a medicine bundle, holding things in a particular, powerful relation to one another and to us'.[42] This act of gathering, with an emphasis not on linear development and heroism but on placing diverse objects and ideas in relation, is central to the artists discussed above, and to this entire project. To understand our world, we have to rethink our attachment to narratives of development and catastrophe. We, and our texts, are known in our relation, in the way we co-constitute each other. We are known in constellation, in what we gather and in what we leave behind; we are known in what comes together and what fails to cohere. Understanding our times, and the relation between human life and environmental concerns, and between life and text, requires new ways of thinking and forms of expression, and these are what this book sets out to explore.

A. Fragmentation and the problem of scale

As is briefly discussed in the Prologue, one of the central problems for critics discussing climate change and the Anthropocene more generally is that of scale. Defined most simply, the Anthropocene is the age or epoch in which human effect on the planet can be measured in geological terms, whether dated from the dawn of agriculture, the Industrial Revolution or the birth of nuclear weapons and power.[43] More recently, however, the term has been widely used in the humanities to refer to both political and poetic ways of conceiving planetary environmental change. The Anthropocene is, for many thinkers, everything that humans do on a planetary scale; as Dipesh Chakrabarty and Bruno Latour have influentially argued, it is a concept that reconfigures our approach to human existence.[44] It is a way to discuss climate change and environmental collapse, the proliferation of industry and the inescapable forces of state and corporate power, the continued separation between human and non-human animals and, in many cases, human writing about these issues. It is, in Farrier's words, 'an event that challenges our sense of what an event might mean'.[45] As Astrid Bracke clarifies, while the Anthropocene is not a synonym for climate change, the terms are frequently linked in the popular imagination as, for many people, climate change is the clearest example of the scope and scale of the Anthropocene.[46] Climate change and the Anthropocene both represent an idea of the real, or the event, that can exceed individual experience. In his influential formulation of the problem, Timothy Clark suggests that 'the Anthropocene enacts the demand to think of human life at much broader scales of space and time': conceptualizing the Anthropocene requires moving from a perspective based on singular action to an almost imponderable planetary scale, while Anthropocenic change may only be manifested as 'innumerable possible hairline cracks' in an individual life.[47]

The challenges of such a scale are not limited to the conceptual. Focusing on global scales at the expense of more local ones may reinforce 'the dominance of neoliberal globalisation' in ways that disempower individual agency: the problem may be seen simply as one of state power or corporations.[48] The converse is also true: the popularization of the 'personal carbon footprint' can be traced to a 2005 BP media campaign in the United States, costing $100 million a year, that deflected responsibility for climate change onto individual consumers, rather than energy producers.[49] As noted by critics such as Rob Nixon, Kathryn Yusoff and Juan Martinez-Alier, the concept of the Anthropocene also fails to differentiate the ways environmental collapse disproportionately affects populations who are already precarious and subject to state, colonial or economic violence, in particular racial and ethnic minorities and the poor. The 'normalization of catastrophe is almost soothing', writes Michael Egan, not only because it presents a tangible, knowable end to a period of great uncertainty and change, but because it relies on the notion that this catastrophe will largely be visited on populations unlike the presumed white, Western reader.[50] If the Anthropocene has been 'world making in epochal pronouncements', as Yusoff argues, it has also been 'put to work as a conceptual grab, materialist history, and cautionary tale' in ways that ignore the legacies of colonial violence and dispossession.[51] Isabelle Stengers likewise suggests that 'the success of this word' does not, in fact, signal a turn from denial to consciousness, and might equally reinforce a 'troubling abstraction' of the human, or 'Man'.[52] The discourse of the Anthropocene can thus potentially become a panacea or an abstraction that ignores questions of both individual and state responsibility for environmental change.[53]

The Anthropocene, as both epochal change and conceptual tool, is thus simultaneously too large and too small, too all-encompassing and too partial. It remains difficult to engage with on the level of the individual, and yet can also be used as a way to deflect responsibility. In emphasizing a 'distant rendering of future ecological change and human anguish', such discussions can often seem remote and unengaging.[54] There is an almost irresolvable tension between the terms 'the Anthropocene', as formulated by Clark and others, and Jamie's 'our Anthropocene', as quoted above. The Anthropocene is simultaneously outside normal human conceptualization and immediate to lived experience. The questions it raises about individual complicity and responsibility are easily placed at a remove. For a number of literary critics, these challenges are ones best addressed by literature. Pieter Vermeulen, for instance, argues that while the Anthropocene cannot be seen as a 'literary problem' as such, the study of literature helps us to consider the Anthropocene 'as a matter of reading and writing, of decoding and inscription'.[55] While Adam Trexler argues, along similar lines to Amitav Ghosh, that contemporary fiction has 'struggle[d] to understand the devastating potential of climatic disaster', Adeline Johns-Putra posits that literature's 'seemingly retrogressive and anthropocentric evocations of reader empathy and inhabitation' remain the best response to these scalar problems.[56] Starting not from environmental science but moral philosophy, Johns-Putra argues that readers' ability to empathize with fictional characters leads to a 'sympathetic acknowledgement of shared vulnerability with others' and a 'desire to address that common vulnerability and promote a common flourishing'.[57] Yet as much as a discourse of common vulnerability is central to this book's argument the fact remains that, in Maggie Kainulainen's words, '[i]n the Anthropocene, it's easy to empathize'.[58] Kainulainen argues instead that climate change must be encountered 'as a sublime object', and that representing climate change requires 'an active rejection of "the malady of the quotidian"'.[59] For each of these critics, and many others, the question of how literature can best represent or engage with ideas of the Anthropocene and climate change rests on ideas of empathy and agency. Despite diverse and often contradictory perspectives, critics are constant in proposing that if literature is to be relevant it must engage with these questions, whether arguing that the Anthropocene must, or should, or has failed to challenge the forms and genres of fiction, or that literature already possesses, whether in terms of empathy or the sublime, the very modes and effects necessary to grapple with planetary change.

The texts discussed throughout this book take a different approach. With only a few exceptions, the work below does not fall easily into a genre of 'climate change fiction' or even 'ecopoetics', although climate and environmental concerns are often paramount.[60] Instead, these are texts that focus on the 'hairline cracks' Clark believes get overlooked, or the idea of the quotidian that Kainulainen rejects. If a story of climate change as such leads either to catastrophe, with all its narrative comforts, or to an overly optimistic resolution, and if an Anthropocene text might struggle to balance individual and collective experiences, attending to the momentary encounter, the daily ritual, and the unexpected friction between people and moments can redress some of the problems expressed above. In moving between fiction, memoir, criticism, poetry and song, I argue that attention to fragmentary form reveals a complicated response to environmental concerns that makes a virtue of uncertainty and accident.[61] Above all, I argue that the fragment – defined variously in terms of literary form, spatial and temporal encounter and material object – is a different way of challenging received narratives of environmental engagement. Rather than telling a story of climate change or the Anthropocene event, these texts illustrate that a gleaned or collected series of fragments is the best way to balance individual and planetary scales.

Few texts better illustrate this argument than Daisy Hildyard's brief essay collection *The Second Body*. The text is divided into four sections, titled '0', 'Ool', a smiley emoticon and a target symbol: the book immediately rejects linear sequencing in favour of principles of similarity and repetition. Although the volume incorporates conversations with climate change scientists and a discussion of Timothy Clark alongside critical readings of Elena Ferrante and William Shakespeare, its primary focus is local and individual at the same time that it challenges any binary division between personal and collective response. Like Jamie, Hildyard begins her collection with a bird, a small brown pigeon she finds on her kitchen floor and for which she briefly cares. Although her description of the pigeon is presented in familiar naturalistic terms, she also foregrounds the idea of text itself: 'Its legs leaned at an angle over its claws: *L*.'[62] Hildyard, and the reader, imagines the pigeon through its textual construction: the division between body and representation is already blurred. This brief encounter leads Hildyard to notice more non-human animals as she reads newspaper accounts and looks at images of mass distress and death. If she feels responsible for the pigeon, she can be no less responsible for the suffering of animals in Norway or Zimbabwe or Fife:

> There is a way of speaking which implicates your body in everything on earth. […] Climate change creates a new language, in which you have to be all over the place; you are always all over the place. It makes every animal body implicated in the whole world.[63]

If humans are accustomed to thinking of their own bodily and experiential boundaries, Hildyard argues, the discussion of climate change necessitates a change in self-conception that acknowledges individual responsibility for seismic change and, just as importantly, forces a reconceptualization of the body itself. In conversations with a local butcher and a criminologist, Hildyard explains how conceiving of the self as an animal body allows for a greater connection with other animals, and a rejection of local boundaries in favour of a sense of being dispersed. Hildyard is clear that she is not writing of concepts or analogies, but actual bodies. The first body is related to your own skin, your own place, your own sense of self, whereas the 'second body' is a larger, unbounded version of you:

> It is not a concept, it is your own body. The language we have at the moment is weak: we might speak vaguely of global connections; of the emission and circulation of gasses; of impacts. And yet, at some microscopic or intangible scale, bodies are breaking into one another. The concept of a global impact is not working for us, and in the meantime, your body has already eaten the distance. Your first body could be sitting alone in a church in the centre of Marseille, but your second body is floating above a pharmaceutical plant on the outskirts of the city, it is inside a freight container in the docks, and it is also thousands of miles away, on the flood plain in Bangladesh, in another man's lungs. It is understandably difficult to remember that you have anything to do with this second body – your first body is the body you inhabit in your daily life. However, you are alive in both. You have two bodies.[64]

We cannot conceive of global climate change, she insists, until we redefine what it means to be an individual, what it means to have an animal body and what it means to occupy a space. Towards the end of the collection she writes of how her own self-conception is challenged when her house floods: while she distracts herself marking essays on Shakespeare, she is also physically implicated and involved in global changes which force her to renegotiate what it means to inhabit a place, or to have ownership of it.

The idea that an encounter with a non-human animal might cause a crisis that reshapes the individual's conception with self and world is a commonplace in contemporary writing, whether in Jamie's essays or novels like Keith Ridgway's *Animals* and, as discussed in Chapter 1, Sara Baume's *A Line Made by Walking*.[65] What makes Hildyard's account particularly important in this context is its formal presentation. The four component parts are not separate essays, but reflections of the same theme, approached from different perspectives. Rather than using subheadings, new subsections are introduced, after a blank space, with a pilcrow. Any given subsection might include an autobiographical reflection, a discussion with an expert in the field, often in a public setting, or an analysis of a literary text. Each textual fragment is open to a form of encounter that is equal to any other: rather than presenting a cumulative linear argument, Hildyard presents a series of textual fragments that accrue meaning in relation to each other and to the reader's own experiences. As in Le Guin's carrier bag, Hildyard emphasizes ideas of collection, repetition and difference over ideas of individual agency and development. Stewart writes, specifically of fiction, that 'repetition is a matter of reframing [where] in the repetition difference is displayed in both directions, just as "identity" is created'.[66] Repetition and quotation, Stewart suggests, does not present the quoted material as secondary, but foregrounds how it creates the original. The same pattern is present in Hildyard's writing: although the observations and reflections in the text originate from one particular individual, their presentation as fragments allows for the creation of a new, dispersed, multi-bodied collectivity.

Hildyard's essay aptly demonstrates the multiple senses of fragment that underpin this book. The fragment can be seen in terms of the momentary encounter with other human or non-human life at the same time that it can be seen as a particular literary form signified by line breaks and blank space. If, as Hildyard writes in relation to Clark, 'it is impossible to relate [the global] body to anything individual because there can be no certain borders between one thing and another', the presentation of fragments allows an approach to these central issues that avoids individual pronunciation or conclusion.[67] This rhetorical shift echoes the work discussed in the opening constellation above: rather than attempting to relate individual experience to global experience in a straightforward way, situating the individual in terms of collective experience, all of these artists trouble the boundaries between individual and collective, local and planetary, to insist that the distinction is already a false one. There is still an individual body, or self, who is responsible for this gleaning, whether walking on the beach, photographing her hands or marking Shakespeare essays. The fragmentary form, however, allows, and even requires, a moment of relinquishing and a recognition that the arbitrary and contingent are our only avenues to understanding the world. As Marc Botha suggests in a discussion of the poet and artist Ian Hamilton Finlay, the fragment is a way of showing 'that existence is fragile, since everything which exists, exists only contingently'.[68] The world is not there to be explained, but experienced, and that experience is momentary, fractured and incomplete.

This use of fragmentary form is, of course, not new to contemporary literature. Philippe Lacoue-Labarthe and Jean-Luc Nancy reflect on how for the Jena Romantics the fragment is 'the most distinctive mark of [their] originality, or a sign of [their] radical modernity'.[69] They trace the genre of the literary fragment back to Pascal and Montaigne, among others, such that the fragment can be seen as a product of the same Enlightenment perspectives I argue contemporary writers reject. Yet the German Romantic definition as framed by Friedrich von Schlegel, Novalis and others in collections of aphorisms such as *Athenaeum Fragments* remains pertinent. *Athenaeum* fragment 206 reads, in its entirety: 'A fragment, like a small work of art, has to be entirely isolated from the surrounding world and be complete in itself like a hedgehog'.[70] As Lacoue-Labarthe and Nancy point out, the fragment is important in its individuality at the same time that it is seen in relation to a larger multiplicity: the 'plural totality' of multiple fragments does not make up the whole, but replicates it, such that the whole is present in each part. As they write: 'Fragments are definitions of the fragment; this is what installs the totality of the fragment as a plurality and its completion as the incompletion of its infinity'.[71] The fragment is both complete in itself and necessarily incomplete: it must be seen in relation to multiplicity – one cannot write one fragment – and yet does not create a homogenous whole.

The wording of *Athenaeum* 206 is particularly productive, however. While Lacoue-Labarthe and Nancy focus on the relation between the fragment and the work of art, they do not reflect on its hedgehogness. Hedgehogs may stand in philosophical terms for completeness and separation, as in Isaiah Berlin's famous ruminations on a fragment of the Greek poet Archilocus: 'The fox knows many things, but the hedgehog knows one big thing'.[72] Whatever it might be that hedgehogs know, however, they are just as entangled in human and environmental concerns as any other creature; in Britain the decline in hedgehog numbers is often taken as one of the clearest evidences of human environmental destruction at the cost of other species' well-being.[73] If the *Athenaeum* fragment seems to posit a separation between the work of art and the natural world, it also demonstrates in that juxtaposition that the two must be taken together: the fragmentary form speaks simultaneously to human and non-human environments. The very thing that is framed as complete in itself is only knowable because it is enmeshed in a human, and a more-than-human, environment.

The Jena Romantics' use of the fragment to navigate questions of totality and individuality can easily be connected to ideas of the monad, as most famously expounded by Gottfried Wilhelm Leibniz. Two decades before Leibniz, the English philosopher Anne Conway stipulated that all creatures, human and non-human, are infinite and unbounded. As she argues, not only is the entire universe infinite, 'but even every creature, no matter how small, which we can see with our eyes or conceive of in our minds, has in itself such an infinity of parts or rather of entire creatures that they cannot be counted'.[74] Each creature, each part of the universe, represents the universe as a whole; as Leibniz writes, the 'interconnection [...] of all created things' means that each substance, or being, 'is a perpetual mirror of the universe'.[75] While the Enlightenment monad and the Romantic fragment might initially seem opposed, their central connection is that both present the miniature, the fragmentary and the individual not as one of a set of component parts that can be combined to generate a whole, but as a whole in themselves. As much as the fragment emphasizes fracture it also presents an 'ethic of finitude' that recognizes the limits of human knowledge.[76]

These concerns are taken up in discussions of the Modernist fragment. Walter Benjamin famously quotes Paul Valéry in distinguishing between the 'patient process of Nature', which is connected to repetition and layering, and the modern short story, which resists retellings.[77] If the processes of miniaturization and repetition were formerly linked to nature, he writes, modern artworks highlight a divorce from a unified understanding of the world framed in terms of authentic experience. The fragmentary form of Benjamin's *The Arcades Project* can be seen as the construction of a totality, combining 'sensory data' with 'abstract knowledge', that itself resists totalization.[78] Just as influentially, Charles Baudelaire defines modernity as 'the ephemeral, the fugitive, the contingent, the half of art whose other half is the eternal and the immutable'.[79] If for the eighteenth- and nineteenth-century thinkers the fragment stands for the whole, for the Modernists the fragment has replaced the whole. Both sets of thinkers, however, focus on the fragment in terms of being, rather than becoming, to use Camelia Elias's important distinction: rather than seeing the fragment in terms of ruin or residue, as something left behind, the fragment is posited as a form in its own right that is particularly reflective of modernity.[80]

Rebecca Varley-Winters's recent account of the Modernist fragment is particularly pertinent here. Varley-Winters shows that while literary fragments emerge through 'indeterminacy and uncertainty', they are also felt and sensed, 'creat[ing] states of conflicted embodiment in which mind and body cannot cleanly separate'.[81] Fragments are experienced phenomenologically, and in relation to the body. They complicate our understanding of gendered approaches to literary history; they challenge mind-body dualisms; above all, they evoke a sense of incompletion that requires the reader to question what kind of text they are reading. In Varley-Winters's account, one of the primary, if often unconsidered, aspects of the fragment is that it requires new conceptualizations of the relation between text, author and reader, in which nothing is stable. As Maria Stepanova writes in a fragmentary account of her family history, the 'fragments of memory and pieces of the old world did create a whole', yet that unity can be seen as a 'twisted body, no longer capable of connecting its memories into a sequence' that she is not sure she wants to be seen.[82] The fragment is caught somewhere between author and reader; it is both partial and whole. The fragment is thus a particularly apt way to discuss the relation between individual, collective and planetary scales that is one of the central challenges of our own time.

The contemporary fragment can be seen in relation to these earlier formulations. For many writers, the fragment is all that is available. Terry Tempest Williams begins her collection *Erosion: Essays of Undoing* with the claim that '[i]f the world is torn to pieces, I want to see what story I can find in fragmentation', arguing that collage and assemblage allow for a new narrative perspective.[83] Moyra Davey, responding to Benjamin and Virginia Woolf, among others, writes that she is 'drawn to fragmentary forms' at the same time she is 'piecing together fragments because I don't yet have a subject'.[84] The fragment is all that we are left with: it has replaced an easy sense of a pre-ordained, accepted unity, and is the only way to approach an incompletely understood world. In *Appendix Project*, a series of talks and essays that respond to her earlier fragmentary memoir *Book of Mutter*, Kate Zambreno discusses her work's 'incompleteness and ongoingness, which connects, for me, to the fragmentary project of literature, and what I long for in writing'.[85] She emphasizes the 'fragmented nature of [her] exhaustion' and the way fragmentation can be connected to mourning and the distortion of time.[86] Zambreno's own work draws on multiple writers and artists not to produce a unitary whole, but rather a diffracted, incomplete idea of selfhood: the fragment is important because it cannot easily be integrated into a new whole, but remains incomplete. And yet, as shown in Jamie's and Hildyard's work, the fragment is also valuable precisely because this sense of incompletion allows for new ways of approaching the world. Fragmentary form limits the need to tell a story about the world, but instead foregrounds the importance of ephemeral, contingent experience. The fragment is not a solution to the problem of scale, as such, but rather a different way of approaching the problem: rather than navigating between a presumably knowable self and a presumably unknowable world, it insists that the world is only known through the self, and the self only known through the world. The fragment suggests that the individual self is less fully understood than we might assume, and yet that this failure of understanding is a necessary foundation for encountering the larger world. At the same time, however, as the quotation from Williams suggests, fragments can also function as a form of storytelling.

B. Fragmentary storytelling

For many thinkers, whether approaching the issue from the world of science or the humanities, the social function of storytelling is ever more important in a time of climate catastrophe. Annika Arnold argues most simply that 'natural sciences only deliver raw facts' while narrative formulations can foreground 'climate change as social phenomenon'.[87] Antonia Mehnert likewise claims that reading novels alongside scientific writing 'provides new insights because [novels] reveal the intimate aspects of human struggles and bring formerly unacknowledged perspectives to light'.[88] Similar discussions are rampant in literary criticism focused on climate change; while sciences are presented as having access to 'facts', the humanities are valued for their ability to encourage readers to relate to those facts. These formulations, while well intended, often present literature as a second-order form of knowledge: scientists understand the world, while writers reflect it. Ursula K. Le Guin is more careful to avoid a strong binary division, arguing that '[s]cience explicates; poetry implicates. Both celebrate what they describe'. She writes that science can 'increase moral sensitivity' while poetry 'can move minds to the sense of fellowship that prevents careless usage and exploitation of our fellow beings, waste and cruelty'.[89] In this formulation science and literature are not presented as two cultures, in C.P. Snow's familiar phrasing, but rather as necessary allies.[90] Le Guin's claim does not go as far as Lawrence Buell's assertion that 'environmental rhetoric rightfully rests on moral and especially aesthetic grounds *rather than* scientific'.[91] Rather, Le Guin proposes that both science and arts possess the ability to reframe environmental discourse in a way that reveals human and environmental interconnections. Anna Lowenhaupt Tsing, who frequently quotes Le Guin in her work, likewise frames storytelling as a way to transcend a simple nature/culture binary that she traces to the Enlightenment. For Le Guin and Tsing, the power of literature is that it troubles our understanding of the world, turning our attention to what the sciences leave out, including our own entanglement with the natural environment and our complicity in its destruction.

Tsing's approach, in terms of both argument and method, is central to any understanding of how contemporary writers approach questions of environmental enmeshment. She most clearly defines, and troubles, the relation between storytelling and science in a passage on the problem of scale:

> To listen to and tell a rush of stories is a *method*. And why not make the strong claim and call it a science, an addition to knowledge? Its research object is contaminated diversity; its unit of analysis is the indeterminate encounter. To learn anything we must revitalize arts of noticing and include ethnography and natural history. But we have a problem with scale. A rush of stories cannot be neatly summed up. Its scales do not nest neatly; they draw attention to interrupting geographies and tempos. These interruptions elicit more stories. This is the rush of stories' power as science. Yet it is just these interruptions that step out of the bounds of most modern science, which demands the possibility for infinite expansion without changing the research framework.[92]

As Le Guin would agree, narrative is not a repackaging of fact, but a form of knowledge in its own right. Tsing's specific focus here on the indeterminate encounter and contaminated diversity is likewise central to all of the writers discussed in this Introduction, and throughout this book. Whether in terms of encounters with human or non-human others, whether in terms of linguistic or material fragments, each of these writers suggests the importance of noticing, and giving weight to particular encounters as a way of redefining questions of temporal and spatial scale. Tsing here builds on her earlier argument that 'a study of global connections shows the grip of encounter: friction. [...] [F]riction reminds us that heterogeneous and unequal encounters can lead to new arrangements of culture and power.'[93] Friction, in Tsing's formulation, is a way to avoid ideas of universal truths and generalization that she sees as a legacy of Enlightenment thought, where Nature can be approached as a separate whole. She draws attention to the planetary scale of climate change models, for instance, which necessitates that 'the local disappear compatibly inside the global'.[94] Tsing's call for a more ephemeral, local knowledge production, a 'rush of stories' does not negate global approaches to environmental change, but draws attention to the experiential encounter, and away from anthropocentric theorizations towards a more inclusive, multispecies approach.[95] Her fleeting image of nesting scales, calling to mind a scaled creature, rather than an abstraction, illustrates the importance of this reimagining.

As much as Tsing's work has been enormously influential, relatively few critics have approached it in literary terms. Tsing's story of mushroom-picking in the Western United States for export to Japan is not only an illustration of ideas of precarity, vulnerability, capitalism and globalization, but is also perhaps more formally experimental than critics have articulated. The volume moves between the autoethnographic and the theoretical, between intertextual allusions and accounts of conversations: in short, it uses very similar strategies to Jamie and Hildyard. While Tsing's text is approached as a work of theory, or anthropology, and Hildyard and Jamie's work is seen in terms of literature, the formal similarities between the three suggest the way self-interrupting fragments provide a way to reconceptualize the relation between the narrative self and planetary change without privileging either. The fragmentary narrative, emphasizing contingency and precarity, is a way of resituating knowledge: the 'contaminated diversity' to which Tsing alludes is not simply a way to discuss interspecies relations, but epistemology. As Alexis Shotwell writes, it is important 'to take seriously the impossibility of telling value-neutral stories about the world, scientific stories or otherwise [...] [W]e might do better science – attend better – if we have better narratives, grounded in arts of noticing'.[96] Like Tsing, Shotwell stresses narrative not as a linear progression, but as an act of attention. Storytelling in this sense is not explanatory, but embedded in a world that is already diverse, partial and contaminated.

Tsing's emphasis on 'the contingencies of encounter' is thus more than a way to discuss interspecies relations, or human complicity in planetary change, as if there could be some formulation of change in which we were not already complicit.[97] It is also simultaneously a way to foreground the ethics of an attentive engagement with the world and a challenge to literary form. If we are used to defining 'persons' as 'protagonists of stories', she suggests, telling stories of a non-human or more-than-human world, and of a landscape, requires a form of noticing that privileges disturbance.[98] One of the central functions of a fragmentary, multidisciplinary approach is that it reminds both reader and writer that there is no pure, disengaged perspective on the world: the scientist or the essayist is not observing the world from a distance, but is noticing the disturbance around them, to which they are contributing. This sense of engagement is not only possible through fragmentary forms, but is certainly highlighted by them: fragmentation suggests a form of storytelling filled with elisions and absence, with contingency and chance, with ghosts and echoes.[99]

Although Tsing's citations of Le Guin draw primarily on her essays, Le Guin's mammoth novel, or collection of fragments, *Always Coming Home*, is just as apt a point of comparison. First published in 1985 and revised and expanded in 2017, shortly before Le Guin's death, the novel concerns a community, the Kesh, who 'might be going to have lived a long, long time from now in Northern California. The main part of the book is their voices speaking for themselves in stories and life-stories, plays, poems, and songs.'[100] The text is an assemblage of fragments, presented with scholarly apparatus such as maps and glossaries, as well as accompanying music and art. Le Guin cautions that a binary division between factual and nonfactual narrative is irrelevant, and there is no clear distinction between a narrative that tells 'what happened' and that which tells a story 'like what happened'; rather, the central distinction is between truth and falsehood: a deliberate lie cannot be considered literature at all.[101] Thus, the assemblage of prayers and songs, fables and histories, human and non-human descriptions all work jointly to illustrate the life of a particular community. Each text can be considered a fragment; each reader will glean different aspects and individual stories in order to reach their own individualistic understanding. The stories are interspliced with the figure of the anthropologist Pandora, echoing mythology but also functioning as an avatar for Le Guin herself, who, when she is first introduced, explicitly 'doesn't want to look into the big end of the telescope and see, jewel-bright, distinct, tiny, and entire, the Valley', but instead privileges '[b]its, chunks, fragments. Shards. Pieces of the Valley, lifesize.'[102] Only an incomplete pattern made from assembled fragments can illuminate the Valley: whatever truth there is is constructed from the relation between observer and observed. Le Guin's method is not only 'a challenge to the often authoritarian narrative practice of the traditional utopia', but also a challenge to any methodology, scientific or literary, that centres on unity and progression.[103] The text requires rethinking both narrative and personhood, as no figure, or story, or theoretical perspective grants comprehensive knowledge.

The new material in the expanded edition, gathered under the title 'Pandora Revisits the Kesh and Comes Back with New Texts', incorporates the short Kesh novel *Dangerous People*, a collection of spiritual or philosophical meditations, another collection of songs, largely focusing on menopause and ageing, and an analysis of Kesh syntax. Chapter 2 of *Dangerous People* appears in the original text as well; here the novel gains two additional chapters, as well as extensive footnotes. While the footnotes have an explanatory function not often found in the earlier version, the difficulty of interpretation is emphasized in the new version of *Dangerous People*, where the character Shamsa struggles to interpret an unsigned manuscript called *Controlling*. The layering is complex: Shamsa's story of her reading is told in a novel by Arravna that is doubly incorporated in Le Guin's own novel, both as fragment and in a complete form, with footnotes presumably by Pandora. The difficulty of interpretation is highlighted in the main body of the text itself:

> All the same, even if the author was deliberately indulging in a compressed allusive mode, the sentence that most troubled her still troubled her. Was it a clear strand across a gap, or a break in the skein, or a knot, a tangle? 'Shattering pressure may induce scattering to find what is traduced.' The chime of *shatter* and *scatter*, *induce* and *traduce*, were much gaudier than this author's usual plain style. Perhaps they signified a sleepy moment, copying out late at night, the mind not in control of the hand, picking up rhymes not reasons. The cracked wheat was done; she stirred it up and left the pot half-open on the stove to cool. Turning back to the counter, thinking of that word *traduce*, she saw the plant of chicory, today's flower now withered shut and tomorrow's buds on the stem mere knots, their promise lost.[104]

The difficult sentence is described before it is reproduced, and remains as mystifying to the reader as it does to Shamsha. Rather than understanding the anonymous author's claim, Le Guin suggests, the text can only be examined for its poetic qualities and for the way that it is situated in a lived environment: what matters is not meaning, but attention. The act of scholarly interpretation does not occur in a vacuum, but while the scholar is cooking and gazing out of the window. Words and flowers echo each other, and it would be misleading to privilege either one. This passage supports Le Guin's much earlier claim, in a lecture from 1980, that

> Fiction in particular, narration in general, may be seen not as a disguise or falsification of what is given but as an active encounter with the environment by means of posing options and alternatives, and an enlargement of present reality by connecting it to the unverifiable past and the unpredictable future.[105]

An encounter with the text cannot be separated from an encounter with the environment. This sentence, allusive and elusive, gains meaning not in interpretation but in incorporation. Noticing the text becomes a way of noticing the world.

Le Guin's work can be framed in relation to Tsing's challenging differentiation between different forms of fragmentation. Artists working from positions of power, she argues, might 'devote their attention to the *form* of fragmentation', while for marginalized artists, the 'eclectic fragments of marginality argue for survival'.[106] The fragment as an aesthetic form that highlights ideas of fracture and ruin, and is conceived of in terms of form itself, speaks to a question of privilege whereas the fragments of marginalized discourses and peoples are a way of refracting that dominance. Le Guin certainly occupies both positions, especially in the figure of Pandora, who must explain, and draws attention to the fragment as form. While the Kesh have never existed, many of their stories and traditions are drawn from real communities in Northern California who were the object of anthropological study by Le Guin's father, and Le Guin has been seen as appropriating Indigenous cultures.[107] Yet in presenting these fragments as fragments, Le Guin also offers a model of resistance to dominant ideas of narrative as both lie and totality. The fragmented narrative is important as it remains open and as it connects the reader to their own environment. While Donna J. Haraway, in framing *Always Coming Home* as 'postapocalyptic', views it as a form of instruction for how we 'can avert inexorable disaster and plant the conceivable germ of possibility for multispecies, multiplacetime recuperation before it is too late', Le Guin's text resists that idea of instruction.[108] While the novel can certainly be viewed as postapocalyptic, it resists the charge that such fictions are, in Claire Colebrook's words, fundamentally anthropocentric, where 'by imagining the end of the world in heroic terms as a battle we must win, it becomes impossible to think of extinction in anything but a narcissistic manner'.[109] Rather than recuperation, Le Guin emphasizes continuance, and the continued value of engagement. *Always Coming Home* does not represent a germ of possibility so much as an open, incomplete, fragmented series of possibilities: even as the novel can be read as utopian, it also suggests that what is perceived as a clear strand may only be a knot. Le Guin's rush of stories suggests a necessary reframing of how we understand narrative; in highlighting the importance of attention and of noticing above that of interpretation, she foregrounds the idea of fragmentation as possibility.

While *Always Coming Home* has largely been examined as a work of science fiction, despite challenging both of those terms, this strategy of fragmentation as possibility can also be found in a contemporary novel such as Olga Tokarczuk's *Flights*. The novel is polyvocal and temporally and spatially disparate: its 116 unnumbered fragments, ranging from a few sentences to the length of a long short story, encompass the diaristic musings of an apparently autobiographical narrative 'I', the story of Kunicki, a man whose wife and child disappear for three days on a Croatian island, and letters from Josefine Solimon, who petitions Francis I, Emperor of Austria, for the body of her father, whose body has been stuffed and put on display, among many others. The stories of Kunicki and Josefine are the closest the novel comes to traditional narratives, and are presented in chronological order, but they often disappear from the text for over a hundred pages. Rather than creating an immersive literary experience, Tokarczuk and her various focalizers draw attention to new ways of knowing. In one of the 'I' sections the narrator pauses in an airport to listen to a series of impromptu lectures from travelling academics, one of whom argues 'that it is impossible to build a consistent cause-and-effect course of argument or a narrative with events that succeed each other casuistically and follow from each other. [...] Constellation, not sequencing, carries truth.'[110] While the narrator grows distracted and bored by this lecture, and soon moves on, this is as close to a technical explanation of her novel as Tokarczuk provides. The idea of constellation is similarly developed by Louise Green, who argues that constellation is a useful method 'because it offers a way of resisting the apparent immediacy of the concept of nature.'[111] Drawing on the work of Adorno and Benjamin, Green proposes a non-hierarchical approach that 'can encompass different orders of knowledge.'[112] This non-hierarchical, synechdochic movement between the part and the whole, between the specific and the universal, is central both to Tokarczuk's work and to this book: rather than telling a story that ends in easy resolution, constellation is a way of keeping multiple elements at play while also emphasizing the importance of their juxtaposition and assemblage.

While Tokarczuk's narrator laments that 'there's too much in the world', *Flights* as a whole tries, much like Le Guin's novel, to capture an entire civilization in parts.[113] At the same time, however, the narrator asks if they are 'doing the right thing by telling stories[.] Wouldn't it be better to fasten the mind with a clip, tighten the reins and express myself not by means of stories and histories, but with the simplicity of a lecture [...]?'[114] The frequent historical scenes of taxidermy and archiving, combined with more contemporary focalizers' discussions of travel and placelessness, foreground the problem of fixity: while knowing something only as it is preserved divorces it from the centrality of encounter, moments of encounter themselves are difficult to enunciate. The novel's Polish title, *Bieguni*, is related to wandering; Tokarczuk discusses the English title as evoking 'movement in general, a shifting perspective and a bit of madness.'[115] The frequent shifts between times, places, narrative forms and characters are disorientating: the stories must function in themselves, but are often incomplete and difficult to parse.

At the start of the novel, the 'I' describes their 'Recurrent Detoxification Syndrome', a version of 'Mean World Syndrome' where patients become obsessed with media coverage of horrendous news. In particular, the 'I' is drawn to 'all things spoiled, flawed, defective, broken'; they take comfort in cabinets of curiosity and anatomical museums, where they can see fragments in terms of ruins and errors.[116] Later, the 'I' discusses being a 'perfect observer', which they exemplify by discussing the experience of looking into apartment windows in Holland, watching the different people therein:

> Standing off to one side. Seeing on the world in fragments, there won't be any other one. Moments, crumbs, fleeting configurations – no sooner have they come into existence than they fall to pieces. Life? There's no such thing; I see lines, planes and bodies, and their transformations in time.[117]

This passage faces one of twelve maps inserted in the text, in this case listed as 'Chinese map (1984)'. The maps are drawn from *The Agile Rabbit Book of Historical and Curious Maps*, published in 2005, and vary as widely in time and space as the narrative elements. The narrator's air of disinterested observation, where the world is seen as a series of disconnected fragments, parallels that of many of the characters discussed in Chapter 1, and supports Kate Marshall's claim that contemporary fiction can respond 'to the pressures of the larger anthropocenic imagination by staging its own temporality within increasing time scales and geologies'.[118] In placing themself as an outside observer of human experience and history, the 'I' can reflect on larger temporal and spatial frameworks without feeling implicated or complicit. In this sense, the 'I' can be seen as an updated version of Benjamin's flâneur, the 'spectator and depicter of modern life', moving through urban spaces with an air of detached observation.[119] The novel in this sense can be seen as cosmopolitan, in emphasizing detachment from a local community in favour of multiple attachments, or emphasizing the relation between rupture and reassemblage.[120] Like Teju Cole, both in his novel *Open City* and his non-fiction writing, the narrator is interested in 'what is everywhere but is everywhere slightly different'.[121] Yet even in comparison to the contemporary examples of flânerie associated with Cole and W.G. Sebald, Tokarczuk's narrator is particularly opaque: they lack not only gender and name, but there is little reason, other than novelistic tradition, to assume that the narrating 'I' is the same in each fragment where they appear. The observing self operates at a substantial remove from the world, and can only observe.

While the reader might be tempted to take this 'I' as particularly central to the novel, especially given that the very first fragment is titled 'Here I Am', other perspectives are available. In a long section where the nameless main character is referred to solely as 'she', Tokarczuk presents an idea of life that parallels Conway's monadism, as discussed above: 'life on this planet gets developed by some powerful force contained in every atom of organic matter. [...] There are no errors.'[122] Fragmentation can be seen either in terms of ruin and preservation or as a state of continual being; it is equally tied to death and life. Near the novel's end, after an interlude where the 'I' reasserts, as in the first fragment, 'I'm here', a fragment presents the origin of a new species, creatures 'that have already conquered all continents and almost every ecological niche'. Initially described as 'airborne anemones' travelling in packs, the creatures are revealed to be 'plastic bags open[ing] up a whole new chapter of earthly existence, breaking nature's age-old habits'.[123] Plastic bags are no longer seen as 'a passive object of reclassification' or a simple sign of environmental pollution that might evoke feelings of disgust or shame; instead, Tokarczuk raises the possibility, in Gay Hawkins's words, that 'plastic bags might move us or enchant us'.[124] This is one of the only explicit discussions of environmental issues in the novel, and can be seen as either fanciful or parodic. In placing it near the novel's end, Tokarczuk might suggest a reframing of the human concerns that have occupied most of the novel. Yet it is only one fragment of many, and to read it as conclusive would be misleading. As Krzystof Hoffman argues, the novel invites a 'catastrophe of interpretation' in the sense both of a 'requirement to abandon the habits of closure, of obtaining a coherent interpretation' and, at the same time, of providing 'a disruption on a well-planned route', recalling the word's original etymology.[125] Much like Le Guin's text, *Flights* poses a series of ends and catastrophes, whether personal, social or environmental, in a framework of possibility. While for the narrator, and many of the other characters, fragmentation speaks to ruin, and what is left behind, for the reader it generates new combinations and ideas.

Tokarczuk herself argues that the form of her novel is typical of Central European literature:

> It is a completely different approach to storytelling. Such a narrative is scattered and non-linear and is revealed as a type of paradox. Chance itself is a driving force for events. I believe the preference for the fragmentary nature associated with the narratives of Central European writers is stronger than among writers in any other place.[126]

While Tokarczuk's work is undoubtedly rooted in Central European traditions, its formal similarity to Le Guin's novel is notable. Both novels, which might be considered examples of the maximalist fragment discussed in Chapter 3, combine multiple fragments not in order to tell one story, but to suggest that there is no one story that can be told. Both use fragments to speak both to ruin and completion. Both gesture towards environmental crisis without seeking to explain it. It is not simply that there is no one way to tell the story of the modern world, or of the Anthropocene: in their temporal and spatial multiplicity, the novels question the idea of modernity altogether. Understanding human entanglement with the world requires radically rethinking ideas of sequencing, causality and emplacement.

These similarities may be coincidental, and yet such coincidences and chance encounters are central to my own thesis and methodology. The act of gleaning suggests both curation and contingency: the selection of elements or objects is a conscious choice, but it is not the only choice that can be made, and the material gleaned is that which comes to hand. Gleaning, as Varda emphasizes, is in part focused on material that has been discarded or abandoned; her film showcases not only gleaners as they move through fields after a harvest, but foragers who find what they can in the refuse of agricultural markets, or in trash left on the side of the road. Gleaning is not only an act of assemblage but transgression, and operates on the boundaries of legality. Gleaning also involves acts of relinquishment: the very material that is taken up may also be discarded. I employ the idea of gleaning because it foregrounds ideas of immanence and encounter, and the way that rather than stipulating a pre-existing relation between subject and object it emphasizes the co-constitution of humans and the material environment, as I explore in more detail in Chapter 2.

I also wish to suggest, however, that this form of gleaning can be taken as a model of contemporary critical practice. The echoes between Varda, Jamie, Hildyard, Spahr, Jetñil-Kijiner, Le Guin and Tokarczuk illustrate, I believe, a central and under-examined thematic and formal focus in contemporary writing. The passages I have selected from these texts support the argument that fragmentation is not simply an aesthetic fashion or a principle of disruption in itself, but meaningful, and suggest a new way to think about concepts such as the Anthropocene. Yet, especially in the case of Le Guin and Tokarczuk, the quotations I have used are gleaned from a much larger piece of work, and are those that seemed particularly significant to one individual on a particular day. This book, like all critical writing, emerges from myriad encounters with texts, and has been clarified by many conversations with colleagues and friends. It has been written in a very particular time and space: rather than seeing this work from a remote, authoritative position, my interpretation has been shaped by my own walks along the sea front and by my own worries and anxieties at a time of planetary turmoil. The work has shaped me as much as I have shaped the work. If this is a common, if under-examined, process in literary criticism, it is important to foreground in the writing of this project. Working with fragmentary or non-linear texts places the reader as the creator of meaning, as they find ways to connect individual fragments into a larger story, or to resist that temptation.[127] At the same time, however, the emphasis on contingency and accident in these texts mean that isolating a particular passage or moment as explanatory is to run the risk of missing the point altogether. These texts resist interpretation at the same time that they invite it: this tension is central to my account of how contemporary writing faces the environment.

C. Fragmentary encounters

As the examples above suggest, *New Forms of Environmental Writing: Gleanings and Fragmentation* concerns texts from a broad geographical range and a much narrower temporal one. The texts discussed below have been published since 2007, one of the possible dates for both 'Anthropocene' and 'cli-fi' entering public consciousness, and the majority have been produced in the last five years. As the discussion of fragmentation above suggests, the fragment as a form is in no way new, and has been a sign of literary modernity for two centuries at least. Yet I wish to argue that in the context of the Anthropocene, the fragment, variously defined, takes on new connotations, and provides a new way of thinking of temporal and spatial questions of human and more-than-human life. As such, I will for the most part not be discussing work that might conventionally fall under the rubric of 'climate fiction', such as novels by Barbara Kingsolver, Maggie Gee or Jeanette Winterson. While Winterson especially does make use of fragmentary form, I wish to avoid reiterating the arguments made by Adeline Johns-Putra, Adam Trexler, Astrid Bracke and many others: rather than examining how novels portray climate change, that is, I am interested in how climate change, and other ideas of the human-environment relation, is refracted in texts that emphasize a much smaller scale. The texts discussed below frame human-environmental encounters at the level of the individual, or many individuals, and any discussion of Anthropocenic scale cannot lose sight of the primacy of individual encounter. This approach also allows a blurring of boundaries between ideas of climate crisis, environmental devastation and local encounters with what might still be called the natural world, as well as questions of human violence and loss. Humans move in, react to and shape their environment in many ways: focusing on fragmentary perspectives permits a more integrated approach that avoids presenting environmental concerns as, in effect, someone else's problem. This is, in part, a retort to Amitav Ghosh's claim, quoted in the Prologue, that climate change has too often been relegated to genre fiction, as well as to Kim Stanley Robinson's argument that 'if you want to write a novel about our world now, you'd better write science fiction, or you will be doing some kind of inadvertent nostalgia piece; you will lack depth, miss the point, and remain confused.'[128] Rather, I would argue that confusion and an apparent lack of depth are productive approaches to understanding or representing our world now: both approaches are necessary and productive, and the insular, fragmented, incomplete or individualistic perspective is as valuable an approach to questions of environmental crisis as is found in texts working on a much larger temporal and spatial scale.

While considerations of the relation between individual and planetary scales are often based in particular environmental encounters, they also gain complexity when placed in a broader social and literary context. As such, this book considers texts from multiple languages and cultures, albeit with an emphasis on works produced in English in the UK and North America. I draw particular attention to works by Scottish writers, including Jamie, Helen McClory, Karine Polwart and Ali Smith, in part because they write from or in relation to the part of the world I know best. However, I resist the temptation to ascribe national characteristics to the work I describe: rather, I believe that studying the sometimes surprising commonalities between works from different traditions reveals new complexities. Likewise, while I focus on novels in Chapters 1 and 3, I also discuss works of poetry, memoir and performance to demonstrate both the flexibility and centrality of the model I am proposing. These cultural and generic emphases are partly in accordance with the limitations of space and my own interests as a researcher, but also illustrate the larger point made above: gleaning, as critical practice, emphasizes a series of connections that are no less meaningful because they are in some sense arbitrary. The novel, or the extended prose text, offers a particularly useful opportunity to examine fragments not in isolation, but as they are juxtaposed, connected and brought into constellation. If, as Jacqueline Rose claims, 'literature remains [...] the place where, as part of the ever more urgent bid to change the world, the unthinkable can still be written and heard', I argue that the fragmentary text is a way of privileging voices, perspectives and thoughts that counter dominant narratives.[129] This book cannot claim to offer an overview of every text that responds to the challenges of the Anthropocene: instead, by placing a selection of texts in sometimes surprising conjunction, it emphasizes those elements of relinquishment, rhythm and chance displayed in Varda's film.

The texts discussed here also can be seen under a rubric of contemporary women's writing, which may seem like an unusual delimitation, given that the concerns of climate change and the Anthropocene are certainly not experienced only by women.[130] The reasons for this focus are twofold. Firstly, if, as Justyna Kostkowska argues, 'fragmentation [has] a powerful ethical and political value of destabilizing the structures of power and domination'; this value can coherently be placed in a tradition of women's writing, including the work of writers from marginalized genders, and feminist thought.[131] Focusing on women's writing does not replicate an essentialist form of ecofeminism where, in Val Plumwood's words, it is 'only women (and perhaps only certain properly womanly women) who can know the mysterious forest' or 'a reign of women [is] the answer to the earth's destruction and to all the other related problems'.[132] Rather, it is a way to emphasize how the environmental fragment in contemporary writing by women is part of a tradition of critique of explanatory narratives associated with Enlightenment ideas of reason and classification. As Spahr writes with Joshua Clover, discourses of the Anthropocene often fail to understand that concept 'as itself constituted by compelled differentials and unfreedoms at every stratum'.[133] Discussions of the Anthropocene, and Anthropocenic literature, must be rooted in anti-sexist, anti-Colonial and anti-racist perspectives and methodologies. Following Rosi Braidotti, whose work is discussed at greater length below, we need to reject 'the residual universalism of a wounded and panic-stricken Eurocentric Anthropocene, and [challenge] the extent to which it upholds all too familiar power hierarchies'.[134] While not all of the work below can be seen as responsive to liberation struggles, I argue that the fragment remains a central form of resistance to dominant narratives, and narratives of domination.

Secondly, if closely related, working on fragmentation in contemporary women's writing permits an emphasis on what Colebrook calls 'the classically feminist question of the *scale of the personal*'.[135] Such claims can be seen, for instance, in Donna Haraway's argument that '[f]eminist objectivity is about limited location and situated knowledge, not about transcendence and splitting of subject and object'.[136] Modern feminist and ecofeminist thought has frequently emphasized the value of situated, bodily knowledge, which leads to an engagement with the ethics of encounter. As I have argued above, environmental awareness or consciousness stems not from theoretical abstraction but lived experience: gleaning does not only draw attention to the object that is gleaned, but to the gleaner. As discussed at greater length in Chapters 2 and 3, individual encounters with place, object and text reshape the world.

The book's three chapters follow a line of expansion that echoes the pattern established in this Introduction, moving from a focus on isolated individuals to more polyvocal narratives and concluding with longer fragmentary fictions. The arc of the book is from individual encounter to multispecies entanglement and finally to ideas of community and care. Chapter 1 draws on affect theory and ecofeminist thought to discuss five narratives of solitary women who feel, to varying extents, removed from both human and more-than-human communities. The novels discussed, by Elin Willows, Helen McClory, Abi Andrews, Claire-Louise Bennett and Sara Baume, feature protagonists who experience the world at a remove and must develop individual strategies of attention. Each novel explores the tension between separation and engagement, and emphasizes the importance of the individual encounter.

The works discussed in Chapter 2 develop this idea of encounter in relation to classificatory systems, performance and memory. The texts considered, by Elizabeth-Jane Burnett, Melissa Eleftherion, Tanya Tagaq and Karine Polwart each, in different ways, can be seen as assemblages and as reflecting the act of assembling. They call attention to the interplay between past and present, between scientific and embodied ways of knowing, and to the importance of audience in the reception of the work. Each of these texts examines, in different ways, how the self is both textually and environmentally entangled, and raises the question of how artwork can lead to change.

Chapter 3 returns to the question of the archive, as discussed in the Prologue, in order to examine ideas of storytelling and intertextuality. Works by Jenny Offill, Bhanu Kapil, Valeria Luiselli, Poupeh Missaghi and Lucy Ellmann, as well as nonfiction accounts of gleaning, are used to challenge dominant conceptions of narrative and explanatory frameworks. These works focus on how the fragment juxtaposes presence and absence, and is used to invoke a nuanced form of care. The Conclusion develops these ideas further, specifically in the context of Ali Smith, to examine how all of the works here can be discussed in relation to a model of literature as a constellation of fragmentary forms, along similar lines to the work by Le Guin and Tokarczuk discussed above. Throughout the book, themes of relinquishment and collection, rhythm and repetition, and bodily encounter are emphasized to suggest that fragmentary knowledge functions as a critique of universalizing discourses. These books challenge conceptualizations of nature or the environment as a knowable whole, and show that formal and thematic multiplicity represents a crucial form of environmental engagement. Rather than a specifically ecological form of writing, these texts not only look at a variety of environments, but also suggest the importance of the text as an environment itself.

The texts discussed below, in part because of their recent publication, may not be familiar to all readers. Rather than making the claim that they should be seen as particularly representative in themselves, however, or that they form a new canon, I explore how encounters with both familiar and less well-known work can reshape our understanding of the relation between literature and the world. As Green explains her own work, 'the assembly of diverse material, fragments that cannot be accounted for in a single system of knowledge, [...] allows for an arrangement of personal experience, public desires, political events, and concrete scientific data'.[137] Working between and through different forms and traditions highlights the role of the reader as gleaner, and suggests the essentially interactive relationship between text and world. Likewise, while this book draws on a wide range of affect theory, posthuman philosophy, ecofeminism and related theoretical models, I do not wish to suggest that the literary texts simply express or instantiate these ideas. Rather, both literary and theoretical examples, if such a distinction can be made, are put into a constellation through which they can illuminate each other.

As Colebrook states in a slightly different context, Anthropocenic thought 'always require[s] a concrete fragment of this world, *lived as fragment,* to enable us to think beyond the fragment, *not towards some unifying whole, nor to some completion of fulfilment of the present,* but to a time in which a different mode of synthesis, beyond our own, might be possible'.[138] This book, in short, takes the challenge of this idea seriously in order to examine how fragmentary texts, and fragmentary lives, can lead to new forms of synthesis and possibility. All environmental thought, I argue, begins in the localized encounter and is known in moments of gleaning and relinquishment. These diverse texts, seen in constellation, suggest new ways of knowing and experiencing the world, and of challenging hierarchical and unifying abstractions in favour of multiplicity, diversity and difference.

Notes

1   Kathleen Jamie, *The Overhaul* (London: Picador, 2012), 3.

2   Alexandra Campbell, 'Atlantic Exchanges: The Poetics of Dispersal and Disposal in Scottish and Caribbean Seas', *Journal of Postcolonial Writing* 55.2 (2019): 205–6.

3   Kathleen Jamie, *Findings* (London: Sort Of, 2005), 59.

4   David Farrier, *Anthropocene Poetics: Deep Time, Sacrifice Zones, and Extinction* (Minneapolis: University of Minnesota Press, 2019), 51. See also Deborah Lilley's argument that Jamie 'uses social, political, historical and ecological ways of seeing to disclose the traces, the means and the effects of these points of intersection between the human and the non-human'. Deborah Lilley, 'Kathleen Jamie: Rethinking the Externality and Idealisation of Nature', *Green Letters* 17.1 (2013): 19. My reading of these passages is also indebted to a long series of conversations with Alan Macpherson when we taught Jamie's work together.

5   Campbell, 'Atlantic Exchanges', 205. Jamie's work can be seen as part of a lineage of environmental writing, reaching back to Rachel Carson, that highlights the connection between terrestrial humans and the sea in order to encourage marine environmentalism. See Stacy Alaimo, 'Oceanic Origins, Plastic Activism, and New Materialism at Sea', in *Material Ecocriticism*, ed. Serenella Iovino and Serpil Oppermann (Bloomington and Indianapolis: Indiana University Press, 2014), 186–203. The Edinburgh-born poet Maya Chowdhry frames similar questions in a broader geographic spectrum, especially in the poem 'Albatross', where the titular bird is 'cursed by your q-tips, skylanders-happy-toys, styrofoam' and dies filled with plastic bottles. Maya Chowdhry, *Fossil* (Leeds: Peepal Tree, 2016), 15.

6   Jamie, *Overhaul*, 50.

7   Rachel Falconer, 'Midlife Music: *The Overhaul* and *Frissure*', in *Kathleen Jamie: Essays and Poems on Her Work*, ed. Rachel Falconer (Edinburgh: Edinburgh University Press, 2015), 160. Louisa Gairn, in the same collection, emphasizes how in *The Overhaul* Jamie 'links together the non-human world with the intimate emotional and embodied world of the family and the self'. Louisa Gairn, '"Connective Leaps": *Sightlines* and *The Overhaul*', in *Kathleen Jamie: Essays and Poems on Her Work*, ed. Rachel Falconer (Edinburgh: Edinburgh University Press, 2015), 139. Likewise Daniel Weston argues that Jamie's writing develops 'a concept of place that recognizes a braiding or entwining of human and non-human forces in the determination of landscape'. Daniel Weston, *Contemporary Literary Landscapes: The Poetics of Experience* (London and New York: Routledge, 2016), 143.

8   Jamie, *The Overhaul*, 50.

9   'brak', *The Online Scots Dictionary*. https://www.scots-online.org/dictionary/scots_english.php [Accessed 21 July 2020].

10 Jamie, *Findings*, 49.

11 Jamie, *Findings*, 60.

12 Jamie, *Findings*, 69.

13 Pippa Marland's extensive reading of this essay positions the doll's head as both 'a necessary corrective to the possible transcendental associations of the orb of white quartz' and a reminder of the 'dissonant kinship of plastic materials'. Pippa

Marland, 'The Gannet's Skull versus the Plastic Doll's Head: Material "Value" in Kathleen Jamie's "Findings"', *Green Letters* 19.2 (2015): 129.

14 Susan Stewart, *On Longing: Narratives of the Miniature, the Gigantic, the Souvenir, the Collection* (Durham and London: Duke University Press, 1993), 145.

15 Sarah Ensor, 'The Ecopoetics of Contact: Touching, Cruising, Gleaning', *ISLE: Interdisciplinary Studies in Literature and Environment* 25.1 (2018): 160.

16 Nicole M. Merola, '"*what do we do but keep breathing as best we can this /minute atmosphere*": Juliana Spahr and Anthropocene Anxiety', in *Affective Ecocriticism: Emotion, Embodiment, Environment*, ed. Kyle Bladow and Jennifer Ladino (Lincoln and London: University of Nebraska Press, 2018), 28. See also Christopher Arigo, 'Notes toward an Ecopoetics: Revising the Postmodern Sublime and Juliana Spahr's *This Connection of Everyone with Lungs*', *How2* 3.2 (2008): asu.edu/pipercwcenter/how2journal/vol_3_no_2/ecopetics/essays/arigo.html [Accessed 13 August 2020].

17 Juliana Spahr, *The Transformation* (Berkeley: Atelos, 2007), 59.

18 Spahr, *Transformation*, 217.

19 Spahr, *Transformation*, 17.

20 Spahr, *Transformation*, 116.

21 Spahr, *Transformation*, 34–5.

22 Meliz Ergin, *The Ecopoetics of Entanglement in Contemporary Turkish and American Literatures* (Cham: Palgrave Macmillan, 2017), 171, 173. See also Rachel Zolf, 'Rachel Zolf on Juliana Spahr: The Transformation Thinks Wit(h)ness', *Lemon Hound*. lemonhound.com/2014/11/14/rachel-zolf-on-juliana-spahr-the-transformation-thinks-withness/ [Accessed 27 July 2020].

23 Spahr, *Transformation*, 47.

24 Lucy Bell, 'Recycling Materials, Recycling Lives: Cardboard Publishers in Latin America', in *Literature and Sustainability: Concept, Text and Culture*, ed. Adeline Johns-Putra, John Parham and Louise Squire (Manchester: Manchester University Press, 2017), 76, 80.

25 Juliana Spahr, *That Winter the Wolf Came* (Oakland, CA: Commune Editions, 2015), 61.

26 Agnès Varda, *The Gleaners and I* (Ciné-tamaris, 2000), *The Agnès Varda Collection Volume 1* (Artificial Eye, 2009).

27 Cole Swensen, *Art in Time* (New York: Nightboat, 2021), 20.

28 Swensen, *Art in Time*, 22.

29 Agnès Varda, *The Gleaners and I: Two Years Later* (C.N.D.P, Canal+, Centre National du Cinéma et de l'Image Animée and Ciné-tamaris, 2002), *The Agnès Varda Collection Volume 1* (Artificial Eye, 2009).

30 See also Samantha Walton's discussion of the importance of tactility, and hands, as a way of understanding the natural world in Nan Shepherd's writing. Samantha Walton, *The Living World: Nan Shepherd and Environmental Thought* (London: Bloomsbury, 2020), 68.

31 Michelle Keown, 'Children of Israel: US Military Imperialism and Marshallese Migration in the Poetry of Kathy Jetnil-Kijiner', *Interventions: A Journal of Postcolonial Studies* 19.7 (2016): 939, 938.

32 Kathy Jetñil-Kijiner, *Iep Jāltok: Poems from a Marshallese Daughter* (Tucson: University of Arizona Press, 2017), 5, 80.

33 Susan Stanford Friedman examines these poems, and the collection as a whole, in terms of 'scalar planetarity', drawing attention to the way the poem's spacetime melds Indigenous craft, with images of the island, the womb and the planet. These questions of scale and spacetime are further developed in Chapter 2. Susan Stanford Friedman, 'Scaling Planetarity: *Spacetime* in the New Modernist Studies – Virginia Woolf, H.D., Hilma af Klint, Alicja Kwade, Kathy Jetñil-Kijiner', *Feminist Modernist Studies* 3.2 (2020): 140.

34 Kathy Jetñil-Kijiner, 'Dome Poem Part III: "Anointed" Final Poem and Video': kathyjetnilkijiner.com/dome/poem-iii-anointed-final-poem-and-video/ [Accessed 2 August 2020].

35 Kathleen Jamie, *The Bonniest Company* (London: Picador, 2015), 41.

36 Kathleen Jamie, *Jizzen* (London: Picador, 1999), 42.

37 Kathleen Jamie, *Surfacing* (London: Sort Of, 2019), 1.

38 Jamie, *Surfacing*, 4.

39 Jamie, *Surfacing*, 244.

40 Jamie, *Surfacing*, 245.

41 Spahr, *Transformation*, 128.

42 Ursula K. Le Guin, *Dancing at the Edge of the World: Thoughts on Words, Women, Places* (New York: Harper & Row, 1990), 168–9.

43 See Will Steffen, Paul J. Crutzen and John R. McNeill, 'The Anthropocene: Are Humans Now Overwhelming the Great Forces of Nature', *Ambio: A Journal of the Human Environment* (2007): 614–21.

44 Dipesh Chakrabarty, 'The Climate of History: Four Theses', *Critical Inquiry* 35.2 (2009): 197–222; Bruno Latour, *An Inquiry into the Modes of Existence: An Anthropology of the Moderns* (Cambridge, MA: Harvard University Press, 2013).

45 Farrier, *Anthropocene Poetics*, 7.

46 Astrid Bracke, *Climate Crisis and the 21st-Century British Novel* (London: Bloomsbury, 2018), 16.

47 Timothy Clark, *Ecocriticism on the Edge: The Anthropocene as a Threshold Concept* (London: Bloomsbury, 2015), 13, 9.

48 Michael Tavel Clarke and David Wittenberg, 'Introduction', in *Scale in Literature and Culture*, ed. Michael Tavel Clarke and David Wittenberg (Cham: Palgrave Macmillan, 2017), 12.

49 Meehan Crist, 'Is It OK to Have a Child?', *London Review of Books* 42.5 (5 March 2020): 12.

50   Michael Egan, 'Culture and Collapse: Theses on Catastrophic History for the Twenty-First Century', in *The Discourses of Environmental Collapse: Imagining the End*, ed. Alison E. Vogelaar, Brack W. Hale and Alexandra Peat (London and New York: Routledge, 2018), 28.

51   Kathryn Yusoff, *A Billion Black Anthropocenes or None* (Minneapolis: University of Minnesota Press, 2018), 1–2.

52   Isabelle Stengers, *In Catastrophic Times: Resisting the Coming Barbarism*, trans. Andrew Goffey (Lüneberg: Open Humanities Press/Meson Press, 2015), 9–10.

53   The term 'Anthropocene' has been supplanted with a number of terms that attempt to represent this responsibility, most commonly the Chthulucene, the Capitalocene and the Plantationocene, many of which are discussed below. While many of these terms have important functions, they have also generated something of a hydra effect; as of May 2020, Franciszek Chałczyk was able to pinpoint ninety-one variants, and there are doubtlessly more in use by the time you read this. For the sake of simplicity, 'Anthropocene' will be used throughout this book except in relation to particular thinkers. Franciszek Chałczyk, 'Around the Anthropocene in Eighty Names – Considering the Urbanocene Proposition', *Sustainability* 12 (2020), article 4458: doi:10.3990/su12114458 [Accessed 5 August 2020].

54   Alexa Weik von Mossner, 'Science Fiction and the Risks of the Anthropocene: Anticipated Transformations in Dale Pendell's *The Great Bay*', *Environmental Humanities* 5 (2014): 205.

55   Pieter Vermeulen, *Literature and the Anthropocene* (London and New York: Routledge, 2020), 25–6. Vermeulen argues that literature is a valuable tool for confronting the Anthropocene in four ways: in terms of the relation between narrative and meaning, the relation between affect and aesthetics, the power of the imagination, and the focus on 'questions of writing, inscription, and action' (p. 20). While the focus of this book is largely on the first two questions, all four of them present a useful framework.

56   Adam Trexler, *Anthropocene Fictions: The Novel in a Time of Climate Change* (Charlottesville: University of Virginia Press, 2015), 233; Adeline Johns-Putra, *Climate Change and the Contemporary Novel* (Cambridge: Cambridge University Press, 2019), 39.

57   Johns-Putra, *Climate Change*, 45.

58   Maggie Kainulainen, 'Saying Climate Change: Ethics of the Sublime and the Problem of Representation', *Symplokē* 21.1–2 (2013): 109.

59   Kainulainen, 'Saying Climate Change', 111.

60   Axel Goodbody and Adeline Johns-Putra examine the popularity and function of climate change fiction, from its roots in the 1970s to its rise in the past two decades, noting that while the term 'cli-fi' was coined in 2007, it became particularly commonplace in 2013. Axel Goodbody and Adeline Johns-Putra, 'The Rise of

the Climate Change Novel', in *Climate and Literature*, ed. Adeline Johns-Putra (Cambridge: Cambridge University Press, 2019), 229–45.

61 A similar approach has been suggested both by Vermeulen, who emphasizes themes of 'excess, waste, entanglement, and multiplicity' (Vermeulen, *Literature*, 155), and Clark, who in a discussion of Timothy Morton highlights ideas of disjunctiveness (Clark, *Ecocriticism*, 184). Neither critic, however, is able to devote space to ideas of fragmentation as such.

62 Daisy Hildyard, *The Second Body* (London: Fitzcarraldo, 2017), 9. Hildyard's first novel, *Hunters in the Snow*, is largely concerned with different forms of political and family history, but ends with the word 'Anthropocene', in some ways setting the stage for her more recent work. Daisy Hildyard, *Hunters in the Snow* (London: Vintage, 2014), 296.

63 Hildyard, *Second Body*, 13.

64 Hildyard, *Second Body*, 25.

65 See Timothy C. Baker, *Writing Animals: Language, Suffering, and Animality in Twenty-First-Century Fiction* (Cham: Palgrave Macmillan, 2019) for an extended account of non-human animals in Ridgway's and Baume's fiction.

66 Stewart, *On Longing*, 20–1.

67 Hildyard, *Second Body*, 33.

68 Marc Botha, 'Precarious Present, Fragile Futures: Literature and Uncertainty in the Early Twenty-First Century', *English Academy Review* 31.2 (2014): 3.

69 Philippe Lacoue-Labarthe and Jean-Luc Nancy, *The Literary Absolute: The Theory of Literature in German Romanticism*, trans. Philip Banard and Cheryl Lester (Albany: State University of New York Press, 1988), 40.

70 Quoted in Lacoue-Labarthe and Nancy, *Literary Absolute*, 43.

71 Lacoue-Labarthe and Nancy, *Literary Absolute*, 44.

72 Isaiah Berlin, *The Hedgehog and the Fox: An Essay on Tolstoy's View of History*, ed. Henry Hard, 2nd ed. (Princeton: Princeton University Press, 2013), 1.

73 Hugh Warwick, *A Prickly Affair: The Charm of the Hedgehog* (London: Penguin, 2010).

74 Anne Conway, *The Principles of the Most Ancient and Modern Philosophy*, trans. and ed. Allison P. Coudert and Taylor Corse (Cambridge: Cambridge University Press, 1996), 17. See Timothy C. Baker, 'Harmonic Monads: Reading Contemporary Scottish Fiction through the Enlightenment', *Scottish Literary Review* 9.1 (2017): 95–113 for a more extensive discussion of the relation between the Enlightenment monad and contemporary literature. For a more thorough discussion of Conway's relation to the scientific revolution, and an argument for the monistic vitalism on Conway and Leibniz as anti-exploitative, see Carolyn Merchant, *The Death of Nature: Women, Ecology, and the Scientific Revolution* (New York: HarperOne, 1990), 253–68; Carolyn Merchant, *Science and Nature: Past, Present, and Future* (New York and London: Routledge, 2018), 157–68.

75 Gottfried Wilhelm Leibniz, *Discourse on Metaphysics and Other Essays*, trans. and ed. Daniel Garber and Roger Ariew (Indianapolis and Cambridge: Hackett Publishing, 1991), 76.

76 Jane Bennett, *The Enchantment of Modern Life: Attachments, Crossings, and Ethics* (Princeton and Oxford: Princeton University Press, 2001), 77.

77 Walter Benjamin, *Illuminations*, trans. Harry Zohn, ed. Hannah Arendt (New York: Schocken, 1969), 92–3.

78 Walter Benjamin, *The Arcades Project*, trans. Howard Eiland and Kevin McLaughlin (Cambridge, MA, and London: Belknap/Harvard University Press, 2002), 417.

79 Charles Baudelaire, *The Painter of Modern Life and Other Essays*, trans. and ed. Jonathan Mayne (New York: Da Capo, 1986), 13.

80 Camelia Elias, *The Fragment: Towards a History and Poetics of a Performative Genre* (Bern: Peter Lang, 2004), 2. Matthew Griffiths further argues that Modernist fragmentation is particularly 'useful in establishing the relationship between human agency and climate change'. Matthew Griffiths, *The New Poetics of Climate Change* (London: Bloomsbury, 2017), 37. While I follow Griffiths's emphasis on the relation between formal aesthetics and ecocritical approaches, however, as well as his interest in reading texts that are not explicitly related to environmental crisis, this book focuses on contemporary work in which Modernist aesthetics are just one of a wide range of formal possibilities.

81 Rebecca Varley-Winters, *Reading Fragments and Fragmentation in Modernist Literature* (Eastbourne: Sussex Academic Press, 2019), 174, 1.

82 Maria Stepanova, *In Memory of Memory: A Romance*, trans. Sasha Dugdale (London: Fitzcarraldo, 2021), 51.

83 Terry Tempest Williams, *Erosion: Essays of Undoing* (New York: Farrar, Straus and Giroux, 2019), xi.

84 Moyra Davey, *Index Cards*, ed. Nicolas Linnert (London: Fitzcarraldo, 2020), 49, 182.

85 Kate Zambreno, *Appendix Project: Talks and Essays* (South Pasadena, CA: Semiotext(e), 2019), 66.

86 Zambreno, *Appendix*, 21.

87 Annika Arnold, *Climate Change and Storytelling: Narratives and Cultural Meaning in Environmental Communication* (Cham: Palgrave Macmillan, 2018), 38.

88 Antonia Mehnert, *Climate Change Fictions: Representations of Global Warming in American Culture* (Cham: Palgrave Macmillan, 2016), 55.

89 Ursula K. Le Guin, 'Deep in Admiration', in *Arts of Living on a Damaged Planet*, ed. Anna Tsing et al. (Minneapolis and London: University of Minnesota Press, 2017), M16.

90 Jesse Oak Taylor frames the relation more strongly, claiming that literature 'now seeks to *change* human/climate relations rather than simply recording or

dramatising them'. Jesse Oak Taylor, 'Atmosphere as Setting, or, "Wuthering" the Anthropocene', in *Climate and Literature*, ed. Adeline Johns-Putra (Cambridge: Cambridge University Press, 2019), 34. Fiction as a form of engagement with climate change tends to be cautionary, but can also foster climate change denialism, as in the work of Michael Crichton; see Eline D. Tabak, 'Science in Fiction: A Brief Look at Communicating Climate Change through the Novel', *RCC Perspectives* 4 (2019): 97–104; Greg Garrard et al., *Climate Change Scepticism: A Transnational Ecocritical Analysis* (London: Bloomsbury, 2019).

91   Lawrence Buell, *The Future of Environmental Criticism: Environmental Crisis and Literary Imagination* (Malden, MA and Oxford: Blackwell, 2005), 46. Original italics.

92   Anna Lowenhaupt Tsing, *The Mushroom at the End of the World: On the Possibility of Life in Capitalist Ruins* (Princeton and Oxford: Princeton University Press, 2015), 37.

93   Anna Lowenhaupt Tsing, *Friction: An Ethnography of Global Connection* (Princeton and Oxford: Princeton University Press, 2005), 5.

94   Tsing, *Friction*, 104.

95   See Thom van Dooren, Eben Kirksey and Ursula Münster, 'Multispecies Studies: Cultivating Arts of Attentiveness', *Environmental Humanities* 8.1 (2016): 2–3.

96   Alexis Shotwell, *Against Purity: Living Ethically in Compromised Times* (Minneapolis and London: University of Minnesota Press, 2016), 100, 106.

97   Tsing, *Mushroom*, 142.

98   Tsing, *Mushroom*, 155.

99   See, for instance, Leanne Shapton's *Guestbook*, which combines photographs and other visual artefacts with brief descriptive texts to tell a sequence of remarkably unsettling stories that resist all the comforts of linear or causal narrative. Leanne Shapton, *Guestbook: Ghost Stories* (London: Particular Books, 2019).

100 Ursula K. Le Guin, *Always Coming Home: Author's Expanded Edition*, ed. Brian Attebery (New York: Library of America, 2019), 7.

101 Le Guin, *Always*, 583.

102 Le Guin, *Always*, 72.

103 Chris Ferns, *Narrating Utopia: Ideology, Gender, Form in Utopian Literature* (Liverpool: Liverpool University Press, 1999), 217.

104 Le Guin, *Always*, 624–5.

105 Le Guin, *Dancing*, 44–5.

106 Anna Lowenhaupt Tsing, *In the Realm of the Diamond Queen: Marginality in an Out-of-the-Way Place* (Princeton: Princeton University Press, 1993), 254. Perhaps the clearest example in recent fiction of this principle is the novel *Noopiming: The Cure for White Ladies*, by the Michi Saagiig Nishnaabeg writer Leanne Betasamosake Simpson, whose work is discussed further in Chapter 2. Told in a series of fragments by a series of seven human and non-human characters, the

novel displaces the reader's sense of a stable material reality, becoming 'a singular organism propelling itself to someplace else whose magnificence is bigger than the sum of its parts'. Leanne Betasamosake Simpson, *Noopiming: The Cure for White Ladies* (Minneapolis and London: University of Minnesota Press, 2021), 231. In a time of ongoing colonial violence, the fragment is the best, or only, path to survival and care. Simpson's novel is an excellent counterpart to Le Guin's, and deserves far more consideration than I have given it here; its relegation to a single footnote reflects both its publication late in the writing of this book and my own hesitancy in pronouncing on a text I am not wholly qualified to discuss.

107 Elyce Rae Helford, 'Going "Native": Le Guin, Misha, and the Politics of Speculative Literature', *Foundation* 71 (1997): 77–88.

108 Donna J. Haraway, *Staying with the Trouble: Making Kin in the Chthulucene* (Durham and London: Duke University Press 2016), 213.

109 Claire Colebrook, 'The Future in the Anthropocene: Extinction and the Imagination', in *Climate and Literature*, ed. Adeline Johns-Putra (Cambridge: Cambridge University Press, 2019), 266. Colebrook draws attention to the aligned comforts of fragmentation and extinction elsewhere: see Claire Colebrook, *Death of the Posthuman: Essays on Extinction, Vol. 1* (Ann Arbor: Open Humanities Press, 2014), 28.

110 Olga Tokarczuk, *Flights*, trans. Jennifer Croft (London: Fitzcarraldo, 2017), 83. Sinéad Gleeson similarly uses ideas of constellation in her series of fragmentary memoirs on embodiment, illness and pain to discuss the way a constellation of influences and relations offers the possibility of a parallel life. Sinéad Gleeson, *Constellations: Reflections from Life* (London: Picador, 2019), 189.

111 Louise Green, *Fragments from the History of Loss: The Nature Industry and the Postcolony* (University Park, PA: Pennsylvania State University Press, 2020), 7.

112 Green, *Fragments*, 6.

113 Tokarczuk, *Flights*, 65.

114 Tokarczuk, *Flights*, 219.

115 Stephen Rojcewicz, 'Olga Tokarczuk: The Right Time and Place', *Delos* 35.1 (2020): 104.

116 Tokarczuk, *Flights*, 22.

117 Tokarczuk, *Flights*, 188.

118 Kate Marshall, 'What Are the Novels of the Anthropocene? American Fiction in Geological Time', *American Literary History* 27.3 (2015): 523–4.

119 Chris Jenks, *Visual Culture* (London: Routledge, 1995), 146.

120 Rebecca L. Walkowitz, *Cosmopolitan Style: Modernism beyond the Nation* (New York: Columbia University Press, 2006), 9; Berthold Schoene, *The Cosmopolitan Novel* (Edinburgh: Edinburgh University Press, 2010), 21.

121 Teju Cole, *Blind Spot* (London: Faber, 2016), 200.

122 Tokarczuk, *Flights*, 293–4.

123 Tokarczuk, *Flights*, 403.

124 Gay Hawkins, 'Plastic Materialities', in *Political Matter: Technoscience, Democracy, and Public Life*, ed. Bruce Braun and Sarah J. Whatmore (Minneapolis: University of Minnesota Press, 2010), 119–20. An even more fanciful version can be found in Company Non Nova's *L'apres-Midi d'Un Foehn*, a 25-minute ballet for plastic bags (staged at Summerhall as part of the Edinburgh Fringe Festival in August 2013), which remains one of the most beautiful performances I have ever seen.

125 Krzystof Hoffman, 'Always towards, Not From-to: Experiment, Travel, and Deconstruction in *Flights* by Olga Tokarczuk', trans. Dorota Mackenzie, *Czas Kultury* 3 (2019): 116–17.

126 Quoted in Hikaru Ogura, 'On New Travel Literature and Central Europe as a Blank Space: Notes on Olga Tokarczuk's Novel *Bieguni* and Her Lecture Series in Japan', in *Perspectives on Contemporary East European Literature: Beyond National and Regional Frames*, ed. Kenichi Abe, Slavic Eurasian Studies 30 (Sapporo: Slavic-Eurasian Research Center, 2016), 14.

127 Although a monograph, by its nature, is structured in a way that frames the author as an arbiter of meaning, and emphasizes linear argumentation, I have tried, where possible, to subvert that, both by the presence of introductory constellations, where I put multiple voices in play, and by a greater emphasis on quotation than I might favour in other works. Looking at these texts both in isolation and in the way they come together is central to the project of this book, but I wish, where possible, to avoid the singular voice of authority that is often associated with such projects.

128 Kim Stanley Robinson, *Green Earth* (New York: Del Rey, 2015), xii.

129 Jacqueline Rose, *On Violence and On Violence against Women* (London: Faber, 2021), 158.

130 In particular, Jon McGregor's two most recent novels, *Reservoir 13* and *Lean Fall Stand*, offer many formal and thematic parallels with the works discussed below.

131 Justyna Kostkowska, *Ecocriticism and Women Writers: Environmentalist Poetics of Virginia Woolf, Jeanette Winterson, and Ali Smith* (Basingstoke: Palgrave Macmillan, 2013), 73.

132 Val Plumwood, *Feminism and the Mastery of Nature* (London and New York: Routledge, 1993), 8.

133 Joshua Clover and Juliana Spahr, 'Gender Abolition and the Ecotone War', in *Anthropocene Feminism*, ed. Richard Grusin (Minneapolis and London: University of Minnesota Press, 2017), 160.

134 Rosi Braidotti, *Posthuman Knowledge* (Cambridge: Polity, 2019), 83.

135 Claire Colebrook, 'We Have Always Been Post-Anthropocene: The Anthropocene Counterfactual', in *Anthropocene Feminism*, ed. Richard Grusin (Minneapolis and London: University of Minnesota Press, 2017), 1.

136 Donna J. Haraway, *Simians, Cyborgs, and Women: The Reinvention of Nature* (New York and Abingdon: Routledge, 1991), 190.

137 Green, *Fragments*, 29.

138 Claire Colebrook, 'Archivolithic: The Anthropocene and the Hetero-Archive', *Derrida Today* 7.1 (2014): 34. Original emphasis.

1

'Edgeless, Sparking, Alone': Solitude and attention

Introductory constellation

A woman finds herself alone. Perhaps she is staying in her room, watching television and taking medication, 'watch[ing] summer die and autumn turn cold and gray through a broken slat in the blinds'.[1] Maybe she is travelling, disorientated, stuck in a 'suppurating suburban hotel to where she herself doesn't know how to get'.[2] Either way, she is alone: most of her encounters are meaningless, and most of her gaze is occupied by the corners of a room she does not particularly like. Maybe she will, like the protagonists of Ottessa Moshfegh's *My Year of Rest and Relaxation* and Eimear McBride's *Strange Hotel*, respectively, find some way out. At the close of Moshfegh's novel the narrator is stopped from throwing herself in front of a train, and the world comes alive. She enters Central Park and finds that '[t]hings were alive. Life buzzed between each shade of green, from dark pines and supple ferns to lime green moss growing on a huge, dry gray rock. Honey locusts and ginkgos aflare in yellows'.[3] Then again, two pages later, the novel's last, it is 9/11, and the final, unexpected and slightly queasy, image of the novel is of someone, beautiful and 'wide awake', diving off of the North Tower.[4] At the end of McBride's novel the narrator grows weary of her own narration, of 'relentlessly reshuffling the deck of pseudo-intellectual garble which, if I'm honest, serves the solitary purpose of keeping the world at the end of a very long sentence'.[5] She seems to embrace the present moment, although the reader can only guess the resolution if they have figured out the code by which the protagonist marks her assignations in the lists of cities that fill the text's pages.

In both novels selfhood is marked by absence and disengagement: the protagonists are unrooted in the world, disconnected from others and themselves, nameless and distracted. As Jhumpa Lahiri writes at the end of *Whereabouts*, her own account of a woman alone: 'Because when all is said and done the setting doesn't matter: the space, the walls, the light. [...] These words are my only abode, my only foothold.'[6] The world of the text is the only world that these characters can fully experience. While they are granted happy endings, of a sort, it is clear that these are not endings at all, but simply changes. All three novels, like those discussed below, can be seen as accounts of individual failure to engage or cope with large-scale questions of planetary or societal transformation. These are not, strictly speaking, stories of environmental encounters or climate change. They do, however, highlight a sense of malaise and disappointment that is an important feature of much contemporary fiction, and in particular of contemporary women's writing.

Deirdre Heddon, writing in the context of Scottish performance studies, has usefully highlighted the importance of disappointment in the context of climate crises and planetary environmental changes. Too often, she suggests, critics have promulgated 'an over-determined focus on "ecology" as a modality of *affective encountering*', which she terms 'ecospectation'.[7] A recurrent focus on embeddedness and integration suggests that all an ecologically minded artwork might need to do is to point towards a relation between humans and the environment, and go no further. Ecological awareness and environmental entanglement, in such cases, can be framed simply as a matter of individual assertion. Heddon is instead interested in what happens when the work does not cohere, or a sense of relation is not fully established. While the texts discussed below – Elin Willows's *Inlands*, Helen McClory's *Flesh of the Peach*, Sara Baume's *A Line Made by Walking*, Claire-Louise Bennett's *Pond* and Abi Andrews's *The Word for Woman Is Wilderness* – are more ecologically focused than Moshfegh's and McBride's, they similarly highlight ideas of incoherence and failed relationality. These novels can be read in terms of ecospectation or, more generally, affect defined in terms of encounter.

Offering one of the clearest definitions of affect theory to date, Gregory J. Seigworth and Melissa Gregg stipulate that affect can not only be seen in terms of the rhythms and modality of encounter, but

> *accumulates* across both relatedness and interruptions in relatedness [...]. Affect marks a body's *belonging* to a world of encounters or a world's belonging to a body of encounters but also, in *non-belonging*, through all those far sadder (de)compositions of mutual in-compossibilities.[8]

If affect can be seen as the body's ability both to affect and be affected, Seigworth and Gregg also draw attention to the failure of that affect. The tension between belonging and non-belonging, or between expectation and disappointment, is central to each of these novels. Fragmentary form allows for a focus on rupture and removal as much as incorporation and engagement. The experience of 'the world's violent and sad intractability', in Linda Tym's words, leads to both negative affect and the apparent loss or flatness of affect.[9] Rather than stories of 'nature healing', where a traumatized or despondent subject achieves some form of clarity through their engagement with the natural world, these fragmentary fictions present feelings of both disassociation and overwhelmedness that often characterize responses to the Anthropocene. The feelings of restlessness, despondency, irritation and fatigue displayed in these novels are closely aligned to what Sianne Ngai calls 'stuplimity', or the combination of astonishment and boredom that greets the sublime. Stuplimity, she writes, 'reveals the limits of our ability to comprehend a vastly extended form as a totality': rather than being rewarded with a 'transcendent feeling', these protagonists are characterized by their 'phobic strivings "away from" rather than philic strivings "toward"'.[10] Rather than experience opening up into something transcendent, the protagonists are left only with words, and failures of expressiveness.

Each of these novels exhibits what Heather Houser calls 'discord' in her discussion of ecosickness in contemporary American fiction. As Houser explains, ecosickness is not limited to discussions of environmental toxicity, but rather is a 'pervasive dysfunction': it simultaneously highlights the co-constitution of the human and more-than-human worlds and the dissolution, both conceptual and material, of 'the body-environment boundary through sickness'.[11] Focusing on ecosickness is thus a way to challenge normative, able-bodied and neurotypical accounts of environmental perception. Houser uses the idea of discord to approach the same feelings of irritation discussed by Ngai. Defining discord as 'a disturbance between immediate response and experience-shaped evaluation', she suggests that 'seeing irritates expectations for the "ideal" appearance and functions of bodies and ecosystems, and this discordant feeling in turn positively irritates understanding of these domains'.[12] Discord and irritation thus become a way to rethink the relation between bodies and environments.

Houser's account of discord, like Heddon's discussion of disappointment, is rooted in the early work of Timothy Morton and his formulation of 'ecology without nature'. As Morton has influentially argued, nature writing, and accounts of 'Nature' as an identifiable whole, has tended to present 'nature as an object "over there" – a pristine wilderness beyond all trace of human contact – [and] re-establishes the very separation it seeks to abolish'.[13] Nature becomes a sublime object that is placed at a remove, outside of human concerns: nature is a monolithic whole that is defined as everything the human is not. Heddon's account of disappointment, Ngai's stuplimity and Houser's discord all seek to combat this Enlightenment account of a nature at once transcendent and distant, drawing attention to the range of affects that come with any environmental encounter. In focusing on negative affects, they challenge ideas that encounters with nature are fundamentally transformative, and instead demonstrate the complexity of such encounters.

The novels discussed in this chapter each draw attention, in different ways, to this range of affects and emotional responses, including, as in Moshfegh's and McBride's novels, the apparent absence or flatness of affect.[14] McClory's and Baume's texts, especially, can be seen in terms of Morton's initial definition of 'dark ecology', which he defines 'not [as] a hippie aesthetic of life over death, or a sadistic-sentimental Bambification of sentient beings, but in a "goth" assertion of the contingent and necessarily queer idea that we want to stay with a dying world'.[15] Recognition of complicity is not an abdication of responsibility: instead, these novels take a cautious response to a broken, or breaking, world, highlighting negative emotions and affects, precisely to demonstrate the centrality of continued engagement with that world. In particular, by emphasizing ideas of solitude and disconnection, they allow for new perspectives on questions of care, attention and engagement with a more-than-human world. Solitude, in each of these novels, allows for the protagonists to interrogate cultural assumptions about the natural world, and to find new ways of placing themselves within their environments, or finding, in Sarah Bernstein's words, 'dignity in [their] loneliness'.[16] While the novels discussed in this chapter are more linear than the texts discussed in the remaining chapters, they also reveal how an aesthetic of fragmentation can be aligned with both cultural and individual precarity and anxiety.

The homogeneity of the novels' protagonists – all are young white women, mostly middle-class, often artists – also deserves consideration, particularly through the lens of ecofeminism. Early ecofeminist accounts are often criticized as binaristic and essentialist, and specific to European conceptions of both gender and nature.[17] In *Woman and Nature: The Roaring Inside Her*, for instance, Susan Griffin frames male desire for knowledge as a form of control, such that 'because of his knowledge, this land is forever changed'.[18] Women and nature, however, are fundamentally aligned, even sisters, such that the earth 'reveals stories to me, and these stories are revelations and I am transformed. Each time I go to her I am born like this. Her renewal washes over me endlessly'.[19] Men impose while women discover and, as such, only women have the capacity to be transformed. For modern ecofeminists such as Sherilyn MacGregor, Griffin's work can be summarized as stipulating 'women's unique connections to nature and their possession of "natural" moral goodness'.[20] Although written with very different aims, Griffin arguably reiterates the dualistic constructions of woman/man and human/nature that later ecofeminists such as Val Plumwood, among many others, seek to challenge.

In calling to break down the dualism of reason and nature, Plumwood seeks to unpick assumptions about the identification of women with nature, the perceived inferiority of both, and the corresponding association of men with reason and culture. Denise Riley has influentially dated this binary separation to the late seventeenth century, where women 'became an ambulant Nature', while nature is coded as particularly feminine.[21] This dualism, Plumwood argues, leads to an 'alienated account of human identity in which humans are essentially apart' from nature, resulting in a 'failure to commit ourselves to the care of the planet'.[22] Instead, she proposes a relational model of selfhood where the flourishing of both nature and non-human others is related to human thriving. Freya Mathews similarly argues for a model of flourishing that 'requires that we be represented within our culture as selves-within-wider-selves, and that our actions be generated in the light of this awareness of our role in the scheme of things'.[23] While critics such as Catriona Sandilands have argued that social ecofeminisms such as Plumwood's still rely on a 'constructed location of women *as if* they were closer to nature', despite their recognition that an association between women and nature is a social construction, the relational model constructed by Plumwood and Mathews allows for a more nuanced view of the relation between selfhood and the wider world, including a more open construction of nature itself.[24]

While the complex history of ecofeminist approaches cannot be fully discussed here, many of the most prominent theories combine emphases on difference and care, allowing for what Stacy Alaimo calls, following Judith Butler, 'constant rifting': 'Feminist theories, politics, and fictions can travel beyond the false dichotomy of rejecting "nature" or valorizing the whole ideological package [to] destabilize the nature/culture divide.'[25] In later work Alaimo goes further to argue not simply for the destabilization of extant binaries and divisions, but for the formulation of an 'environmental ethics in which the flows, interchanges, and interrelations between human corporeality and the more-than-human-world' can be framed as an act of resistance.[26] Rather than simply aligning women with nature, contemporary ecofeminism challenges both categories, and the entire relational framework, to move towards a more nuanced account of how humans and non-human others inhabit the earth. Samantha Walton has more recently noted that while 'a false division between the human and "nature" has created the conditions for the Anthropocene', any meaningful response to our current crises 'demands a recognition that ecology has shaped and will determine the success of all rights and justice struggles, gender-based and otherwise'.[27] To that end, environmental and feminist thought can be framed in terms of intersection and solidarity. Lola Olufemi's feminist definition of solidarity, for instance, as 'a strategic coalition of individuals who are invested in a collective vision for the future', emphasizes the importance of 'mutual aid' and recuperation.[28] This sense of potential recuperation across species lines is central to much contemporary ecofeminism. Astrida Neimanis, for instance, argues that 'posthuman feminism provides understanding of bodies as operating simultaneously across different interpermeating registers': bodies, both human and more-than-human, must be understood in terms of both difference and what they hold in common.[29] Contemporary ecofeminism, and Anthropocene feminism, does not return to an overly essentialist discourse, in either praise or censure, but instead offers new models of relationality and care.[30]

I begin with Griffin's work, however, because as much as her argument is often grounded in an essentialist, dualistic framing, the form of her text privileges fragmentation and intertextuality. *Woman and Nature* is constructed from myriad fragments, often headed by epigraphs from a variety of authors: the quotation above is printed underneath a sentence from Simone Weil.[31] Topics range from Cartesian philosophy to cows, while the assorted fragments encompass poetry and prose, autobiographical accounts and philosophy, catalogues and aphorism. In praise of Griffin's work, Patrick D. Murphy writes that she 'exposes the monological character of masculinist normative discourses' through a 'postmodernist meta-narrative structure'.[32] Alaimo likewise highlights the way Griffin's text 'not only resists the imposition of order, but opens up paths of escape', even as she laments the presentation of a monolithic voice of women that is ultimately too utopian.[33]

Griffin's opening discussion of 'Matter', for instance, highlights repetition and the passive voice: 'It is decided that matter is transitory and illusory [...]. Matter is transitory and illusory, it is said. [...] It is decided that matter is passive and inert'.[34] The voice of received, and presumably masculine, authority, is itself passive and inert, capable only of repeating the same stale assertions. While Carolyn Merchant and Val Plumwood devote substantial space to charting the development of dualistic or mechanistic constructions of nature, particularly in the Enlightenment, Griffin takes this approach as given, and easily challenged: the presentation of masculinist philosophies in fragments divorced from any particular social or historical context allows for polemical critique. When she returns to 'Matter' in the text's final section she begins with italicized sentence fragments: '*Because we know ourselves to be made from this earth. See this grass. The patches of silver and brown. Worn by the wind.* [...] *Because we know ourselves to be made from this earth. Temporary as this grass.*'[35] Human, and specifically female, enmeshment in the earth can be asserted straightforwardly through a string of fragmented observations. There is no fundamental separation between fungi, bacteria, fish, blackbirds, plants and humans. The 'she' who speaks these passages, which dominate the book's final pages, represents all women, now able to see with their own eyes, free from masculine reason. This transformation is also personal, however: Griffin alternates between the italicized voice of 'she', presented in italics and fragments, and an 'I', represented in normal type and often in run-on sentences. The text ends with the I's Joycean, orgasmic declaration of oneness with the earth and all other creatures, anticipating Greta Gaard's contention that 'gender and eroticism are entangled with my love of this earth'.[36]

As much as Griffin's philosophical approach might now fairly be seen as outdated or essentialist, her work remains important for highlighting how textual experimentation becomes a way to challenge traditional constructions of both gender and nature. In refusing methodological contextualization or normative syntax and constructing a polyvocal, intertextual assemblage, Griffin shows that formal fragmentation is a way to rethink questions of interaction, or even separation, between body and nature. As Rosi Braidotti notes in a discussion of Luce Irigaray, these questions are often rooted in a history of feminist philosophy, where '[f]ragmentation of the self [is] woman's basic historical condition'.[37] The way fragmentation creates space for entangled multiplicities will be further discussed in the following chapters, but Griffin's work remains important here for illustrating how rethinking environmental encounter requires not only new conceptual tools, but also formal and aesthetic strategies.

While my argument hews more closely to Alaimo's approach than that of earlier ecofeminists, the concerns raised by Griffin remain germane to contemporary writing of and by women. As suggested by Moshfegh's text, and at much greater lengths by the work below, Griffin's model of unity and enmeshment in nature is no longer available: the world is already corrupted, perhaps has always been, and nature cannot be seen in terms of unity. One of the most perplexing scenes in recent fiction comes in the final sentences of Rachel Cusk's *Kudos*, the third volume of her autobiografictional trilogy beginning with

Outline. Throughout the trilogy, constructed as a series of episodic encounters, Cusk follows Virginia Woolf's suggestion that shorter, fragmented fiction can be seen as a productive form of women's writing, 'for interruptions there will always be'.[38] The encounters that fill the novels are rarely contextualized, but are treated as whole in themselves, while at the same time refusing explanatory metanarratives. As such, the trilogy can be seen in terms of the maximalist fragment discussed at the end of this book. The novel's protagonist, named only in passing, is often pictured in hotels, or at writing workshops, mainly in continental Europe, although sometimes at home in the UK. Despite this emphasis on a realist description of place and encounter, the trilogy generates a sense of unease. Sophie Collins begins her hybrid, fragmentary volume of poetry and essays *Who Is Mary Sue?*, for instance, with an account of reading Cusk's work, while not naming it:

> At the foot of these stories – at once ludicrously vague and full with detail – is a frayed hole, a conspicuous lack of identity in the very space that has most often been tasked with generating readerly incentive.
>
> Threadworms, stray hairs: loose threads surround the hole, invading it. They are disturbing: they are unruly, and they emphasise a persisting absence.[39]

Collins draws attention to the way Cusk's use of fragmentation is used not to create an assemblage, like the works discussed in Chapter 2, but to reveal an absence. Rather than portraying the protagonist as embedded in the world, these fragments reveal the failure of her integration.

In *Kudos*'s final pages there is a moment of apparent escape, where nature is briefly seen as a 'liberatory wilderness'.[40] Finishing a telephone call home, the narrator walks to the beach, both 'wild and strewn with litter', and happens across a group of mostly naked men, who turn to look at her 'like animals surprised in a grove'.[41] There is no clear nature/culture divide here: the beach is no less wild for being littered, while the humans seem to have no sovereignty. The narrator immerses herself in the sea, echoing, more positively, the end of Kate Chopin's *The Awakening*, and for a brief moment the novel seems to gesture towards the healing powers of nature and the possibility of oneness. Moments later there is a turn, however, where the protagonist sees a 'huge burly man' walking towards her as she swims:

> He came to a halt just where the waves broke and he stood there in his nakedness like a deity, resplendent and grinning. Then he grasped his thick penis and began to urinate into the water. The flow came out so abundantly that it made a fat, glittering jet, like a rope of gold he was casting into the sea. He looked at me with

black eyes full of malevolent delight while the golden jet poured unceasingly forth from him until it seemed impossible he could contain any more. The water bore me up, heaving, as if I lay on the breast of some sighing creature while the man emptied himself into its depths. I looked into his cruel, merry eyes, and I waited for him to stop.[42]

While the man does not stop, the novel does. If the narrator's irritation is not explicitly voiced, it is replaced by the reader's irritation at the way this anonymous male figure despoils both sea and story: after three volumes tracing an individual consciousness, the reader might expect more resolution than the appearance of a urinating man. If men are not aligned with reason here, they are still aligned with the power to dominate and disrupt. The narrator and the sea become one, subject to the whims of a godlike, if ridiculous, male power. The scene is not an allegory for the Anthropocene, nor a straightforward account of sexual power, but it gestures towards the way interruption is not only a positive act of reclamation, but can be forced upon the subject. Cusk suggests that the question of who tells a woman's story, and a story of the natural world, is still central to any contemporary imagining. If fragmentation can be seen as an answer to male dominance, whether in philosophical or physical forms, it can also be a sign of the inability of a woman to tell her own story, or have it be listened to. While nature may not offer respite, however, such scenes of dominance and threat, or human-made devastation, also suggest the importance of rethinking ideas of nature and the environmental encounter.

Cusk's combination of anger and passivity in this passage is paralleled in some of the texts discussed below, in combination with other affects. These five novels, however, are united not just in telling similar stories, but in indicating the importance of foregrounding affect in any depiction of a nature/culture divide, and women's encounters with the natural world. These are not simply stories of women immersing themselves in nature, but rather accounts of why such immersion may not be possible, even as it is still longed for. While texts in the following chapters, from a wider variety of cultural perspectives, emphasize new approaches to relation, these texts are important for the way they emphasize the fragility of relation, and its possible failure. The three sections of this chapter highlight a variety of intertwined areas of focus. Willows's and McClory's novels use fragmentary form to portray flat affect and the failure of integration. Nature is presented as an undifferentiated whole, or a transcendent other to which the protagonist has no access. Themes of grief and trauma in both novels reappear in Bennett's and Baume's novels, which also include a focus on material presence of non-human matter, whether physical objects or non-human corpses. Finally,

Andrews's novel critiques ideas of wilderness through a similar theoretical lens to the one I am using throughout this book, drawing on Anna Tsing, Donna Haraway and others. All of these novels are united in their focus on solitude and precarity, and in presenting fragmentary form as a way of thinking through the difficulty of environmental encounter. Comparing this narrow selection of novels by Swedish, Scottish, English and Irish authors, all first published between 2015 and 2018, demonstrates their thematic and formal continuity. While their conclusions are somewhat different, the similarity of their approaches demonstrates a prevalent and sometimes overlooked feature in recent fiction.[43]

A. Forms of remove: Elin Willows and Helen McClory

Elin Willows's *Inlands* and Helen McClory's *Flesh of the Peach* share a surprising number of formal, thematic and narrative features. Originally published one year apart, in 2018 and 2017 respectively, the novels depict a young woman's sojourns in a remote part of the world – northern Sweden and the southwestern United States – at the time of a failed relationship. The novels are both told in numbered fragments: *Inlands* is separated into eighty-four short chapters, most of which are broken into smaller fragmentary sections, while *Flesh of the Peach* is divided into 102 numbered chapters, alongside eight unnumbered chapters titled 'What She Would Spend Her Money On' and one called 'What She Would Say Later'. The sequential numbering of chapters is juxtaposed with frequent repetition of particular emotions and themes: both novels can be seen simultaneously as accounts of progress and stasis. Given that each revolves around a death, as well as the end of a relationship, the novels can easily be read in relation to theories of trauma and testimony: like many trauma texts, the narratives are 'composed of bits and pieces of a memory that has been overwhelmed by occurrences that have not settled into understanding or remembrance'.[44] Past and present appear as broken fragments that both reader and protagonist must seek to make coherent. The novels can particularly be positioned in terms of the relationship between place and trauma discussed by Anne Whitehead, who writes that the

> traumas of the recent past profoundly challenge our ability to position ourselves in relation to them or to find our bearings. The question of positioning that landscape evokes can be regarded as crucial within the current discourse of trauma, for all efforts to confront and remember the past must be preceded by a consideration of the perspective from which we, as belated witnesses, view the event.[45]

The difficulty in positioning is reflected in the frequent feeling of alienation the protagonists experience. *Inlands* opens with a fragmented discourse of place: 'In a place where people look at you. A place where it's apparent that I'm new.'[46] Before either place or character can be enunciated, Willows establishes a sense of unbelonging. The fragmentary syntax foregrounds this sense of displacement: in eliding the presumed 'I am' that would begin the first sentence, Willows illustrates the narrator's inability to connect herself with her place. The subject is already missing, unmoored. *Flesh of the Peach* similarly opens: 'She stood out on the observatory of the Empire State Building in failing light, felt delicate and underslept, and waited for something decisive to occur.'[47] Although the subject is more centred, grammatically, the protagonist is likewise poised in a liminal space, anxious for change, and again, unbelonging. Before either character can consider their traumas, or themselves, they begin with place. Place both defines and overwhelms individual character. As in Whitehead's analysis, perspective must be situated in physical space before it can be understood in psychological, human terms.

The characters' reactions to these moments, however, are very different. The unnamed protagonist of *Inlands* has moved to a small town in northern Sweden for a relationship that dissolves instantly on her arrival. She is not entirely sure why she stays. Her clearest enunciation of the situation is that while '[f]ailure is the wrong word', her choice to remain in the town opens her to a new form of reality, or unreality: 'There are so many different realities. My life now which has nothing to do with my previous life. What I experience here, which almost no one back home can understand. But nobody here either.'[48] Later she says again that it is 'as if my reality mainly feels unreal.'[49] Her condition evokes a combination of freedom and stasis that is similar to the repeating present of a fugue state, where a subject makes strange and unexpected trips in a state of obscured consciousness, at the same time that it is almost the opposite: rather than a compulsion to travel, she feels compelled to remain behind.[50] Her positioning in this remote village troubles the relation between real and unreal: it is not a form of escape from a previously established 'real' tied to her previous life so much as it is a rejection of dominant models of the 'real' overall. She is neither healed nor hindered in her removal, but rather is able to disengage from narratives of emotional progress and distress. Just as the village she lives in is unnamed and barely described, her own emotional and social life is based in repetition rather than forward movement: as in Ngai's analysis quoted above, she is always striving away from, not towards. The novel is not without incident, nor is the protagonist completely alone: she encounters other people at work, suffers a loss and, like Frankie in Baume's *A Line Made by Walking*, does learn to cry at the novel's end. The vast majority of the novel's short paragraphs and fragmented sentences, however, reiterate her feeling of removal from the world and a continuing sense of unreality, even as her 'self-chosen loneliness cross[es] over into unwanted isolation'.[51]

This combination of expectation and removal experienced in a state of mild confusion or disengagement might best be described as what Kathleen Stewart calls, in a discussion of Lauren Berlant, 'pockets'. As Stewart explains:

> A space opens up in the ordinary. There is a pause, a temporal suspension animated by the sense that something is coming into existence. The subject is called to a state of attention that is also an impassivity – a watching and waiting, a living through, an attunement to what might rind up or snap into place. The subject finds itself in a situation. Events and outcomes are immanent, unknown but pressing.[52]

Like Moshfegh's, McBride's and Cusk's narrators, Willows's protagonist is suspended but attentive, both to herself and to the world around her, even as she is unable adequately to explain her situation. She is, in Stewart's words, 'a subject troubled by the world's potential for event, and culling the current precarity of life itself into a new object of analysis'.[53] This attention to individual and collective precarity is perhaps the central theme of the novels discussed in this chapter. Each of the protagonists is precarious in the sense of being ungrounded: being connected neither to a particular place or to other people, they become unsteady in themselves. Here, however, precarity is not straightforwardly, in Anna Lowenhaupt Tsing's words, 'a state of acknowledgement of our vulnerability to others' nor, in Berlant's terms, 'a condition of dependency'.[54] Rather, especially in Willows's novel, precarity can be seen as an inability to acknowledge conditions of vulnerability or dependency. The protagonist's precarity is not fundamentally economic, as she easily finds a job, and not entirely social. Precarity is experienced as a form of remove and an inability to integrate oneself with others. It is known in terms of solitude and the rejection of emotional outpouring, or what Berlant would term 'flat affect'.

'Flat affect' is a term drawn from psychiatric discourse, where it signals 'a kind of emotional opacity in which affective display [...] has little range, intensity and mobility, and subjectively, it is not clear to the patient what the feelings they experience mean'.[55] Berlant expands this definition to focus on 'underperformativity', which deviates from melodramatic norms of expressive emotion to foreground 'the obstacles to immediate reading, without negating the affective encounter with immediacy'.[56] Flat affect is a mode of recession and apprehension: it is a way to avoid the excesses of emotional performance, deemed interpretable and sincere. Rather than responding to an event, the subject remains apprehensive of an event that 'remains to be sensed'.[57] The subject, in this sense, disassociates themselves from the present while remaining attentive to it. This is the condition of *Inlands*'s protagonist. Her declarations of emotional flatness often appear as straightforward disassociation: 'I'd like to remember my emotions. Like how something hurts the body, like how it feels to be pleasantly surprised, like the intense fatigue after something fun happens. But I don't remember, I don't feel.'[58] This suspended state is highlighted by appearing, in a paragraph of its own, at the start of a chapter, which then goes on to describe, in scenes familiar from the rest of the novel, the protagonist's ordinary domestic life. While she is divorced from her emotions, they remain an object of analysis. If her disassociation can easily be read as a sign of trauma, it is also, following Berlant, a refusal to engage with discursive forms that prioritize the intensity of private feelings and vulnerability. The narrator does not divulge her complicated patterns of grief either to other characters or to the readers: instead, her withdrawal can be seen as a form of defensive suspension. In the repeated, fragmentary assertions of emotional withdrawal and unreality, Willows constructs a dynamic of attentiveness and withdrawal that stands in stark opposition to traditional narratives of both overcoming trauma and immersion in nature.

The concept of 'nature' is central to *Inlands* without ever wholly being explicated. From the novel's opening, nature is poised as something remote, if still identifiable: 'Nature surrounds this place, but I still don't make it out there.'[59] Nature, at the start, is precisely where the narrator is not: it is not associated with women or with wildness, it is not transcendent or sublime and it is not indicative of human domination. It is simply what surrounds the narrator and the village. The narrator's changing relationship with this amorphous, undefined nature is key to understanding what emotional development the novel presents. Midway through the text she ventures into the surrounding nature and finds herself in a forest. Crucially, her journey, or her decision to enter the woods is not recounted: she is in bed looking at her phone, and then she is outside.

> The forest is an empty space. A breathing room, a break, even if it does not offer me anything like that. Yet. I guess that it will happen, that I'll end up coming across paths, that are not visible, aren't even paths, between the trees, know my way, place my feet in the right places and feel at home. Now I'm only visiting. […] Being here is to leave reality.[60]

This is perhaps the most undifferentiated account of a natural encounter to be found in any of the texts discussed in this book: nature is entirely divided from anthropocentric notions of reality. The protagonist does not see the forest as landscape to be viewed, or land as a place of work, and does not perceive individual trees or non-human others. There is, she says, 'just the forest and nature left now'.[61] If 'self-landscape encounters' can be seen 'to integrate a psychotherapeutically derived, relational conception of self with an ecological conception of place', Willows's novel is distinctive in refusing both principles.[62] The narrator seems to have little, if any, relational concept of self, nor a concept of ecological enmeshment. If the forest is a *terra nullius*, she is what we might call a *hominem nullius*. The insertion of 'yet' in the passage, however, indicates a possibility of renewal and engagement, an anticipation of an emotion that is yet to come, familiar from Berlant's and Ngai's affective theories. The forest is not home yet, but contains the possibility of home, or of a situated perspective. The narrator repeatedly raises this possibility: while other characters know 'the name of the plants that actually thrive here' in a way that she does not, she comes to see '[t]he place as a unity of nature and village. Me as an observer.'[63] Her longing for social and environmental integration is paralleled: the environmental encounter is not yet, but always still to come.

By the end of the novel, the narrator realizes that while she does not want to leave the village, she no longer wants to remain there either. She still sees nature as a blank whole, but not entirely alien to her: 'The silence of nature doesn't feel nearly as aggressive or insistent.'[64] If earlier in the novel she has lamented that 'nearby nature [...] does not open itself to me when I visit', by the end she has learned to venture out on the ice, as the local residents do, and to accept the freshness brought by the snow, in the absence of the more vibrant forms of life she is used to in the south.[65] This change is occasioned by both personal loss and acclimation: over the two years or so that the novel describes she comes to feel, if not at home, at less of a remove. If, as Tim Ingold claims, 'it is only because we live in an environment that we can think at all', Willows's novel raises the question of how one thinks of an environment at a point where thought itself is troubling or alien.[66] The narrator's reticence, combined with the repetition of fragmentary declarations which often refuse the familiar comforts of narrative and character development, can certainly be compared with recent novels such as Jeremy Cooper's *Ash before Oak*.[67] Willows's novel is particularly distinctive, however, in using fragmentary form to trace the desire for environmental encounter, rather than describing the encounter as such. The combination of stuplimity and underperformativity that mark the novel illustrates how fragmentary narratives can resist transformative encounter, and that turning away from the natural world at the very same time as being attentive to it is, in itself, a form of engagement.

These questions of reticence, irritation, anticipation and disappointment are more fully developed in *Flesh of the Peach*. The combination of the collapse of an affair with a married woman in New York and the death of her estranged mother in Cornwall presents the protagonist Sarah Browne with two possible paths, '[o]ne home across the pond, and another unseen in the American interior beckoning her'.[68] Sarah's journey to New Mexico is precipitated by the desire for '[u]ntempered land': she is attracted by internet images of 'an undulating golden plain and pine forested mountains' and sees, in this *terra nullius*, the possibility for individual renewal.[69] While, like Willows's protagonist, Sarah seeks remote places for their own sake, she is drawn to a familiar construction of the American southwest as uncharted territory, a fitting place for self-reinvention. Even on her journey west, however, Sarah begins to recognize 'her complicity intersecting at too many points': in her hotel room, listening to a report on war, she is reminded by the foreign correspondent of 'your obligation to a western world. To follow the narrative. The narrative of a book that is so often just the word death death death in the footnote'.[70] If her journey is only implicitly a colonial one, she still recognizes the prevalence of a construction of 'cultural landscape' that is in itself reductive.[71] To view the land as untainted wilderness would be to ignore her own complicity, while to dwell on that complicity would be to reassert her own agency at the expense of both Indigenous and non-human others. Her desire for reinvention and nature healing is both cynical and intentional: 'Sentimental. Spirit of the land rubbish. Touch the stones and ground the body, whatever. She was here for reinvention, and she was here to be self-sufficient and to get over those sorts of stupidities'.[72]

McClory's novel juxtaposes England and America to illustrate the tension between Sarah's desire to begin again, which she sees as endemic to the American wilderness, and her combined longing for and fear of stasis, which is tied to England and home. Midway through the novel, in a two-paragraph chapter, Sarah discusses the beauty of different landscapes in terms of both their possibility for renewal and her own, more negative, affective response, as she recovers from an episode of self-harm:

> The most beautiful place she had ever seen was a land crossed while under the influence of a blank disgust where love and her crimes were seared away from her. That most beautiful place, it was in Devon, passed through solo on foot pushing her bike, an open field with hard furrows and a pale sky and her breath ghosting in front. She took sterile to be best. When she forgot her body that was best. [...] This was the beautiful place. All around. A halo of it, separating her from her from herself. [...]

You are prepared to do away with yourself, but will avoid that for the time being while the kind English hills absolve you. Until they don't and you need a changed landscape. A fresh continent, if the old is that seeped through and encrusted. That's the point. To walk forever being forgiven by whatever's outside because your insides keep leaking your disgust and that holds you together.[73]

Nature is beautiful because it is both distinct from the self and envelops the self. Being alone in nature is, simply, a way not to die. While this is not a scene of pathetic fallacy, the open, undifferentiated land reflects Sarah's own flatness: it provides a way of seeing herself at the same time that she turns away from the self. Importantly, the fields in Devon are not wilderness, but worked agricultural land that is simply unoccupied: what defines the natural is the absence of embodied others, although the land is still marked by human activity. The landscape still, however, permits Sarah to attend to her surroundings in a new way. Earlier in the novel she has stated simply that '[t]his was the American desert and she had begun again, okay'.[74] The American desert and the English countryside both offer the prospect of renewal precisely because that is the script they have already been assigned: one goes into nature to find oneself because that is what people have already done. And yet, in this passage in Devon, and later scenes in New Mexico, renewal is also a process of self-estrangement. McClory's account is diametrically opposed to, for instance, Terry Tempest Williams's characterization of the American wilderness – in the specific context of New Mexico, Utah and Montana – as 'a place where we experience the quiet and sometimes violent unfolding of nature [... and] where we feel the rightness of relationships, where we sense our true place'.[75] In McClory's novel the natural world is perceived as sterile and dispassionate: it shows you the wrongness of your relationships, both with others and with yourself. Beauty is revealed not in terms of unity, but separation, not in terms of wonder, but disgust.

Although somewhat different in tone from the works on which Nicole Seymour focuses, *Flesh of the Peach* also raises Seymour's question: 'How are we *supposed* to feel in our relations with environments and living creatures [and] what happens when we do not feel that way?'[76] The novel's dedication to 'unlikeable women', reiterated in the final sentence of the acknowledgements, suggests the way McClory positions Sarah as interesting precisely because she has the 'wrong' reactions to both other people and environments. Her irritation with the world, and herself, does not neatly fit into an account of nature healing. Seymour draws on the work of Sara Ahmed to discuss how such reactions to environments can be seen in terms of queer discomfort. As Ahmed writes, '[d]iscomfort is hence not about assimilation or resistance, *but about inhabiting norms differently.* […] Queer feelings may embrace a sense of discomfort, a lack of ease with the available scripts for living and loving.[77] Sarah's discomfort with the world is not solely a feature of her queer sexual identity, but can also be seen in terms of queerness as bodily disorientation. She not only is never at home in a given landscape, but is unhomed in her body. Relationships with others, whether romantic or familial, are only a source of distress. Sarah's attempts at integration, including a disastrous affair with a man, illustrate the importance of 'staying with the trouble', in Donna Haraway's terms, or with the sense of discomfort and separation. As Haraway defines the phrase, staying with the trouble requires 'learning to be truly present, not as a vanishing pivot between awful or edenic pasts and apocalyptic or salvific futures, but as mortal critters entwined in myriad unfinished configurations of places, times, matters, meanings'.[78] While Sarah certainly can be seen to pivot between equally terrible pasts and futures, the novel's emphasis on unfinished configurations allows McClory to show how the 'available scripts' are always insufficient. Whether in presenting place in terms of placelessness and loss, or combining multiple genres – including Gothic horror – to signify unease with narrative conventions, McClory illustrates the necessity of focusing on discomfort and incompletion.

This discomfort can be seen not only in terms of environment and narrative, but physical embodiment. Ahmed draws on Drew Leder's argument that the body 'often seizes our attention most strongly at times of dysfunction' to argue that intense feeling, such as pain, recalls the self to the body.[79] In McClory's novel, bodily discomfort is frequently discussed in scenes of self-harm. While in the Devon scene quoted above Sarah is able to focus on the landscape in order to ignore her own physical pain, in America the sequence is reversed. Sarah begins by considering the post-apocalyptic nature of an imagined America, where a 'small neat cabin is the only comfort' before dismissing her 'vague immigrant thoughts' in favour of an unanchored list of perceptions that range from physical description to metaphysical musings, while emotions are not only '[h]ard to pick out' but '[p]ossibly parasitic worms'.[80] Like Haraway, she turns from questions of the past and future to focus on the present, but it is a present that is still marked by trauma. Attention to the world, without emotion, presages attention to the body, as she draws a knife against old scars. Physical pain is presented as a form of engagement, even as Sarah knows that it only offers a temporary respite. The act ultimately seems superfluous to her, as she wonders '[h]ow long can you calmly sit putting this gutty collage together sticking the bits back on when they fall off'.[81] At the same time, this 'American you', emotionless and bleeding, is still 'art', 'better than what she had ever attempted before'.[82] Sarah's act returns her attention to the body, and is indeed a process of self-transformation, that stems, in some ways, from her attention to the world. Crucially, however, this attention is not a form of integration or belonging, but one of separation. The 'American you' is one who resists narratives of redemption or forgiveness, and who does not see herself as part of nature. Whether in terms of sex, self-harm or the rehearsal of traumatic memories, each of Sarah's attempts to understand herself is also self-destructive. Staying with the trouble comes at great personal cost and, unlike in Haraway's formulation, cannot necessarily be seen as a model of engagement.

The novel does, however, present a form of solution. As the novel continues the timelines become increasingly muddied and the traumatic events multiply: Sarah grows increasingly unmoored. Towards the novel's end she attempts to leave America, her partner Theo and her self-conception behind, running away in an unpunctuated sentence:

> Make it basic take it naïve So long Theo So long golden So long grass So long old road tracks heading uphill So long the scents of vanillin and juniper and the flowers whose names you never learned [...] Goodbye knowing there is no end, and you straighten yourself freer under the rising sunlight painted on leaning mountains and you hope with weighted tenderness you will never see any of this again.[83]

The hope for self-renewal is based not in arrival, but departure. Like *Inlands*, *Flesh of the Peach* positions remove as a way of relating to the world. McClory's protagonist, however, is far more attentive than Willows's: while both resist the narrative scripts they have been handed, for Sarah this resistance is often a conscious choice, a refusal to adhere to conventions or ideas of the normative. Even as, in the novel's final pages, she returns home, in a scene peculiarly reminiscent of Daphne Du Maurier's *Rebecca*, Sarah's journey is one not of renewal, but petrification. In America she imagines coating the world with salt, preserving the trees, and the bacteria, fungi and beetles that eat them: 'She would kill and make perfect.'[84] This is the world she finds in Cornwall, where in the novel's final sentence she walks through 'the blackout shapes of trees and the mass of petrified flowerbeds'.[85] The preserved, dead world becomes, ironically, a source of renewal, or a form of relation. In refusing narratives of progress that rely on a transcendent or sublime view of the natural world, Sarah comes to fashion or encounter a world that she can understand and inhabit.

While both McClory's and Willows's novels can be read as trauma narratives, they upend the expected trajectory of recovery and incorporation. In many ways, perhaps surprisingly, both protagonists find themselves, at the start, asking the same questions Richard Mabey begins with in *Nature Cure*, his account of depression and nature healing: 'Where do I belong? What's my role? How, in social, emotional, ecological terms, do I find a way of *fitting*?'[86] Like Mabey, too, they find that they are unable to 'submit to nature' in order to see themselves as part of a larger whole; Mabey writes that when he attempts this form of integration he finds himself 'too disconnected': 'all I felt was a kind of rebuke, a clear statement that I was no longer part of that world'.[87] Instead, Mabey discusses, in cautious terms, how his 'cure', such as it is, comes from taking nature into himself through imaginative acts, which then allow a physical rejoining with the world. In McClory's and Willows's novels, on the other hand, this imaginative act is impossible, at least for most of the novels' durations. The protagonists may attempt to imagine themselves as part of the world, but this imagination is insufficient and, in the case of *Flesh of the Peach*, precipitates self-harm. The novels raise the question of what happens when these questions simply cannot be answered, and nature remains distant and lacks vibrancy. Instead, the novels highlight fragmentation, both of self and of narrative, as a form of engagement itself. Rather than becoming integrated in the world as a whole, the protagonists find what solace they can in moments of attention. Rather than tracing a journey from distress to healing, they show how distress can, itself, be a form of encounter. Nature, for the most part, remains other, and yet in considering their relation to the natural world, the protagonists are forced to confront their own identities. This form of fragmentary attention, coached in flatness and underperformativity, is also visible in Bennett's and Baume's texts, which focus much more specifically on the material object.

B. Fixing things: Sara Baume and Claire-Louise Bennett

The similarities between Bennett's *Pond* and Baume's *A Line Made by Walking* are even more pronounced than those between *Inlands* and *Flesh of the Peach*. In both texts, a young woman leaves Dublin to recuperate in a small Irish village. Direct attention to the physical world, whether in terms of domestic objects, in Bennett, or dead animals, in Baume, brings a form of understanding of the relation between embodiment and emplacement. Both texts are presented in fragmentary form. Bennett's work is told in a series of short stories, ranging from two sentences to seventeen pages, such that it is not entirely clear that it is a novel at all. While my analysis rests on the assumption that the protagonist of the stories is the same person throughout, and that the ordering of the stories presents a connected narrative, this is ambiguous in the text itself. Baume's novel is more linear in construction: the ten chapters are named after, and incorporate photographs of, ten dead non-human animals the protagonist Frankie finds and discusses. Each chapter, however, is filled with multiple narrative fragments, including Frankie's discussion of seventy-four separate artists, whose works she brings to mind in an attempt to understand her own experience. Both texts reach out to the world through intertextual reference, but also highlight attention to immediate physical surroundings, rather than a transcendent or removed view of nature, as a response to solitude and precarity.

Frankie, in *A Line Made by Walking*, is the most direct example of 'ecosickness' as discordance in the novels discussed in this chapter. While the death of her grandmother precipitates the grief that leads her to withdraw from the world, her concerns oscillate between the personal and the planetary. The novel's opening fragments discuss, in order: a newspaper photograph of 'the last "uncontacted" tribe'; the discovery of a dead robin which leads to Frankie's decision to create a photographic series 'about how everything is being slowly killed', along with a photograph of that robin; the anthropomorphic shapes of clouds; her solitude and her distrust of pathetic fallacy; the death of her grandmother; the felling of a tree; the work of the Dutch conceptual artist Bas Jan Ader; her domestic cleaning routine; her memories of her childhood; and the remembered sight of a jackdaw flying alongside a bus.[88] Past and present are completely intertwined, as are human and non-human experience. What unites these fragments, if anything, is Frankie's sense that they each in some way reflect both global death and her own solitude. At the end of the first fragment she expresses surprise 'that there are still. People. Out there. And almost immediately, I forget.'[89] Two pages later she is '[a]ll on my own. Except for the creatures'. By the eleventh fragment, she is able to situate herself:

> I understand how it can be that I am being killed when it is spring. I am being killed very slowly; now is only the outset. My small world is coming apart because it is swelling and there's no place for me any longer, and I still want to cry out but there's no point because I am a grown individual, responsible for myself.[90]

Her sense of this global, if gradual, death is framed in relation to watching Werner Herzog's documentary about the South Pole, *Encounters at the End of the World*, echoing the importance of Herbert Ponting's earlier South Pole documentary, *The Great White Silence*, in Andrews's novel. The film ends, as Frankie notes, with a 'deranged penguin' who wanders away from its peers towards the mountains. Frankie feels an overwhelming sense of empathy, commenting that: 'The world is wrong, and I am too small to fix it, too self-absorbed.'[91] Frankie both identifies with and laments the impossibility of taking responsibility for the penguin: its almost-certain death reminds her of her own, as well of her powerlessness to save even one animal. Photographing the remains of various non-human animals becomes a form of mourning and remembrance that also allows her to mourn herself.

Frankie clearly manifests the increasingly familiar association between awareness of climate change and negative emotional responses, most simply termed 'climate change anxiety'. While both national surveys and psychological studies have shown that a majority of respondents in many countries experience emotions of worry, grief and stress related to their awareness of climate change, this cannot easily be correlated to behavioural change.[92] Awareness of climate change can revive childhood fears of damage, undermine hope in the future and make the subjects feel that they are not cared for by their leaders, a combination which becomes, according to Sally Weintrobe, 'the biggest psychic barrier to facing the reality of global warming.'[93] Frankie's concerns are not limited to global warming, but encompass a range of behaviours common to contemporary life, from the exploitation of both human and non-human others to her own growing sense of alienation. She retreats into a narcissistic self-absorption, avoiding the world rather than engaging with it. Indeed, at the end of the novel she declares that she misled the reader, and herself, in her earlier description of the film, wanting 'to believe it was the deranged penguin because this is a better reason for being inconsolable, a so-much-more interesting and complicated and quixotic thing to be disturbed by than the banal reality.'[94] Whether she turns away from planetary-scale change or uses it to excuse her own emotions, however, she still places her own sense of precarity in relation to that of others. Her anxiety and grief for herself, her grandmother, the animals she finds and the animals she sees on television all work towards the central question posed by Allyse Knox-Russell, in response to Judith Butler:

> How do we grieve, or encourage others to grieve, that which does not fit into normative conceptions of the 'grievable', particularly when our unwillingness to acknowledge loss may be the greatest obstacle we face in advocating for social change?[95]

Frankie's identification with the penguin, and the animals she photographs, comes from the notion that neither is grievable, and yet both must still be grieved. She cannot acknowledge her own losses, or her removal from the world, and yet must do so in order to move onwards.

Frankie's solution, like that presented in many of the texts discussed in Chapters 2 and 3, is attention as a form of care. Attention is a form of attentiveness that recognizes the world as it is, without judgement or intrusion. Attention is not an insertion of the self, nor an active withdrawal; instead, attention can be framed as a way of being with the world.[96] The novel is filled with fragments where Frankie simply observes the plants and animals around her, noting their differences. This is as much of an artistic practice as her recollection of more canonical artworks:

> I make an effort to appreciate even the most ubiquitous bits of nature. Not just the exquisite infestations of white blossom, but the elegance of each black thorn. Not just the petal-packed dandelion buds, but the hollow stalks from which their yellow bursts. Not just the swallows and song thrushes, but every different kind of crow as well.[97]

Attending to the world in its multiplicity and difference is a way to anchor the self. Frankie's self-worth, or self-conception, comes from these acts of observation, which do not enmesh her in the world so much as they demonstrate that she is still capable of caring about the world at all. Frankie's attention echoes that of Ray, the protagonist of Baume's earlier *Spill Simmer Falter Wither*, who defines himself, in part, through his gleaning. He celebrates his 'junk-treasures': the exoskeletons of crabs, driftwood, bass lures and glass pebbles he has found on the beach, and 'all the dead things' he gathers in his garden.[98] These objects do not suffice, however; Ray comes to 'realise that all these particles of matter don't matter, that not one is capable of expressing grief'.[99] If Frankie does not glean to the same extent, her narrative reinforces the idea that observation is itself a form of collection. She refuses to kill animals in order to use them for her photographs, but instead sees the significance of each animal in their encounter. Both Frankie and Ray see their acts of gleaning and observation as a way to reclaim the natural world, and integrate themselves within it, at the same time that they recognize the futility of their actions. In Ahmed's words, the texts exemplify both the act of bringing 'objects to life in their "loss" of place' and 'the failure of gathering to keep things in their place'.[100] Gleaning, as presented by Baume, is not a simple act of preservation or containment; instead, as in Ahmed's formulation, attending to the world means attending to loss, to the failure of creatures and things to cohere or to tell a story. It means accepting loss and grief as organizational principles, and so redefining what it means to attend. Both characters look to what has been discarded or ignored as a way to tell a story about the world, even as they inevitably make themselves central to that story.

As much as Frankie explicitly sees her animals as signs of the 'sublime', however, and frequently speaks of the countryside around her as 'my wilderness', the natural world is always marked by human interference.[101] Midway through the novel she sees a fox, a 'birthday gift from the capricious countryside', and is momentarily elated until she realizes that there is 'something not-quite-right about it, something misshapen': the fox has a tin can stuck on its head.[102] Like the birds Kathleen Jamie finds on the beach, the very creature that signifies the wild is shaped by human actions and refuse. The fox reappears later in the chapter, twisted and 'writhing with flies': the tin can has obscured its vision, so that it has been struck by a car and killed.[103] Before she photographs the fox, Frankie removes the can from its face, as an act of restoration, and yet the implication is already raised that her actions are as much a sign of human interference as the car and the can. While Sarah in *Flesh of the Peach* argues simply that an 'animal stupid enough to die by reversing car is a piteous thing', Frankie's reaction is more complex.[104] Throughout the novel her reactions to the dead animals she finds combine pity and empathy. A dead, mangled hare leads her to think that '[t]his is how it will be for all of us [...]. Even the ones who do no harm.'[105] The inevitability of human destruction affects not only non-human animals but also individual humans: mourning these creatures thus becomes a way of mourning for herself. Following the work of Iris Murdoch and Simone Weil, Elise Aaltola argues that attentiveness to non-human animals 'emerges out of unselfing': it is a process of eradicating the ego that is often achieved in solitude and wilderness experiences.[106] These experiences may evoke 'awe and elevation', and recognition of the vital presence of other animals.[107] Yet as much as Frankie's solitude does open her to the presence of other animals, her focus on dead animals, and specifically roadkill, challenges ideas of integration into a more-than-human world. Instead, Frankie sees herself, like the animals, as a victim of the human world.

The topic of roadkill is itself growing in prominence in a variety of disciplines. In Jane Desmond's definition, roadkill is 'ultimately attributed to an animal being in the wrong place at the wrong time, not the driver'; although the animal dies because of human actions, the human is assumed not to bear any responsibility for these actions.[108] The idea of roadkill cements ideas of certain animals being disposable or anonymous, or what McClory terms '[s]tuck gravy of broken mammal'.[109] Roadkill is commonly seen not as an act of violence, but simply as a consequence of non-human animals' inability to adapt to a human world. In asking '[d]oes roadkill have a face', Matthew Calarco argues that roadkill cannot be reduced to narratives of decay or pessimism, but neither can the human-roadkill encounter easily be framed as ethical encounter, since the vast majority of people do not acknowledge the roadkill at all.[110] Considering roadkill, he claims, is 'not simply to recognize an objectless existence [...but] also to catch a glimpse of the innumerable life-worlds that exist within, alongside, and beyond our own'.[111] In defining roadkill as an event rather than an object, he stresses that animal corpses trouble categories of both vitality and decay: the animals certainly cannot be seen as companion species, say, or capable of interaction with humans, and yet they cannot be reduced simply to objects, as they have, as in Baume's novel, the power to unsettle or engage the viewer, or to act as a force of interruption. Neither substance nor life, neither belonging wholly to the wild nor the human world, roadkill presents a way of examining both the incommensurability of the human and non-human worlds and their close relationship. While the roadkill in Baume's novel is a sign of Anthropocenic power and devastation, then, it also raises questions about the nature of attentiveness, and the value placed upon other lives and forms of material being.

Baume's novel, in both its catalogue of remembered artworks and its portrayal of dead animals, shows how gleaning and attention can combine into an act of witness. Witnessing the death of others is, according to Deborah Bird Rose, an ethical necessity: any account of life must recognize death as 'a necessary partner'.[112] Rose differentiates between the way in which, particularly in Indigenous perspectives, 'death binds living beings into an ecological community' and what she calls 'double death', or the amplification of death through contemporary environmental devastation, so that 'the balance between life and death is overrun, and death starts piling up corpses in the land of the living'.[113] Throughout her work, Rose emphasizes the ethics of encounter and integration: ethical time, in this sense, is a way of opening the self to the non-human world, and recognizing that each creature is a component of a longer multispecies ancestry, or part of a continuous cycle of death and rebirth. The contemporary period of human-made mass extinction is a refusal of this interface. As Rose writes, this requires an individual responsiveness:

> If we choose silence in response to the unmaking of all this exuberance, we ourselves become deader than dead, for without an ethical sensibility we lose our capacity to be responsive to the dynamic exuberance of life. Along with all the multispecies double death, we also start to degrade the future of our own lives and deaths.[114]

This, in many respects, is Frankie's dilemma (as well as being a central concern of the next two chapters): if writing, or other creative responses, seems to uphold the idea of human individual supremacy, silence can seem like complicity in the ongoing slaughter of our time. Frankie's empathy is not sentimental, but is a way to recognize both her own embeddedness in a multispecies sphere and the overwhelming nature of modern mass death, leading to a degraded future. At the same time, however, her artwork also raises the possibility of reification, or treating the animals she encounters as things.

Frankie's photographs are ultimately a way of incorporating the wild within her own domestic routines. Earlier in the novel she reflects on the limitations of her world: 'Only clouds. Only pigeons. Only the green slime and brown moss which grows between the panes. The world within my sight span remains precisely as it was.'[115] Her domestic routine is similarly unwavering: 'I measure out my breakfast things, select my implements. Tear a square of tissue from the roll, pour milk from carton to jug, arrange it all on a tin tea tray.'[116] The natural and domestic worlds are both measurable and known in their repetition. As with Calarco's discussion of roadkill, Baume's novel raises the possibility of distinguishing between objects and things. Thingness, in the words of Bill Brown, 'inheres as a potentiality within any object', and is precipitated by the object-event.[117] Things are known through encounter: as Brown writes, they force 'the subject's attention: as fact, as interruption, as summons'.[118] While objects are complete in themselves, things, according to Arjun Appardurai, 'are congealed moments in a longer social trajectory'.[119] Things can be seen in terms of potential, in terms of movement between animacy and inanimacy, and in their relation to the dynamics of encounter. Frankie's encounters with things, whether man-made material or non-human corpses, consistently have the possibility of being transformative: rather than simply observing objects, she knows the material world through embodied participation. These encounters collapse distinctions between the human and non-human world: even while taking the stance of an outsider, Frankie is always implicated in, and transformed by, her encounters with the physical world.

The idea that encounters with things can be a way of experiencing the world is clarified by comparison to Bennett's *Pond*. The setting of the text is largely restricted to the protagonist's cottage, especially her kitchen, and the garden and pond outside. Early in the text the protagonist states that while she might 'have the appearance and occasionally emanate the demeanour of someone who grows things', she has 'only a polite curiosity for horticultural endeavours'.[120] Even in comparison to *Inlands*, there is a limited sense of the natural world in Bennett's text. Instead, like Baume, the primacy of encounter is revealed in acts of attention, and this in turn troubles easy assumptions about how humans are situated in their environment. In the story 'The Big Day' the protagonist is asked to speak at a party at her neighbours' house. She considers discussing the stones that make up her cottage, as revealed in a photograph taken by her landlady. She is especially interested in a congruence of smaller stones in one corner: she describes the way 'one's attention is drawn back to these gatherings of smaller stones in much the same way as the minor constellations beguile the stargazer'.[121] This discussion of the importance of attention to material things goes on for several pages, and indeed the text largely consists of such discussions.

This quality of attention is, in many ways, inherently solipsistic. The narrator does not attend the party, or give her speech, despite imagining it being rapturously received. After the party has happened, however, she walks, holding a bowl of potato peelings, over to a sign that is left over from the party, adjacent to the neighbours' pond:

> There were some slugs along the edges of it, and some woodlice too. It was completely soaked and the plywood was coming apart. Pond. I lifted it up carefully and carried it over to where the ivy grows round and round and jiggled it in behind the entwined trunk of a tree. It will surely outlive the pond in any case. It's not a very deep pond after all. I always believed they were endlessly deep. But when I took something down there one day that I needed to get rid of fast, a broken, precious thing, I dropped it into the water and it did not sink and go on sinking. It just sort of wedged itself and was horribly visible. And within moments lots of very small things, some of them creatures I suppose, collected and oscillated, slowly, along the smooth crevices of its broken precious parts.[122]

The scene is ambiguous and disturbing. Even as the narrator, counter-intuitively, asserts the permanence of the already-decaying sign against the natural world of the pond, the insertion of 'pond' in the middle of the description emphasizes, at the very least, the close relationship between the two. The thing which is seen in a state of decay is upheld, and the thing which is seen as potentially vital is framed as subject to inevitable decay. As in Frankie's pictures of roadkill, there is not a simple assertion that the human environment is hostile to non-human elements, or an opposed praise of the wild, but rather the suggestion that the relation between the two is convoluted, overlapping and always transformed in individual encounters. The second half of the paragraph is more troubling. The narrator's refusal to specify the exact nature of the 'precious thing' raises a host of interpretive possibilities.[123] There is no clear differentiation between 'thing' and 'creature', between what properly belongs to nature and what is only inserted there, or what is transcendent and what is simply horribly visible. The passage illustrates the futility of categorization: there is no 'nature', nor 'human', but only things as they are encountered and attended to.

Both texts can be framed in the tension between remove and attention. While attention is often placed in relation to distraction, in these novels attention can more specifically be defined as attending to the world. Attention is a form of encounter and engagement with the other. Alice Bennett, like Calarco and Rose, draws on Emmanuel Levinas's ethical formulation to describe this relationship. For Levinas, the relationship between the I and the other does not result in collectivity or 'a common concept': the other is simultaneously 'the Stranger who disturbs the being at home with oneself' and 'the free one'.[124] As Bennett interprets this relationship, the self 'is constituted by this ethical encounter at the threshold', such that attention to the stranger troubles the boundary between self and world.[125] While in Levinas's and Bennett's discussions this stranger is implicitly human, in Bennett's and Baume's novels the other can be non-human, and even inanimate. This expansion of alterity is possible in part because the protagonists are in multiple senses already not 'at home' with themselves. Both characters create, or attend to, what Baume elsewhere calls the 'glorious, crushing, ridiculous repetition of life' in part because any idea of home must be formed through attention.[126]

The novels illustrate how a position of solitary remove necessitates an active engagement with and construction of the world. While Bennett's protagonist declares that her 'head is turned by imagined elsewheres', the majority of the text is occupied with what she calls 'domestic flutterings': attending to the control knobs on her cooker, for instance.[127] Baume's Frankie likewise draws attention to the repetition of her days, of the sense that 'only what I make' – whether in terms of art, domestic tasks or self-fashioning – will be left behind.[128] As Baume writes in *Handiwork*, a philosophical, fragmentary memoir about her own processes of making, most of her time as an artist is spent 'in the approach': the threshold between self and other is central to the relationship.[129] The objects she makes – in this case a series of small wooden birds – are known as if they are 'a part of my body'; at the same time, she frames herself as an Audubon, 'making a lifeless replication of the world I know'.[130] Making is insufficient, and yet in each act of making the self encounters the other, and so comes to know the world.

Bennett's and Baume's focus on domestic space can be placed in a tradition of Irish writing about the home, where, as Rhona Richman Kenneally writes, space is known in terms of its 'agential capabilities': 'a house co-determines, in tandem with its human inhabitants, the interactions, experiences and thought processes of its human (and nonhuman) residents'.[131] The house is 'material as well as metaphorical', in Susan Fraiman's words, or a juxtaposition of 'dispersed images and a body of images at the same time', in Gaston Bachelard's.[132] The house, like the things in it, oscillates between states of being: attending to the house becomes a form of understanding the dynamics of encounter. While Bennett's and Baume's protagonists are as removed from the world as Willows's and McClory's, then, this removal functions in a very different way: rather than moving away from, or indeed moving towards, Bennett's and Baume's protagonists move with and through. In isolation, they come to understand the world as a series of encounters and acts of making, where the material fact of the other alters their sense of self. Late in Baume's novel Frankie finds an injured sparrow, which dies, and which she buries, rather than photographs. She cries 'indecently hard', asking, in a line that stands on its own: 'Have I cried out my deadness now?'[133] When she wakes she can 'begin, at last. To fix things.'[134] If the phrase is vague and ambiguous, the sense of 'things' here is important: Frankie turns her attention to photographs, to the house she lives in, to putting things in their place. Knowing things becomes a way of knowing the world without seeing it as transcendent, or even threatening; as she writes in a description of the artist Tom Friedman, the solution is to 'make the blank [the] artwork.'[135]

Baume's novel is certainly not optimistic: the final line is simply: 'Art, and sadness, last forever.'[136] The line is partly a description of Frankie's philosophy, but also of Joseph Beuys's work *7000 Oaks*, begun in 1982, where Beuys began a series of planting oaks, alongside a basalt standing stone: the artwork continued after Beuys's death, juxtaposing '[t]he oaks which grow. The stones which don't.'[137] The stones and oaks are both things in their place, combining animacy and inanimacy, the I and the other. Making, and planting, becomes a way of engaging with the world that refuses the sublime, but also accepts the world as more than the self. If Frankie is still isolated at the end of the novel, she has found a form of encounter that signifies continuity as well as rupture.

The end of *Pond* is more ambiguous. Like Frankie, Bennett's protagonist frames her life in relation to pre-existing artwork. In particular, she draws attention to 'that book I read recently' about 'the lone survivor of this impenetrable catastrophe [who] has only a very restricted area within which to work out the rest of her existence.'[138] The narrator recounts the story of this book for six pages, noting the relation between the fictional protagonist's life and her own: both navigate their domestic solitude carefully, preserving what they can. The novel is clearly important to the narrator, and the echoes between the two are clear. As the narrator later notes, she makes several errors in her account, having lent the book to a friend, but this is not particularly concerning, since 'it's the impression that certain things made on me that I wanted to get across, not the occurrences themselves.'[139] The description of this novel is one of the most sustained discussions in the entirety of *Pond*; in sharp contrast to Frankie, however, Bennett's narrator never names it. The unnamed book is, quite clearly, Marlen Haushofer's 1963 novel *The Wall*, and the vast majority of the summary in *Pond* is accurate. There are significant differences between the two texts: not only is Haushofer's protagonist the victim of a global catastrophe in which she is the only apparent survivor, limited to her house and the surrounding lands, but she is also able to form a community. For most of the novel she is surrounded with a dog, a cat and a cow: she is affected 'more by the concern for my animals than by my own desperate situation'.[140] Haushofer's novel contains all the elements that Bennett's avoids: engagement with the natural world and with non-human animals, the spectre of misogyny, and the insidious violence and cruelty that corrupts people. Yet the texts are strikingly similar in their portrait of solitude and loneliness, of responsibility and of attention to the world. Haushofer's novel is not a key to explain the ambiguities of Bennett's text, but the sustained discussion suggests an avenue for interpretation. *The Wall* suggests the way integration with the environment, and care for others, can be a respite from a failing world, if only, and tragically, temporarily. *Pond* goes a step further to look at what happens when even these avenues for solace have been removed, and enmeshment with nature no longer seems possible. If Frankie, in *A Line Made by Walking*, can come to know the world through making and observing what is made, Bennett's protagonist remains slightly more removed. The imperative in both novels, as in Haushofer's, remains the same, however: it is only in engaging with the world as material that it can be known.

Bennett's text ends, curiously, with a two-page story with, presumably, a different protagonist, told in the third person. In the story a woman, or more likely a child, buries a set of green papers in the earth, and in that moment realizes that '[l]ove can be surprising'.[141] An apple sits on the lawn, and the protagonist imagines throwing it against the house just as her brother is throwing snails, but does not. The text ends:

> After a short time there was a shift – the apple held her in its fluent green gaze as all thoughts and awarenesses in her began to softly trickle out across the garden. The windowpane flinched beneath its white sash. And then, of course, it was time for them both to go indoors and wash their hands.
> Morning stands on its high swing and waits, shunting the dirt back and forth beneath its nails with a bare piece of card.[142]

If the relation of this fragment to the rest of the text is opaque, its challenge to a separation between people and things is clear. Bennett is not indulging in an easy anthropomorphism here. Rather, the apple and the windowpane are presented as vital, agential things known through their mutual encounter. This is, Bennett suggests, how we know the world. If Bennett's work does not easily fall under the rubric of environmental literature, it instead reshapes our notion of what constitutes an environment. The world she constructs is vibrant and limited at the same time: this immediacy, or immanence, becomes a way to reframe worldly dwelling. Both Bennett and Baume suggest, in slightly different ways, that when the world is too vast or horrific to be imagined, the best hope for continuance and integration is to attend to daily encounters with material form. This constraint in turn becomes a way of re-opening the world.

C. Willed solitude: Abi Andrews

Abi Andrews's *The Word for Woman Is Wilderness* might initially seem something of a departure from the four novels discussed above. The protagonist is not only slightly younger, at nineteen, but does not bear the signs of trauma and grief that mark the other texts. While the novels just discussed can be characterized in terms of movement away from a situation, Erin Miller's journey in Andrews's novel is defined by movement towards: she frames her journey from England to Mount Denali in Alaska, via Greenland and Canada, as 'an Odyssean epic, [...] a female quest for *authenticity*'.[143] Her models for her journey are Jack London, Henry David Thoreau and, more surprisingly, Theodore Kaczynski, known more popularly as the Unabomber: she is playing '*what I conceived to be a MAN's game*'.[144] She also takes inspiration from women's writing, ranging from Ursula K. Le Guin and Elizabeth Bishop to Laura Ingalls Wilder and, at greater length, Rachel Carson, but her explicit purpose in her journey is to reclaim the idea of wilderness for women. Her journey is both a nod to earlier ecofeminist discussions of wilderness or wildness and more recent popular accounts of self-reinvention through travel such as Cheryl Strayed's *Wild*. Like earlier women's travel narratives, too, an emphasis on gender is apparent from the start: while, as Bénédicte Monicat argues, the topic of masculinity is rarely commented on in men's travel writings, 'women's travel narratives [begin] with the use of an autobiographical voice which develops itself around and from the proclaimed femininity of the author'.[145] Erin begins her account detailing how women are 'excluded from, and banished to, nature'.[146] As such, her travels are designed to reflect women's experiences of wilderness more generally, as seen through the experience of one individual.

The gender and environmental politics of Andrews's novel are more explicit than those of the other authors: the novel draws from familiar ecofeminist and ecocritical texts, as well as other works of feminist theory. I am considering it in relation to these other more ambiguous texts, however, because Andrews's focus on solitude and attention is, at times, surprisingly similar. Like the other protagonists discussed above, Erin is, in McClory's words, 'edgeless, sparking, alone'.[147] Just as importantly, the novel uses a similar fragmentary presentation. The text is divided into very short sections, each given a fairly lengthy title that often does not directly pertain to the events described: the titles are drawn from a wide range of relevant authors, including Jack Kerouac, Donna Haraway and, at the novel's end, Anna Lowenhaupt Tsing. The text is filled with illustrations: photographs, handwritten diagrams and various styles of illustration. If travel writing, in Giuliana Bruno's terms, can be seen as 'a "way" to know, transforming knowledge into a geographical matter', Andrews's text illustrates how that geography can also be reflected in the material text.[148] A text that seeks to incorporate the multiplicity of women's experience, and multiple geographical places, must itself be multiple. The text thus, in keeping with its own sources, creates a form of 'embodied objectivity' in Donna Haraway's terms, where 'feminist objectivity means quite simply *situated knowledge*'.[149] As Haraway explains:

> Gender is a field of structured and structuring difference, where the tones of extreme localization, of the intimately personal and individualised body, vibrate in the same field with global high tension emissions. Feminist embodiment, then, is not about fixed location in a reified body, female or otherwise, but about nodes in fields, inflections in orientations, and responsibility for difference in material-semiotic fields of meaning.[150]

This approach, which is closely aligned with standpoint epistemology, underpins Andrews's novel in terms of both theme and form.[151] The text is oriented around Haraway's 'politics and epistemologies of location, positioning, and situating': Erin's narration draws equal attention to how she is situated in the geographical world and the intellectual world. As much as the novel recounts travels through different physical environments, it is equally a story of travel through different intellectual and literary environments, presented in terms of inflection and difference. This approach is equally employed in the memoirs and poems examined in Chapter 2, but is of particular interest here in terms of the attention Erin gives not only to the physical world, but to the world she knows through textual encounters.

Erin repeatedly asserts the centrality of a relation between wilderness and women in uncritically essentialist terms, arguing that the 'relationship we need with the natural is one that is feminine' and lamenting 'the unfair and ungrounded exclusion of women' from philosophies of wilderness.[152] She draws links between cetaceans and human women as both being oppressed by patriarchy, claims that 'owning a vagina is mystical' and, following an essentialist and dualistic argument familiar from the early days of ecofeminism, concludes that 'Woman is closer to the mountain and the wolf than man even if only because he put her there'.[153] Indeed, she characterizes her own quest as a reaction to gender norms, asking: 'if running into the wild is so often a wounded retreat from societal constraints and oppressions, then shouldn't anyone *but* straight white men be doing it more?'[154] In terms of its explicit statements of the relationship between women and nature, then, Andrews's text, or at least Erin's narration, initially seems to reiterate arguments such as those posed by Griffin above, as well as other early ecofeminist thinkers such as Mary Daly.

Although Erin often positions wilderness writing in terms of a tradition dating back to Thoreau, she also comments on the urgency of her trip in the context of the Anthropocene, arguing, in relation to nuclear waste, that 'how to convey invisible death to the future is a problem unique to our age'.[155] Her account echoes Merchant's more recent emphasis on 'the place of women and gender' in Anthropocenic literature: Merchant herself argues for the construction of the Gynocene in place of the Anthropocene, 'an age in which women can contribute policies and power to help resolve climate change'.[156] Andrews's text is thus firmly anchored in a second-wave, materialist examination of how traditional, patriarchal approaches to ideas of wilderness have led to catastrophic planetary developments. It is also, in a more self-critical mode, anchored in ideas of North American wilderness that are associated with settler colonialism. While Erin discovers the solipsistic nature of her desire to find an unexplored, uninhabited wilderness, the novel makes relatively sparing reference to Indigenous cultures or perspectives. In framing gender in binaristic terms, and in highlighting a largely white body of scholarship and intertextual references, the novel only briefly gestures towards any significant consideration of how its themes might be approached from a decolonized perspective.[157]

Yet if these formulations are themselves familiar, Andrews's text adds to this discourse by privileging ideas of textual, as well as environmental, encounter. As much as Erin's journey is a physical one, it is also constructed by her reading and writing. Her search for solitude, for instance, is framed in reference to Marianne Moore, who 'said that solitude is the cure for loneliness, which was very crafty of her, and perhaps my trip's whole mantra'.[158] Yet she also frequently expresses irritation and frustration with the premise of her expedition and its reliance on diary entries in both written and video form:

> How do you really *front the essential facts of life authentically*? Probably it is not even possible in our time of saturation. I can only try my best. Maybe writing is less inauthentic than the audience of a camera. But even then I am writing to be read, so again the 'solitude' is tainted by the inverse voyeurism. Go tell that to Thoreau and Heidegger and the Unabomber.[159]

The transcripts of her video logs are filled with false starts and scenes she repeats in order to make them seem more authentic to her presumed audience. Similarly, she worries that the ghosts of famous writers she begins to see around her, ranging from Rachel Carson to Adam Smith, are a corruption of solitude. This anxiety both echoes and expands Patrick D. Murphy's statement that ecocriticism is 'a critical method that both evokes the responsibility of the critic and reinstates referentiality as a crucial and primary activity of literature'.[160] Erin's account is filled with ruminations about her own practices of literary, as well as spatial, referentiality: she worries that constructing a text about her experience is as much an act of inscribing herself upon the landscape as the works she seeks to repudiate. In an interview, Andrews speaks about how her own inspiration comes from the film *Into the Wild*, which depicts the death of Chris McCandless in the Alaskan wilderness, stating that '[a]ny documentary on the themes I wrote would have to be about the unmaking of the documentary' and that her novel is a form of 'writing the unmaking'.[161] This idea of unmaking is reflected in Erin's anxiety. Much of the novel's second half is concerned with her discovery of a series of writings by a man named Damon that have been left in the Alaskan cabin she stays in. Reading these documents, she decides that all forms of inscription are damaging. A map is 'a corrupting thing'; a text ignores the way 'pure wildness is the absence of words'; a documentary film suggests that to 'document is to litter, to litter photographs of the tundra in the tundra behind you'.[162] While Baume's Frankie takes photographs in order to integrate herself with the world, Andrews's Erin, even as she takes photographs, argues that such acts of making are impositions that force a separation between women and wildness. The fragmentary form is thus necessary for the novel because it allows Erin simultaneously to make and unmake the world at the same time.

Throughout the novel Erin argues that this form of fragmentation leads to multiple perspectives: this move, she argues, is gendered, and resists the dominant narratives of individual freedom she finds in the works of the men

she reads, in particular Kaczynski. A 'feminine perspective', she writes, is one
that admits 'there is not one truth, there are many narratives'.[163] While Damon's
and Kaczynski's writings are a product of 'forgetting existence was a mosaic of
beauty', her own work is to recognize that mosaic quality.[164] The novel ends with
two long letters Erin writes. In a letter to Kaczynski she argues that he should
replace individualism with 'a more collectivist sentiment', while in a letter to her
future self she draws on Virginia Woolf to argue for the importance of what I
am calling gleaning: 'Not collection as possession but a collection like that of
the reverent bowerbird'.[165] These ideas of fragmentation, gleaning and collection
are continuously framed as feminine pursuits: while men see their relation to
the wilderness as one of individual power or control, women are able to move
within it and recognize it in terms of difference. While Erin emphasizes her own
affect much less than the protagonists described above, and indeed passages of
attention to the world are more limited, her belief that she can only arrive at
these conclusions from a position of solitude is itself revealing. As Ngai writes,
'the desire for detachment is a direct consequence of the kind of interest our
feeling about the object has fostered'.[166] Remove from the world is, for both
Kaczynski and Erin, a direct response to it, as she herself notes. Kaczynski's
error is in believing that this remove can be permanent, however, whereas Erin
comes to recognize her own implication in the human activities around her.
This is most clearly presented not in Erin's letters, but in her signatures. Her
letter to Kaczynski ends: 'Reform over revolution. / Down with patriarchy, /
Erin Miller (QUEEN OF THE WILD)'.[167] In writing to Kaczynski she frames her
ideas as a manifesto, in a style that echoes his own. She ends her letter to herself,
and the novel: 'From Erin in the cabin in our wilderness, / Denali, / Alaska, /
Earth'.[168] This signature echoes children's ways of writing their address, but in
its recognition of scale, and the idea that wilderness is shared between past and
future, also reflects a greater understanding of her own responsibility for, and
limited agency in, the world at large.

Perhaps the most important aspect of Erin's concluding letters, however, is
that they are unlikely ever to be read. Her record of her experience is framed
in terms of outward expression, but instead reveals how her self-conception
changes through her encounters with the natural environment, which are often
boring and sometimes terrifying. This, perhaps, is the greatest commonality of
the five novels discussed in this chapter: attending to the world changes the self,
but not in a way that can be considered transcendent or sublime, or that reifies
the individual. Instead, willed solitude becomes itself a form of engagement.
There is no possibility of retreat from the world. Rather, isolation creates a space

where the world is impressed on one in its multiplicity and complexity. Each of the novels, as discussed above, illustrates the way the individual body belongs to, and is revealed through, a multiplicity of encounters. These encounters must, however, be known as themselves, and can only be recounted in fragmentary form.

Each of these novels, in slightly different ways, resists the lure of explanatory narrative. As such, it would be reductive to situate them straightforwardly as examples of environmental literature; certainly Andrews's novel is the only one explicitly to engage at length with questions of climate change or use a term such as 'Anthropocene', while the physical environments in the others are often restricted, partial and incomplete. These environmental encounters must, in turn, emphasize partiality and incompletion. Global catastrophe or change is, as I have argued in the Introduction, rarely experienced at planetary level, although it can certainly be conceived of in terms of collective experience. Rather, these novels illustrate an affective uneasiness or dissatisfaction with the world that is manifested through differing forms of attention to the world. Being attentive to the world does not itself serve as a catalyst for change, whether individual or global. Instead, attending to the world in continual processes of making and unmaking allows the protagonists to understand their own relational selfhood. The world is what affects the self, and fragmentary form allows those myriad reflections to be presented without an overdetermined interpretation.

These five novels are notable in the way they present fragmentation as a form of thinking with and through the world, and of resisting the lure of a unified story. Their emphasis on solitude is particularly important: while the texts in the remaining chapters also emphasize collective experience, these novels illustrate the simultaneous difficulty of and need for establishing a relationship with the natural world as an individual. Although this chapter was planned before, and revised after, the height of Covid-19 anxiety, the first draft was written during a period in which Aberdeen was in localized lockdown, such that I was not only alone in my flat, but forbidden from travelling more than five miles away, throughout my time reading these books. In my own seclusion every encounter, whether seeing dolphins in the sea or slugs coupling on the pavement outside my house, whether seeing the lilacs bloom and fade or the arrival of a small flock of goldfinches nearby, seemed both more and less significant than in my previous life. Solitude draws your attention to the world and shows how you are situated in an environment that is co-constituted by myriad other forms of life. It also shows the limits of your agency. Solitude troubles, both positively and negatively, received notions of how humans exist in the world. Each of these novels emphasizes that trouble without seeking wholly to resolve it. Instead, fragmentation is a method of presenting a world that is known through trouble, incomplete and partial. Whether one seeks to arrange the pieces or simply collect them in order to relinquish them again, solitude shows a world that is already in pieces. Restriction, grief, loneliness and confusion are in themselves a way of understanding the world, and resisting the lure of mastery. This emphasis on negative affect is not, of course, the only potential use of fragmentation in contemporary literature, and it is to questions of integration and performativity that I turn in the next chapter.

Notes

1   Ottessa Moshfegh, *My Year of Rest and Relaxation* (London: Jonathan Cape, 2018), 3.

2   Eimear McBride, *Strange Hotel* (London: Faber, 2020), 6.

3   Moshfegh, *My Year*, 287.

4   Moshfegh, *My Year*, 289.

5   McBride, *Strange Hotel*, 147.

6   Jhumpa Lahiri, *Whereabouts* (London: Bloomsbury, 2021), 153.

7   Deirdre Heddon, 'Confounding Ecospectations: Disappointment and Hope in the Forest', *Green Letters* 20.3 (2016): 333. Original emphasis.

8   Gregory J. Seigworth and Melissa Gregg, 'An Inventory of Shimmers', in *The Affect Theory Reader*, ed. Melissa Gregg and Gregory J. Seigworth (Durham and London: Duke University Press, 2010), 2. Original emphasis.

9   Linda Tym, 'Perilous Boundaries: Affective Experience in Three Scottish Women Writers' Short Fiction', *Journal of the Short Story in English* 61 (2013): 3.

10 Sianne Ngai, *Ugly Feelings* (Cambridge, MA, and London: Harvard University Press, 2007), 11. As Ngai notes, texts that discuss what she calls 'negative feelings' and avoid melodrama or strong emotion tend to be canonically minor, 'as if minor or ugly feelings were not only incapable of producing "major" works, but somehow disabled the works they do drive from acquiring canonical distinction' (10–11). While the texts discussed in this chapter are perhaps too recent to be enshrined in a canon, their relative lack of critical attention perhaps reflects this paradigm.

11 Heather Houser, *Ecosickness in Contemporary U.S. Fiction: Environment and Affect* (New York: Columbia University Press, 2014), 11, 3.

12 Houser, *Ecosickness*, 68, 71.

13 Timothy Morton, *Ecology without Nature: Rethinking Environmental Aesthetics* (Cambridge, MA, and London: Harvard University Press, 2007), 125.

14 Moshfegh and McBride's novels draw attention to the loneliness of urban spaces, which, as Olivia Laing writes, 'shows that loneliness doesn't necessarily require physical solitude, but rather an absence of paucity of connection, closeness, kinship'. Nevertheless, the mainly rural or unpopulated spaces of the novels considered below highlight a particular form of loneliness that comes from social remove. Olivia Laing, *The Lonely City: Adventures in the Art of Being Alone* (Edinburgh: Canongate, 2016), 3–4.

15 Morton, *Ecology*, 184–5.

16 Sarah Bernstein, *The Coming Bad Days* (London: Daunt Books 2021), 36. Bernstein's narrator's later claim that '[t]he process of seeing is also the process of saying, and so what is required is an intervention into the grammar of looking' (213) similarly echoes many of the texts discussed below.

17 bell hooks, for instance, argues in discussing the Black communities in Kentucky where she was raised that: 'No one talked about the earth as our mother. They did not divide the world into the neat dualistic gendered categories that are common strategies in both reformist feminist movement and in environmental activism.' bell hooks, *Belonging: A Culture of Place* (New York and London: Routledge, 2009), 46. Melanie L. Harris, in a Womanist intersectional analysis derived from the work of Alice Walker, similarly argues that the material and spiritual interconnectedness with the earth is a hallmark of African and African American experience. Melanie L. Harris, *Ecowomanism: African American Women and Earth-Honoring Faiths* (Maryknoll, NY: Orbis Books, 2017), 29.

18 Susan Griffin, *Woman and Nature: The Roaring inside Her* (London: The Women's Press, 1978), 48.

19 Griffin, *Woman*, 219.

20 Sherilyn MacGregor, *Beyond Mothering Earth: Ecological Citizenship and the Politics of Care* (Vancouver and Toronto: UBC Press, 2006), 26. Catriona Sandilands likewise argues that Griffin's work emphasizes 'an ongoing feminine embodied knowledge of nature that is a source of patriarchal jealousy and domination'. Catriona Sandilands, *The Good-Natured Feminist: Ecofeminism and the Quest for Democracy* (Minneapolis and London: University of Minnesota Press, 1999), 13.

21 Denise Riley, '*Am I That Name?': Feminism and the Category of 'Women' in History* (Basingstoke: Macmillan, 1988), 18.

22 Val Plumwood, *Feminism and the Mastery of Nature* (London: Routledge, 1993), 71.

23 Freya Mathews, *The Ecological Self* (London: Routledge, 1991), 111.

24 Sandilands, *Good-Natured Feminist*, 65.

25 Stacy Alaimo, *Undomesticated Ground: Recasting Nature as Feminist Space* (Ithaca and London: Cornell University Press, 2000), 136.

26 Stacy Alaimo, *Bodily Natures: Science, Environment, and the Material Self* (Bloomington and Indianapolis: Indiana University Press, 2010), 142.

27   Samantha Walton, 'Feminism's Critique of the Anthropocene', in *The New Feminist Literary Studies*, ed. Jennifer Cooke (Cambridge: Cambridge University Press, 2020), 113. See also Claire Colebrook's argument for a 'multiple' Anthropocene feminism that raises the question of who might constitute a 'we'. Claire Colebrook, 'We Have Always Been Post-Anthropocene: The Anthropocene Counterfactual', in *Anthropocene Feminism*, ed. Richard Grusin (Minneapolis and London: University of Minnesota Press, 2017), 10.

28   Lola Olufemi, *Feminism, Interrupted: Disrupting Power* (London: Pluto Press, 2020), 136.

29   Astrida Neimanis, *Bodies of Water: Posthuman Feminist Phenomenology* (London: Bloomsbury Academic, 2019), 23.

30   As Neimanis argues, questions of 'coloniality, race, gender, species, class, culture, [and] taste' are not only inseparable from each other, but, 'importantly, none of them is separate from us'. Neimanis, *Bodies of Water*, 165. Despite the significant differences between contemporary ecofeminist, posthuman feminist and Anthropocene feminist approaches, all of these works are united not only in moving past essentialist discourses of both gender and environment, but also in refusing to treat them as separable from other social questions.

31   Weil's fragmentary, aphoristic writings remain a central influence on contemporary women's writing. While particularly notable in the work of poets such as Anne Carson and Jorie Graham, Weil is taken as an inspiration by writers such as Terry Tempest Williams and many others.

32   Patrick D. Murphy, *Literature, Nature, and Other: Ecofeminist Critiques* (Albany: State University of New York Press, 1995), 43, 40.

33   Alaimo, *Undomesticated*, 181–2.

34   Griffin, *Woman*, 5.

35   Griffin, *Woman*, 223. Original emphasis.

36   Greta Gaard, 'Toward New EcoMasculinities, EcoGenders, and EcoSexualities', in *Ecofeminism: Feminist Intersections with Other Animals and the Earth*, ed. Carol J. Adams and Lori Gruen (New York and London: Bloomsbury, 2014), 226.

37   Rosi Braidotti, *Patterns of Dissonance: A Study of Women in Contemporary Philosophy*, trans. Elizabeth Guild (Cambridge: Polity, 1991), 122.

38   Rachel Cusk, *Coventry* (London: Faber, 2019), 174. See Abi Andrews's use of Woolf to make a similar point below.

39   Sophie Collins, *Who Is Mary Sue?* (London: Faber, 2018), 7. The use of a central intertext that remains unnamed also occurs in Bennett's *Pond*, as is discussed below.

40   Alaimo, *Undomesticated*, 16.

41   Rachel Cusk, *Kudos* (London: Faber, 2018), 230–1.

42   Cusk, *Kudos*, 232.

43 All five writers are published by small, independent presses and, with the exception of Sara Baume, are debut novelists. While some of their work has received critical attention, their experimental approaches are less visible than some of the authors discussed below, due in part to the dominance of a handful of major publishers in the British market.

44 Shoshana Felman, 'Education and Crisis, or the Vicissitudes of Teaching', in *Testimony: Crises of Witnessing in Literature, Psychoanalysis and History*, ed. Shoshana Felman and Dori Laub (New York and Abingdon: Routledge, 1992), 5.

45 Anne Whitehead, *Trauma Fiction* (Edinburgh: Edinburgh University Press, 2004), 48.

46 Elin Willows, *Inlands*, trans. Duncan J. Lewis (Whitstable: Nordisk Books, 2020), 11.

47 Helen McClory, *Flesh of the Peach* (Glasgow: Freight Books, 2017), 1.

48 Willows, *Inlands*, 127.

49 Willows, *Inlands*, 164.

50 Ian Hacking, *Mad Travellers: Reflections on the Reality of Transient Mental Illness* (London: Free Association Books, 1999), 8.

51 Willows, *Inlands*, 39.

52 Kathleen Stewart, 'Pockets', *Communication and Critical/Cultural Studies* 9.4 (2012): 365.

53 Stewart, 'Pockets', 367.

54 Anna Lowenhaupt Tsing, *The Mushroom at the End of the World: On the Possibility of Life in Capitalist Ruins* (Princeton and Oxford: Princeton University Press, 2015), 29; Lauren Berlant, *Cruel Optimism* (Durham and London: Duke University Press, 2011), 192.

55 Robbie Duschinsky and Emma Wilson, 'Flat Affect, Joyful Politics and Enthralled Attachments: Engaging with the Work of Lauren Berlant', *International Journal of Politics, Culture, and Society* 28 (2015): 185.

56 Lauren Berlant, 'Structures of Unfeeling: *Mysterious Skin*', *International Journal of Politics, Culture, and Society* 28 (2015): 193.

57 Berlant, 'Structures', 195.

58 Willows, *Inlands*, 143.

59 Willows, *Inlands*, 19.

60 Willows, *Inlands*, 132.

61 Willows, *Inlands*, 132.

62 David Conradson, 'Freedom, Space and Perspective: Moving Encounters with Other Ecologies', in *Emotional Geographies*, ed. Joyce Davidson, Liz Bondi and Mick Smith (Aldershot and Burlington, VT: Ashgate, 2005), 107.

63 Willows, *Inlands*, 73.

64 Willows, *Inlands*, 219.

65 Willows, *Inlands*, 111.

66   Tim Ingold, *The Perception of the Environment: Essays on Livelihood, Dwelling and Skill* (London and New York: Routledge, 2000), 60

67   See Timothy C. Baker, 'The Gender Politics of Trees', in *Nonhuman Agencies in the Twenty-First-Century Anglophone Novel*, ed. Yvonne Liebermann, Judith Rahn, and Bettina Burger (Cham: Palgrave Macmillan, 2021), 169–86.

68   McClory, *Flesh*, 3.

69   McClory, *Flesh*, 54, 8. The geographic journey Sarah takes is the same as in Valeria Luiselli's *Lost Children Archive*, discussed in Chapter 3, albeit for very different purposes.

70   McClory, *Flesh*, 49, 48.

71   Val Plumwood, 'The Concept of a Cultural Landscape: Nature, Culture and Agency of the Land', *Ethics and the Environment* 11.2 (2006): 120.

72   McClory, *Flesh*, 56.

73   McClory, *Flesh*, 96.

74   McClory, *Flesh*, 50.

75   Terry Tempest Williams, *Erosion: Essays of Undoing* (New York: Farrar, Straus and Giroux, 2020), 41. Williams is specifically writing in defence of the Wilderness Act of 1964; as Carolyn Merchant has noted, in defining wilderness as an area where 'man is a visitor who does not remain', the act 'reads Native Americans out of the wilderness'. Carolyn Merchant, *Science and Nature: Past, Present, and Future* (New York and London: Routledge, 2018), 210.

76   Nicole Seymour, *Bad Environmentalism: Irony and Irreverence in the Ecological Age* (Minneapolis and London: University of Minnesota Press, 2018), 21. Original emphasis.

77   Sara Ahmed, *The Cultural Politics of Emotion*, 2nd ed (Edinburgh: Edinburgh University Press, 2014), 155. Original emphasis.

78   Donna J. Haraway, *Staying with the Trouble: Making Kin in the Chthulucene* (Durham and London: Duke University Press, 2016), 1.

79   Drew Leder, *The Absent Body* (Chicago: University of Chicago Press, 1990), 4; Ahmed, *Cultural*, 26.

80   McClory, *Flesh*, 131–2.

81   McClory, *Flesh*, 133.

82   McClory, *Flesh*, 133.

83   McClory, *Flesh*, 218.

84   McClory, *Flesh*, 143.

85   McClory, *Flesh*, 227. McClory's subsequent novel, *Bitterhall*, ends more optimistically, perhaps, with the claim that while '[y]ou can't save anybody', you can 'keep trying'. Helen McClory, *Bitterhall* (Edinburgh: Polygon, 2021), 355.

86   Richard Mabey, *Nature Cure* (London: Pimlico, 2006), 10. Original emphasis.

87   Mabey, *Nature*, 224.

88 Sara Baume, *A Line Made by Walking* (London: Heinemann, 2017), 1–6. The three original editions of the novel present different reading experiences. In the British version, cited here, the photographs Frankie takes are embedded in the text in a variety of aspect ratios; in the simultaneous Irish publication they are used as section headings, and closely cropped; in the slightly later American edition, the photographs are not included at all.

89 Baume, *Line*, 1.

90 Baume, *Line*, 6.

91 Baume, *Line*, 27.

92 Susan Clayton and Bryan T. Karazsia, 'Development and Validation of a Measure of Climate Change Anxiety', *Journal of Environmental Psychology* 69 (2020): 101434. doi.org./10.1016/j.envp.2020.101434 [Accessed 18 August 2020].

93 Sally Weintrobe, 'The Difficult Problem of Anxiety in Thinking about Climate Change', in *Engaging with Climate Change: Psychoanalytic and Interdisciplinary Perspectives*, ed. Sally Weintrobe (London and New York: Routledge, 2013), 46.

94 Baume, *Line*, 295.

95 Allyse Knox-Russell, 'Futurity without Optimism: Detaching from Anthropocentrism and Grieving Our Fathers in *Beasts of the Southern Wild*', in *Affective Ecocriticism: Emotion, Embodiment, Environment*, ed. Kyle Bladlow and Jennifer Ladino (Lincoln and London: University of Nebraska Press, 2018), 214. Although widely adopted by thinkers in ecocriticism and animal studies, Butler's argument is specific to humans: she is interested in the way that 'a field of would-be humans, the spectrally human, the deconstituted, are maintained and detained'. Judith Butler, *Precarious Life: The Powers of Mourning and Violence* (London and New York: Verso, 2006), 91. See also Catherine Keller's discussion of the way '[a]nthropocentric individualism has accompanied the denial of mourning'. Catherine Keller, *Cloud of the Impossible: Negative Theology and Planetary Entanglement* (New York: Columbia University Press, 2015), 235.

96 While Simone Weil, in defining attention as a form of prayer, frames attention in far more religious terms than the novelists here, her formulation of the term remains a basis for many discussions since. See Simone Weil, *Gravity and Grace*, trans. Emma Crawford and Mario von der Ruhr (London and New York: Routledge Classics, 2002), 117. In particular, see Julia Bell's use of Weil's ideas of attention to reflect on contemporary life. Julia Bell, *Radical Attention* (London: Peninsula, 2020), 29–34.

97 Baume, *Line*, 105.

98 Sara Baume, *Spill Simmer Falter Wither* (Dublin: Tramp Press, 2015), 84, 92.

99 Baume, *Spill*, 101.

100 Sara Ahmed, *Queer Phenomenology: Orientations, Objects, Others* (Durham and London: Duke University Press, 2006), 165.

101 Baume, *Line*, 127, 212.

102   Baume, *Line*, 147.

103   Baume, *Line*, 164.

104   McClory, *Flesh*, 51.

105   Baume, *Line*, 217.

106   Elise Aaltola, *Varieties of Empathy: Moral Psychology and Animal Ethics* (London and New York: Rowman and Littlefield, 2018), 148–9.

107   Aaltola, *Varieties*, 150.

108   Jane Desmond, 'Requiem for Roadkill: Death and Denial on America's Roads', in *Environmental Anthropology: Future Directions*, ed. Helen Kopnina and Eleanor Shoreman-Ouimet (New York and London: Routledge, 2013), 48. See also Sandra Swart, 'Reviving Roadkill?: Animals in the New Mobilities Studies', *Transfers* 5.2 (2015): 81–101; Kate Rigby and Owain Jones, 'Roadkill: Multispecies Mobility and Everyday Ecocide', in *Kin: Thinking with Deborah Bird Rose*, ed. Thom van Dooren and Matthew Chrulew (Durham and London: Duke University Press, 2022), 112–34.

109   McClory, *Flesh*, 51.

110   Matthew Calarco, 'Claimed by Roadkill', in *Feeling Animal Death: Being Host to Ghosts*, ed. Brianne Donaldson and Ashley King (London and New York: Rowman and Littlefield, 2019), 77–8. Calarco draws on the work of Emmanuel Levinas, who defines the face as 'a fundamental event' or an ethical demand. For Levinas, this face-to-face encounter is necessarily limited to humans. Tama Wright, Peter Hughes and Alison Ainley, 'The Paradox of Morality: An Interview with Emmanuel Levinas', in *The Provocation of Levinas: Rethinking the Other*, ed. Robert Bernasconi and David Wood (London and New York: Routledge, 1988), 168–9.

111   Calarco, 'Claimed', 79.

112   Deborah Bird Rose, 'Multispecies Knots of Ethical Time', *Environmental Philosophy* 9.1 (2012): 127.

113   Deborah Bird Rose, 'What If the Angel of History Were a Dog?', *Cultural Studies Review* 12.1 (2006): 75.

114   Rose, 'Multispecies Knots', 139.

115   Baume, *Line*, 69.

116   Baume, *Line*, 69.

117   Bill Brown, *Other Things* (Chicago and London: University of Chicago Press, 2015), 5. I am indebted in the following discussion to Elizabeth Anderson, *Material Spirituality in Modernist Women's Writing* (London: Bloomsbury, 2020), 6–7, as well as many conversations we have had.

118   Brown, *Other*, 23.

119   Arjun Appadurai, 'The Thing Itself', *Public Culture* 18.1 (2006): 15.

120   Claire-Louise Bennett, *Pond* (Dublin: Stinging Fly, 2015), 6.

121 Bennett, *Pond*, 35. In an Irish context a long discussion of stones inevitably evokes Samuel Beckett's *Molloy*; in constructing a tonally similar passage but having the narrator not only neither suck the stones nor place them in her pockets but only observe them from the outside, and indeed encounter them through photographs, Bennett gestures both to the text's Modernist lineage and its sharp contrast from its predecessors.

122 Bennett, *Pond*, 37.

123 In the years I have been teaching this text, student interpretations range from it being the bowl of potato peelings just mentioned to a miscarried foetus, and everything in between.

124 Emmanuel Levinas, *Totality and Infinity*, trans. Alphonso Lingis (Pittsburgh, PA: Duquesne University Press, 1969), 39.

125 Alice Bennett, *Contemporary Fictions of Attention: Reading and Distraction in the Twenty-First Century* (London and New York: Bloomsbury Academic, 2018), 127.

126 Sara Baume, *Handiwork* (Dublin: Tramp Press, 2020), 215.

127 Bennett, *Pond*, 140, 46.

128 Baume, *Line*, 178.

129 Baume, *Handiwork*, 55.

130 Baume, *Handiwork*, 155, 171.

131 Rhona Richman Kenneally, 'I am Off-White Walls': Exploring and Theorizing Domestic Space', in *The Vibrant House: Irish Writing and Domestic Space*, ed. Rhona Richman Kenneally and Lucy McDiarmid (Dublin: Four Courts, 2017), 16–17.

132 Susan Fraiman, *Extreme Domesticity: A View from the Margins* (New York: Columbia University Press, 2017), 35; Gaston Bachelard, *The Poetics of Space*, trans. Maria Jolas (London: Beacon, 1994), 3.

133 Baume, *Line*, 251.

134 Baume, *Line*, 251.

135 Baume, *Line*, 276.

136 Baume, *Line*, 302.

137 Baume, *Line*, 302. Indeed, the project continues near where I write, in Huntly, where Caroline Wendling's *White Wood* consists of plantings from acorns taken from Beuys's original oaks. See Alan Macpherson, 'Art, Trees, and the Enchantment of the Anthropocene: Caroline Wendling's *White Wood*', *Environmental Humanities* 10.1 (2018): 241–56.

138 Bennett, *Pond*, 65.

139 Bennett, *Pond*, 78.

140 Marlen Haushofer, *The Wall*, trans. Shaun Whiteside (San Francisco: Cleis Press, 1990), 62.

141 Bennett, *Pond*, 147.

142 Bennett, *Pond*, 148.

143 Abi Andrews, *The Word for Woman Is Wilderness* (London: Serpent's Tail, 2018), 7. Original emphasis.

144 Andrews, *Word*, 251. Original emphasis.

145 Bénédicte Monicat, 'Autobiography and Women's Travel Writings in Nineteenth-Century France: Journeys through Self-Representation', *Gender, Place and Culture* 1.1 (1994): 65.

146 Andrews, *Word*, 4.

147 McClory, *Flesh*, 89.

148 Giuliana Bruno, *Atlas of Emotion: Journeys in Art, Architecture, and Film* (New York: Verso, 2018), 191.

149 Donna J. Haraway, *Simians, Cyborgs, and Women: The Reinvention of Nature* (London and New York: Routledge, 1991), 188. Original emphasis.

150 Haraway, *Simians*, 195.

151 See Sandra Harding, 'Rethinking Standpoint Epistemology: What Is "Strong Objectivity?"', in *Feminist Epistemologies*, ed. Linda Alcoff and Elizabeth Potter (New York and London: Routledge, 1993), 49–82; D.Lynn O'Brien Hallstein, 'Where Standpoint Stands Now: An Introduction and Commentary', *Women's Studies in Communication* 23.1 (2000): 1–15.

152 Andrews, *Word*, 291.

153 Andrews, *Word*, 240, 252.

154 Andrews, *Word*, 150. Original emphasis.

155 Andrews, *Word*, 55.

156 Carolyn Merchant, *The Anthropocene and the Humanities: From Climate Change to a New Age of Sustainability* (New Haven and London: Yale University Press, 2020), 87.

157 For an overview of the relation between settler colonialism and feminism, see Maile Arvin, Eve Tuck and Angie Morrill, 'Decolonizing Feminism: Challenging Connections between Settler Colonialism and Heteropatriarchy', *Feminist Formations* 25.1 (2013): 8–34.

158 Andrews, *Word*, 232.

159 Andrews, *Word*, 166. Original emphasis.

160 Patrick D. Murphy, *Ecocritical Explorations in Literary and Cultural Studies: Fences, Boundaries, and Fields* (Lanham, MD and Plymouth: Rowman and Littlefield, 2010), 1. Murphy's critique of Thoreau's work which he argues promotes an 'illusory kind of simplicity' that 'precludes the possibility of widespread social transformation' closely parallels Erin's own (19).

161 Abi Andrews, 'Q+A with Abi Andrews about *The Word for Woman Is Wilderness*', *Two Dollar Radio* (2018): twodollarradio.com/blogs/radiowaves/q-a-with-abi-andrews-about-the-word-for-woman-is-wilderness [Accessed 22 August 2020].

162 Andrews, *Word*, 219.

163 Andrews, *Word*, 214.

164 Andrews, *Word*, 215.

165 Andrews, *Word*, 286, 299. Erin quotes Woolf's dictum to '[a]rrange whatever pieces come your way', although she elides the following sentence from Woolf's diary: 'Never be unseated by the shying of that undependable brute, life, unsettled as she is by my own queer, difficult nervous system'. Virginia Woolf, *The Diary of Virginia Woolf, Volume III: 1925–30*, ed. Anne Olivier Bell (Harmondsworth: Penguin, 1982), 39.

166 Ngai, *Ugly Feelings*, 85.

167 Andrews, *Word*, 292.

168 Andrews, *Word*, 302.

2

'How It Had All Connected': Assemblage, classification and performance

Introductory constellation

The long-awaited release of Fiona Apple's *Fetch the Bolt Cutters* in April 2020 was immediately hailed not only as a welcome re-emergence of the artist after eight years of silence, but as an album that spoke immediately to a world fundamentally altered by pandemic-related lockdowns.[1] The album's relevance to the present situation was reflected less in its thematic material than many of its aural components: largely recorded in Apple's home, the album includes many homemade and domestic percussion instruments and effects, while the title song includes 'backing barks' from Apple's dogs.[2] The album's affectual resonance was captured not only in its sense of anger and frustration, but in its fragmented production that reflected Apple's own living situation: it was received as an album about isolation. I listened to the album for the first time on one of my daily walks along the River Don in Aberdeen, and the sudden shift between feeling as if I were in Apple's own kitchen and assuming the barking dogs were behind me in the park, not on my headphones, was thrilling and disorientating. When the album finished, the normal sounds of birds and river and passing children seemed new: my aural environment had been reshaped by my encounter with Apple's music. Apple's sudden tonal shifts, including tempo changes, idiosyncratic approaches to verse-chorus structures, surprising vocal effects including the frequent layering of her own voice and the use of non-traditional instrumentation all created a sense of fractured becoming that easily resonated with my own experiences of the world, and that of thousands of other listeners.

The album that carried me through that summer, though, was Phoebe Bridgers's *Punisher*, released two months later. The final track, 'I Know the End', contains three distinct parts. It opens with a first-person narrative describing the speaker's own disorientation in place and time, with an ambient accompaniment. Midway through, drums and electric guitars kick in, and the lyrics become focused on an unspecified, if apocalyptic, collective threat: 'It's a government drone or an alien spaceship / Either way we're not alone.'[3] This lyric too gives way to a new section, a roar of guitars, horns and screams, as well as an ominous chorus, that is finally replaced simply with Bridgers's heavy breathing and a small cough at the song's end. Although the song has a clear arc, and a cathartic momentum, it is up to the listener to make sense of the relations between its constituent parts. There is no stable narrative persona; rather, the self becomes absorbed in collective upheaval. Both Apple's and Bridgers's albums, I want to suggest, were particularly moving to me because of their sonic fragmentation: in resisting familiar song structures and instrumentation, they made the world wider. Unlike Taylor Swift's *folklore*, which was released at the same time and similarly seen as particularly relevant to the lockdown experience, Apple's and Bridger's albums resist familiar song forms and sonic effects in order to present an assemblage of sounds and images that are fundamentally disruptive at the same time they point to new possibilities for collective experience.[4] Neither album, unlike the works of art discussed below, engages directly with environmental concerns. They both, however, can be seen as examples of the ideas of fragmentary encounter and multiplicity that govern this chapter.

Calls for the importance of emphasizing multiplicity in any account of the world can be traced, in modern theoretical contexts, at least back to the work of Gilles Deleuze and Claire Parnet, who argue that the 'minimum real unit is not the word, the idea, the concept or the signifier, but the *assemblage*.'[5] An assemblage, as Deleuze specifies, is 'a multiplicity which is made up of many different ages, sexes and reigns – different natures': it can be understood in terms of symbiosis and sympathy.[6] Assemblages involve non-human actors and technological media and can be framed, following Rosi Braidotti, as a form of subjectivity that 'flow[s] across and displace[s] binaries' of nature/technology, male/female, local/global and so on.[7] Deleuze's original term 'agencement' contains both active and passive senses: it is not only what is gathered, but also the act of gathering or, in my terms, gleaning.[8] Assemblage is not a wilful act of collection and classification, but a form of relation between multiple actors, human and non-human. For Braidotti, it is a form of knowledge production that 'is always multiple and collective': she frames her own essay as an assemblage of the work of a multiplicity of scholars.[9] In its simplest definition, assemblage is a way to understand that knowledge is not generated by a single voice, nor does it rely on or instate a familiar subject-object binary. Rather, knowledge is created – the world is known – through myriad voices working in concert. This approach has particular pertinence to modern ecological and environmental philosophies since, as John Law and Marianne Lien argue, nature 'is neither given nor made, but rather the stubborn outcome of myriad practices that together conjure and confirm its existence'.[10] While the texts discussed in Chapter 1 often privileged, albeit in complex ways, a relation between subject and object, and in so doing suggested the possibility of nature as a knowable other, the texts discussed below focus on immanence, multiplicity and co-constitution.

Focusing on assemblage and multiplicity, as Braidotti suggests, allows for a redefinition of the human. As she writes, 'the human needs to be assessed as materially embedded and embodied, differential, affective and relational'.[11] The human subject is not transcendent or universal, but known in and through their material relations with other agents, both human and non-human. This perspective is closely allied to Tsing's definition of precarity, where she argues that '[u]npredictable encounters transform us; we are not in control, even of ourselves. Unable to rely on a stable structure of community, we are thrown into shifting assemblages, which remake us as well as our others'.[12] In Tsing's formulation, encounters are mutually transformative; as in the work of Alexis Shotwell, as discussed in the Introduction, emphasizing multiple encounters enables a discourse that emphasizes contamination over purity, collectivity over individuality and becoming over fixed identities. Encounters, in this sense, create the space for what Braidotti terms 'a sort of epistemological humility' that emphasizes the ethical, democratic foundations of knowledge.[13] Both Tsing and Braidotti begin their accounts with an emphasis on encounter as embodied: knowledge does not proceed from an abstract, ethereal plane, but is always immanent and known through the encounter. Encounter is how bodies are known in relation to each other. Such a focus on materiality is endemic to feminist criticism where, as Anna Fisk writes, critique and reinvention are 'not just a matter of scavenging and rebuilding' but dismantling and reassessment.[14] Particularly within posthuman feminism, however, encountering the world as an embodied self does not necessarily imply the pre-existence of that self. The human subject, as Braidotti clarifies in relation to Donna Haraway's concept of the cyborg, does not occupy a 'unitary subject position', but is 'multi-layered, complex and internally differentiated', as well as differentiated in relation to others.[15] That is, it is not only that the world must be dismantled and rebuilt, but that the self is transformed and known through this relationship.

My reading of assemblage and multiplicity in some senses parallels, and derives from, Karen Barad's work on entanglement. In the first sentences of *Meeting the Universe Halfway*, in the 'Preface and Acknowledgments', Barad writes:

> To be entangled is not simply to be intertwined with another, as in the joining of separate entities, but to lack an independent, self-contained existence. Existence is not an individual affair. Individuals do not preexist their interactions; rather, individuals emerge through and as part of their entangled intra-relating.[16]

Like Braidotti, Barad emphasizes that even the most theoretical or academic productions are products of myriad encounters, and in themselves can be seen as forms of entangled assemblage. The work of theory is not separate from the world of lived encounters: both Barad's academic writing and her web of interpersonal relations can be seen, as in her discussion of Niels Bohr, as 'specific physical arrangements'.[17] There is no unified, unitary subject position from which to proceed: all thought and action – a distinction Barad would perhaps not endorse – emerge from 'material practices of intra-acting within and as part of the world'.[18] The material world does not exist independently, waiting to be discovered; neither does the observant subject emerge into the world wholly formed, ready to pronounce on what it finds. As the theologian Catherine Keller, whose work draws on Barad as well as many of the other thinkers discussed below, articulates:

> *From our own entangled relations, we may infer infinite complications.* [...] If the separateness of our lives is a sham, then the work of our civilization to produce us as discrete subjects vying to emulate, master, know, and consume external objects succeeds only through its systemic repression of that site of active relationship.[19]

For both Barad and Keller, there is not an 'I' that pre-exists a 'you' on which it can then pronounce: echoing some of the contemporary ecofeminist perspectives discussed in Chapter 1, both thinkers, from radically different disciplinary perspectives, argue that any understanding of difference comes only in relation.

As Barad clarifies, this does not mean that knowledge is inherently subjective, as this would be to repeat a subject-object distinction, but rather knowledge emerges from an attentiveness to material becoming, as I explored in Chapter 1. This approach to embodiment allows for a reconsideration of the 'givenness' of bodily boundaries, as seen in other thinkers in postcolonial, feminist, disability and queer studies, as well as in a number of Indigenous thinkers, as will be explored below.[20] Bodies, as Barad writes, 'are not objects with inherent boundaries and properties; they are material-discursive phenomena.[21] Although Braidotti, Keller, Tsing and Barad write from different disciplinary backgrounds, and there are clear distinctions in their arguments, they each focus on an opening of the world that emphasizes encounter and multiplicity rather than the acceptance of givenness, or the reaffirmation of a subject-object distinction. I return to Braidotti and Barad's work throughout this chapter not only because their texts have been central in my own understanding of the topic, but also because they are rooted in, if very different from, the feminist approaches discussed in Chapter 1.[22] Braidotti's call for contemporary feminism to embrace 'multiple transversal alliances across communities' echoes much of the following argument.[23]

The longing for a new form of transformative encounter is often found in nonfiction works of nature writing or travel writing. Jini Reddy's *Wanderland*, for instance, opens with a discussion of her desire not simply to travel, but to experience the world in a new way: 'Call me sentimental but I wanted something more than to walk through an alluring landscape and admire its beauty. I wanted somehow to be more *porous*.'[24] Reddy writes of her ambition to 'connect with the Other in the land'; while she frames this in terms of mystical or magical experiences, and meets with a variety of religious and spiritual seekers, this question of Otherness is also related to her own feelings of isolation.[25] Born in London to Indian parents, themselves raised in South Africa, Reddy was raised in Canada and her book is in part a documentation of what it means to return to England as someone already considered Other. She concludes the book by speaking of her 'need to retrieve those lost, mute and unloved parts of myself', which is only possible in encounters with the land.[26] While Reddy certainly maintains familiar ideas of a human self that encounters the world in space and time in a far more linear way than Barad, her text also opens up the possibility that selfhood is constituted in this 'porous' engagement with the material world, such that the relation between self and other, or self and Other, is created and revealed in intra-action. In seeking mystical experiences, Reddy opens herself to different ways of knowing, and being known by, the world.

Reddy's work also exemplifies Braidotti's discussions of nomadic writing as an inherently political form of resistance to mainstream communication and hegemonic formations. Embracing 'radical nonbelonging' is a way to resituate the self in the world, through the immediacy of encounter.[27] Nomadism, Braidotti explains, 'is not fluidity without borders, but rather an acute awareness of the nonfixity of boundaries', while the nomad is a 'multiple entity, functioning in a net of interconnections'.[28] Nomadism, in this sense, is not a way to frame the movement of a human subject through the material world, but a way to understand the way both are co-constituted. As Barad, Reddy and Braidotti all emphasize, however, these ideas of multiplicity and assemblage do not entail a complete fluidity where all relations are ambiguous, and there can be no final distinction between subject and object or self and other. Rather, these relations are created in and through encounters.

This chapter traces three approaches to encounter, in a variety of different genres and styles. I begin with a discussion of poetic works by Melissa Eleftherion and Elizabeth-Jane Burnett. Both authors examine the relation between memory and embodiment in terms of both their material encounters with the natural world and their relation to received forms of classification and description. I then turn to a variety of texts, including song, prose and performance, by Tanya Tagaq and Karine Polwart. While Tagaq and Polwart are certainly very different artists, both combine traditional forms of music and performance with an intermedial approach, such that both written texts and recorded or performed music become forms of collective enunciation of personal loss and planetary environmental change. Finally, I turn back to Burnett's memoir *The Grassling*, which incorporates each of these elements in an experimental assemblage to open new possibilities for thinking about the relation of self and world. Each of these artists, while working from distinct cultural and aesthetic traditions, emphasizes ideas of assemblage, multiplicity and encounter to create challenging new forms.

The mixture of forms and genres in each of the works discussed below can be considered in terms of not only assemblage but bricolage, or 'the construction or creation of an artwork from a diverse range of available materials'.[29] Lisa Kay's account of bricolage in creative arts therapy begins with the twin foundations of her gathering and assembling of found objects to create artworks, and her research practices, where using multiple methodologies and theoretical constructs can generate novel insights. Both aspects can be seen in many of the works below, and indeed throughout this book: the unexpected combination of material objects, forms and genres, or theoretical frameworks is endemic to the work of fragmentation and gleaning. Bricolage, however, can be seen as a process that leads to a completed project: the term can refer to both the construction of a work of art and the resulting artwork. Assemblage and gleaning, however, are differentiated by their focus on relinquishment and incompleteness: assemblage is a form of becoming, rather than the creation of a particular object. While both bricolage and assemblage foreground the juxtaposition of multiple, often unlikely, materials, I want to emphasize the qualities of multiplicity and embeddedness that are central to these texts and performances. Each of these works in various ways highlights ideas of loss, relinquishment and incompletion. This changes not only the resulting artwork, but also how we think of the relation between the work of art and the subject who produces it, and ultimately undoes that distinction. The artist does not only produce the work, but is produced by it in a ceaseless network of encounter and exchange. While I cannot go as far as Barad's argument for a form of agency that is not ascribed to individual intent or action, but is solely about the 'possibilities for changing the configurations of spactimematter relations', I argue that a focus on fragmentation as a form of continuously opening possibility changes the role of the artist and the observer.[30]

As will be explored at greater length below, this focus on encounter, multiplicity, fragmentation and assemblage leads to new approaches to embodiment, as can again be seen in relation to Braidotti and Barad. For Braidotti, differentiation and actualization can only be seen in terms of multiplicity: individuation and embodiment can only occur 'through networks of natural, social, political and physiological relations'.[31] Braidotti argues that we are 'deeply steeped in the material world' at a structural level.[32] This statement does not imply a homogeneity of matter, but rather allows differentiation, as in her repeated credo 'we-are-(all)-in-this-together-but-we-are-not-one-and-the-same'.[33]   Difference and individuation are made possible because any 'we' is not limited to the human, but already is enmeshed in interaction with others. Embodiment and individuation are possible precisely because any material self is already bound up and interacting with myriad others. Barad goes further to claim that:

> The world is an ongoing intra-active engagement, and bodies are among the differential performances *of* the world's dynamic intra-activity, in an endless reconfiguring of boundaries and properties [...]. *Embodiment is a matter not of being specifically situated in the world, but rather of being of the world in its dynamic specificity.*[34]

Bodies, again, are not given, or seen as end products. Embodiment cannot be seen either as cause or effect, but rather as the intra-action of matter. For Barad, bodies, like words and things, do not pre-exist or have determinate meanings, but must be understood in relation to their material becoming.[35]

This approach to bodies is clearly challenging, and perhaps counter-intuitive: I am writing, and you are reading, from the perspective of an embodied self, and it is easy to take that embodied selfhood as consistent, even if it is formed through discursive practices. Barad, whose work is frequently interpreted through a feminist or even ecofeminist lens, is in part responding to Judith Butler; Butler approaches the materiality of bodies in terms of the way bodies can be seen 'as the effect of a dynamic of power', while performativity, as she clarifies, 'is the reiterative power of discourse to produce the phenomena that it regulates and constrains'.[36] For Butler, in Barad's reading, matter is ultimately produced by discursive practices, whereas Barad argues that matter is always becoming, '*not a thing but a doing*'.[37] Yet Butler's argument that language 'emerges from the materiality of bodily life' reveals her own attempts to rethink both distinctions between matter and discourse and ideas of cause and effect.[38] Both thinkers, like Braidotti, trouble the distinction between body and discourse, and in doing so redefine those terms in very different ways.

What is important here, however, is the way this argument is itself already formed in relation to ideas of discourse and embodiment. The mutual citation between these thinkers reveals the way their ideas are shaped by and through discourse, and how that matters, in the dual sense that all three of them employ. If the body does not pre-exist, nor does a thinking of the body: such thinking is, in itself, always multiple and referential. If this is in some ways a truism, it is also central to the texts below, in a range of registers, as well as those discussed in Chapter 3. Understanding embodiment, in the majority of these texts, is in part a process of coming to recognize oneself not as a fixed point, but as known in relation to encounters with others, human and more-than-human, and as sharing that material reality. At the same time, however, these embodied encounters are also understood in relation to texts: the works in this chapter are frequently concerned with maps, field guides and other forms of discursive knowing that are both regulatory and, ultimately, liberating. The self is constructed in relation to material immanence and to texts and discursive practices: any understanding of the embodied self must take into account its engagement with a multiple, material world and at the same time the way knowledge of that world is reached not solely through material encounter, but discursive, and even classificatory, practices. The use of fragmentary form becomes a way to keep these elements in play: rather than charting a linear progression towards understanding, these texts show how body, world and text are all always known in and through each other. The textualized body is not simply a metaphor, in Elizabeth Grosz's terminology, but a form of encounter that reveals texts and bodies as mutually co-constituted in their entanglement.[39] This focus on the relation between body, world and text can be seen not only in the thematic and formal strategies of the work below, but in the way their authors all stress the importance of their works' reception. It is not sufficient to state the existence of these relationships; rather, textual performances must equally be seen in relation to their audience.

As such, these works can be situated in relation to ideas of becoming as formulated by Deleuze and Félix Guattari. As they introduce the concept, becoming is not a process of identification or a stable state of being: becoming is not a transition from one identity to another. Becoming has no outcome other than itself. Rather becoming, as Braidotti clarifies, is 'a process of redefining one's sense of attachment and connection to a shared world' that 'expresses multiple ecologies of belonging'.[40] Each of the authors discussed below employs a variety of textual and performative strategies to reveal these multiple ecologies and the complete entanglement of discursive and material relations. In her discussion of Deleuze's ideas of becoming Braidotti writes that becoming is 'an affect that flows, like writing, it is a composition, a location that needs to be constructed together with, that is to say, in the encounter with, others'.[41] The texts discussed below take each of these elements – affect, writing, composition, location and encounter – as constituting the fundamental network in relation to which the embodied self can be understood. The self is always caught up in, and formed by, its entangled encounters.

A. Lists and erasures: Melissa Eleftherion and Elizabeth-Jane Burnett

Melissa Eleftherion's *field guide to autobiography* opens with a brief, untitled poem, nestled in the bottom right corner of the page:

          i made myself from rocks

shells   birds   trees   insects

         mountain and   ocean

i made myself   as you have   carapace

this is an autobiography of fractures

this is a field guide to a field guide

to identity   that muscular slap of light[42]

The poem is an invocation and a set of instructions for how to read the rest of the volume. The self is, from the first line, constructed and assembled in relation to a more-than-human world; as in Braidotti's account, differentiation is only possible within a material network. The poem is both constrained and freewheeling: even as the poem burrows into the corner of the page, the words themselves separate and make room for absence and exploration. Matter and identity are known together, in their becoming, in their reference to textual form and their own fragmentation. The spacing allows for multiple interpretations: it is possible to read the fourth line both as 'i made myself [just] as you have [a] carapace', where the 'you' signifies some sort of arthropod, and as 'i made myself as you have', with 'carapace' being an echo of the list above, in which case the 'you' might refer to the human reader. This essential ambiguity drives much of the collection: the poems do not simply detail a human subject's encounters with the non-human world, but a continual, and unresolved, process of becoming that includes both humans and non-humans without privileging either.

Unusually for a first collection, the book includes a lengthy interview with Eleftherion where she clearly enunciates her vision for the volume, which emerged from her practice as an archivist and her use of field guides as source texts. She writes:

> With *field guide*, I wanted to explore the inter-relatedness of various species and in so doing, tell a story about the larger body of which they are fragments. Autobiographies are rife with fractures and missing pieces – fragments as form, then. [...] I've had this intuition that we're all fragments of one magnificent, multi-cellular organism and that was the impetus for this book.[43]

As Eleftherion explains, the collection is at once autobiographical and universal: it is about the becoming-woman of teenagers, about dissociation after sexual abuse and trauma, and about the need for all humans to relinquish a hierarchical model of the world. Burnett notes that innovative poetics, especially 'those engaging with indeterminacy', are often criticized as not 'result[ing] in any "meaningful" environmental action'.[44] This in part explains the remarkably clear connections Eleftherion and Burnett make between their poetic work and larger environmental concerns in a number of interviews and other sources. *field guide* is not simply invested in ideas of the construction of the self as materially embedded in the world, but provides a pathway for the reader to consider these themes in relation to their own life and activism. Like Tanya Tagaq, too, whose approach to these same themes will be discussed in the next section, Eleftherion employs fragments precisely as a way to showcase multiplicity and assemblage. Fragmentation becomes a way of knowing that does not simply approach things in themselves, but leads to change and revisioning. Fragmentation thus signals difference and inclusion: it creates the space for a new way of imagining the self in relation to the world.

Eleftherion's approach is clarified through her formal innovation. While some poems employ stanzaic structures, others let their individual words spread across the page, creating a material environment out of blank space.[45] The first thing to note about *field guide*, then, is that while it gestures towards the title form, and some poems are very clearly titled after and descriptive of assorted birds, shellfish and other creatures, the volume also initially appears to resist the classificatory organizational principles that underlie most field guides. In a survey of assorted modern field guides, John Law and Michael Lynch identify four commonly shared features: naturalistic accountability, authority, a picture theory of representation and a strategic use of texts.[46] Whether field guides employ schematic representations, photographs, diorama or naturalistic illustration, each emphasizes the interplay between text and image. This combination, deployed correctly, makes the text authoritative for a novice birdwatcher for instance, who may attempt to identify or locate a particular animal on the basis of having first encountered it in a field guide. A field guide should, they argue, emphasize 'essential' details and not include 'gratuitous' ones: its function is not to present non-human life exactly as it might be seen in a given encounter, but to give the observer a set of tools that permit correct identification.[47]

Field guides, in this sense, privilege ideas of vision as collection, as seen in the discussion of MacGillivray in the Prologue. Textual encounters precede and define material encounters. As the authors clarify in a revised version of their paper, however, field guides can be understood as a situated practice of reading that 'requires an active consultation of texts as part of the embodied performance of a socially organized activity'.[48] As such, on the one hand classifications can be seen as a form of abstracted, authoritative knowledge: classifications can be seen either as ordering the world in their own image or responding to local situations, but they cannot be considered simple representations of what the observer might see. On the other hand, however, the encounter between reader, field guide and natural environment is a situated performance that depends on both physical and social interactions. As Claire Waterton has shown in experiments combining natural observation and choreography, acts of classification themselves 'can be seen as performances'.[49] Like Burnett's accounts of performance below, Waterton emphasizes the way performances show that classificatory systems include elements of contingency and surprise.

field guide to autobiography, perhaps inevitably, avoids the interplay of text and image, and in doing so, resists declarations of authority, especially those that rely on classification systems often connected to patriarchal and cultural normatives. The text's meaning does not pre-exist the reader's own encounters with the world, but is formed in relation to it. At the same time, however, especially in early poems that draw on and combine phrases from various field guides, Eleftherion's work begins to suggest a network of multiple ecologies that are not only contingent, but resistant to explanation. One brief untitled poem opens 'acolyte elytra / occipital petal / fecal parietal cloacal'.[50] While the reader might know some of the words, they are unlikely to be familiar with them all, and may have no way to contextualize them. Instead, Eleftherion draws attention to assonance and consonance, to the visual and aural rhymes and repetitions that become their own way of ordering. Another untitled poem presents a series of descriptions that are only attached to non-human creatures in the footnotes: the line '[u]sually lamellate, sometimes flabellate' is enjoyable for its rhymes, for the way the words roll in the reader's mouth, but discovering it applies to the superfamily *scarabaeid* may not be illuminating for many readers.[51] Yet Eleftherion's approach does not emphasize language at the expense of understanding. The poem 'winged, stalked' begins simply '[c]ommon, common, uncommon / Distinguished from other wrens / Distinguished from the loon', without at any point revealing what birds are being described. The poem ends, however, much like Kathleen Jamie's work discussed in the Introduction, with the invitation to '[l]isten'.[52] The reader is invited not to identify a particular species, replicating a subject-object binary, but to immerse themselves in a linguistic network of signs and words that do not refer to pre-existing entities, but are known in themselves. The first function of the field guide, then, is to suggest the world's multiplicity: even as it resists understanding, it is immersive and often beautiful.

Burnett's *Swims* similarly opens with an invitation to the reader contextualized in relation to a classificatory system, in this case dictionaries. The first poem, which is untitled and not listed in the table of contents, opens with an epigraph from Georges Bataille: 'A dictionary would start from the point at which it would no longer give the meanings but the tasks of words.' Words, like Barad's definition of matter, are not things but doings. The poem begins with a set of infinitives ranging down the middle of the page, while 'To Swim' appears to their left, not quite a title but still a common reference point. The injunctions range from the abstract to the specific, from activities easily associated with swimming to those completely distinct. The reader is invited to 'disappear', 'float', 'be lichen'; they are told '[t]o appear / in *Vanity Fair* before breakfast. / To afterwards destroy the economy of Greece' and, in the centre of the page, '[t]o be an assemblage'.[53] The meaning of the lines is revealed solely in their relation. While the form is different from Eleftherion's opening, and Burnett elides, temporarily, the 'I' with which Eleftherion begins, both poems similarly gesture to a self that is known in assemblage, and to a resistance to classificatory norms that nevertheless acknowledges their persistence. Both poets write to and from a system of knowledge in order to challenge and expand it.

Eleftherion and Burnett's presentation of assemblages can be clarified in relation to the idea of constellation that Louise Green borrows from Theodor Adorno and Walter Benjamin. In Green's reading, a constellation 'juxtapose[s] elements from different orders of knowledge, refusing a hierarchical ordering of the general and the particular'.[54] The constellation is a non-hierarchical ordering that avoids universalization, but rather combines or makes adjacent particular phenomena that become intelligible in their relation. As Green writes:

> The constellation allows seemingly incommensurable things to be placed alongside each other without reducing them to a relationship of equivalence. It makes visible the contradictory aspect of the real, introducing awkward material complexity into the smooth logic of any systematic organization. Constellations of phenomena are always provisional.[55]

If these juxtapositions are visually represented in Eleftherion's poetry, they are more clearly enunciated in Burnett's work. In 'Preface', for instance, she stipulates the way swimming, and the writing of that swimming, creates a new form of relationship:

Not that   *the river is like* the body
or   *the river is* the body
but   both have gone
and what is left is something else.[56]

The relation between body and world, or more specifically between human body and river body, is not one of equivalence or influence or even understanding. Instead, it is a provisional encounter that creates a space for transformation and complexity. While Alice Oswald's *Dart*, *Swims*'s clear predecessor, privileges human experience, even as Oswald cautions that the recorded conversations that appear in the poem should not be attributed to particular real people but 'read as the river's mutterings', Burnett makes a space for unenunciated or inarticulable forms of knowledge.[57] Burnett and Eleftherion use the familiar forms of field guides and dictionaries not simply as a challenge to received forms of authority, but rather to indicate the way a focus on fragmentary material encounter can expand and transform our understanding of the more-than-human world that privileges multiplicity and interaction.

Like Eleftherion, Burnett takes care to explain to the reader what they are encountering and its implication for larger considerations of environmental embeddedness and change: she describes the volume as 'a long poem documenting twelve wild swims across England and Wales [...]. Each swim is conceived as an environment action, testing the ways in which individuals might affect environmental change.'[58] The twelve swims – in Devon, Somerset, Sussex, Cumbria, London, Snowdonia and Cornwall – are presented as records of performance, often with the involvement of other people, both living and dead. Burnett's second poem titled 'The Ouse', for instance, begins with an e-mail sent to collaborators where she invites them to write messages on her swimsuit. A photograph of the swimsuit itself was featured in 'The Trembling Grass' exhibition at the University of Exeter/CCANW in 2014 (which Burnett also curated) and is included in Burnett's academic monograph, but is not included in *Swims*. Instead, the left-hand margin of the poem is titled 'suit-text before water' and the right-hand margin is titled 'suit-text after water'. In her discussion of the work, Burnett discusses how it can be seen as a collaboration between poet, collaborators and river:

> The text itself is collaborative in multiple senses, since I invite participants to contribute their own words to the swimming costume (on the theme of their current environmental hopes and fears) and the river then adds its changes to it. This scenario provides possibilities for the artwork, and those producing and receiving it, to connect more closely with the natural world since the distance between practitioner, artwork and the natural world is decreased. In a poignant act of erasure in this piece, the phrase 'GAZA, may you not be a war zone' became 'may you not be a war zone' – the word GAZA having disappeared from the costume at the end of the swim. To interpret this erasure as the river's comment on a specific environmental and humanitarian issue is, of course, to anthropomorphise, but this kind of contact can nevertheless be helpful in considering the non-human as capable and deserving of a response.[59]

The text of the poem is not simply a record of a performance, but an embodiment of a multiform exchange between human and non-human agents. In the main body of the poem, between the original and erased lines on Gaza, themselves in miniscule italics, Burnett writes:

I, the rhythm of river
part-nature, part-poem, part-kin

I, the collaboration
part-nature – parts nature
collapses
the shoulders[60]

The 'I' is not simply a poetic persona, but the emergent product of this collaboration, and the collaboration itself: it is not bounded by an individual body, but is defined in relation to what Barad would call spacetimemattering, or the interplay between space, time and matter that does not privilege any one aspect, but views them in mutual relation. The collaboration does not depend on separate, pre-existing entities: rather, those elements or phenomena are known only in their relation. The use of repeated words that shift meaning and grammatical function – 'part' as modifier and 'parts' as verb, for instance – does not simply replicate the rhythms of the river, but instantiates them. The poem employs multiple approaches to lineation and stanzaic structures, and moves from straightforward declarations of love for the world to, like Eleftherion, lists of natural elements praised for the sound they make – 'nettles nettles rush / lemon loosestrife thyme' – to discussions of violence in Mosul to breathless, overwhelming overflows of words and feeling.[61] It ends, finally, with words as creatures in their own right: 'little throbs of words beating and smell of / fur and / feathers wet on the wing of words wetting the air tongue wet on the air'.[62] To isolate any one poetic technique, or one frame of reference, would be to miss the point, although readers may seize on any number of individual elements. Instead, just as Burnett immerses herself in the river so that both are changed by the encounter, the reader must immerse themselves in the poem and come away changed. The poem enacts Burnett's desire to see nature as informing a sense of self in a way that dissolves 'the distance between human suffering and environmental degradation'.[63]

In Eleftherion's poetry, like Tagaq's songs and prose, the relation between human suffering and environmental degradation is often framed in terms of sexual assault and violence. The six couplets in 'elytra meat' juxtapose adolescent girlhood with field guide descriptions of beetles: 'That little girl already a slut to you on roller-skates / Elytra truncate and not much taller than wide.'[64] Both girl and beetle are classified and observed, positioned as objects: rather than framing beetle life as an analogue for human life, Eleftherion demonstrates the potential violence in classificatory systems. If 'a group of soft bones breaking' is 'a history of capitalism', Eleftherion's work presents a way of reframing the imperial, patriarchal drives behind many modern classification systems, where the 'imperial impulse to archive knowledge' has simply been replaced by fantasies of global information networks.[65] As Eleftherion describes her chapbook *little ditch*, which uses language drawn from mineral field guides to explore 'sexual abuse, rape culture, & internalized misogyny', she sees connections between the vocabulary of field guides and 'the oppressive vocabularies of patriarchy', which 'reinforce this hegemonic palimpsest'.[66] The chapbook ends with 'ammonite sonnet', which begins: 'the ammonite an index of sutures / I got tired of cataloguing them / hermetically sealing little traumas'.[67] Individual pronouncement becomes a form of control. While the imagery of sexual violence is far more prominent in *little ditch* than in *field guide*, both collections raise the question of knowledge as a form of control.

In Eleftherion's work the shifting assemblages of human and non-human lives and bodies resists easy categorization. In 'catalpa', for instance, the referential descriptions of a tree in bloom, with 'heart leaf' and blossoms like a 'radial star' give way to 'the thing / that used / to hit me'.[68] The three lines, almost but not quite justified to the right margin, are most easily readable as the intrusion of human violence, as the penultimate line 'the tree her bruised shadow made' supports. Natural description partly gives way to autobiographical, or at least human, experience. I grew up with a catalpa outside my childhood home, however, a tree so old that it marked a turning point in the road before most of the houses were built, and most autumns I would be hit by the tree's falling seed pods, surprisingly heavy. As a reader I am able to approach the poem both in terms of human and more-than-human violence and as an invitation to reflect on my own encounters with non-human life. As Burnett writes, poetry 'is not entirely retained by the poet but is partially given to its readership'.[69] The poem is not simply a record of encounters, but itself a form of encounter with the reader as well. The spacing of 'catalpa', which has a great hollow at its centre, provides a space for the reader to insert themselves: Eleftherion's poems do not straightforwardly juxtapose environmental and human concerns: rather, they present them as part of a complicated network that invites the reader in.

These acts of invitation are central to Burnett's poetics as well. In 'The Teign' an unattributed voice in bold inserts itself into a fisheries survey:

	Salmon	Sea Trout
1951	118	592
1952	45	**this is not solving anything**

Biological examination of this area has shown that **I am too old**.[70]

While Alexa Weik von Mossner makes the straightforward argument that 'intimate knowledge of and personal passion for [an] environment' enable authors to convey 'the material qualities and sensual feel of a natural environment in a way that enables readers to imaginatively experience them', Burnett raises the possibility, like the authors discussed in Chapter 1, that this imaginative experience might sometimes fail, and that such failure is intrinsic to understanding the world as multiple.[71] Frustration and negative affect are central to these experiences of encounter, and can mimic the reader's own sense of confusion or lostness. Encounters, as Lauren Berlant and Kathleen Stewart write, 'are not events of knowing, units of anything, revelations of realness, or facts'.[72] Instead, the encounter can be disruptive and incomplete: as much as it suggests integration, it can also highlight disconnection. Negative affect becomes a way of approaching the 'dissolution' of familiar frames of knowing, and highlighting the complexity of the assemblage.[73]

As Burnett writes in her own poem on the Dart, however, feelings of 'sadness' and 'de-connecting' can still, in material encounter, give rise to 'open possibility'.[74] Such possibilities are in part generated by the wealth of literary and cultural reference points scattered throughout the volume. Burnett's first poem on the Ouse acknowledges it as the site of Virginia Woolf's drowning, but asserts that the poetic persona is 'learning / through the fact / of my being here'.[75] The river is experienced equally through discursive and material encounters. Likewise, 'Grasmere' not only evokes the Romantics but Elizabeth Bishop's 'One Art' as the speaker reflects on 'all the lost things / bits of lost time and heart' at the same time that they consider 'debris from Fukushima'.[76] Burnett does not simply juxtapose Anthropocene exhaustion with personal renewal or nature healing, nor intertextual allusions with accounts of material encounter. Rather, she suggests, in this constellated form, that each of these elements can be held in tension and give rise to new possibilities. Like Eleftherion, Burnett makes space for the individual reader and includes them in her assemblages. The reader's imaginative experience is not controlled by the poet, but rather included in the interaction.

The complexity of Burnett's approach, and the possibilities it opens, is made most clear in two poems late in the volume. 'The English Channel' opens with a dedication to named humans and an unnamed pelican, a lengthy epigraph from Arthur Ransome's *Swallows and Amazons*, and directions for a swim where the reader or swimmer is invited to receive and remember a 'non-human identity', in reference to Ransome's character Titty, who occupies herself with being a cormorant.[77] The eight sections that follow depict these non-human identities and the human responses: Rosie is a mackerel, Florence a plastic bottle cap, Sam 'at first a whale shark and then actually a horseshoe crab', while 'someone' is 'a pelican that wasn't happy, or a piece of litter'.[78] The tone is light-hearted, even as Anthropocene anxiety sneaks in: the process of identification is less, as Burnett writes in a discussion of John Clare, 'about the human voice wishing to dominate, or to translate those other voices into human experience, than about interacting with the environment so as to articulate a faithful expression of self as experienced in a particular environment and a given time'.[79] The human selves are not pretending to be non-human animals, but are experiencing the environment from a more-than-human perspective. In each case the human experiences difficulty and confusion in their new material form, and yet is open to new ways of becoming. While this approach is inherently anthropocentric, perhaps, Burnett clarifies her perspective in the following poem, 'Porthmeor', which opens with a list of non-human animals brought back from extinction, with the instructions that their sounds be played into the sea. On the following page the speaker describes how

> the sea snail and mackerel pulse to gorilla
> and the surfers meld bright bodies to the tide
> as brine-bashed and salt-skinned I rise and I rise
> and all of us glimpse a better way that we could be
> living.[80]

The interplay between species creates a more-than-human assemblage that exceeds any one body or perspective. Imaginative identification with other species does not simply allow for empathy, but for new forms of living that recognize the particularity of each creature and phenomenon. This is exemplified in the swirl of lines over the page, as the page itself becomes an inclusive environment that permits different forms of encounter.

The emphasis on encounter and assemblage in the work of both poets suggests new possibilities for knowing that often parallel Barad's thinking. Barad explains at length that a given experiment cannot be seen as a record of a particular phenomenon taken by a detached observer. Rather, the experiment itself changes the nature of that phenomenon.[81] This means, quite simply, that the world is not there to be known, and knowledge does not pre-exist the encounter. She clarifies: 'Knowing is a direct material engagement, a practice of intra-acting with the world as part of the world in its dynamic material configuring, its ongoing articulation. The entangled practices of knowing and being are material practices'.[82] The various human and non-human bodies and presences in the work of both poets must be seen in their relation because neither pre-exists the encounter. Donna Haraway makes a similar point in arguing that '[b]eings do not preexist their relatings' and that consequently there 'are no pre-constituted subjects and objects, and no single sources, unitary actors, or final ends'.[83] Both Eleftherion and Burnett use varying formal and textual strategies to demonstrate the importance of knowing the world only in and through the material encounter, or as what Eleftherion calls 'the melting of classification'.[84] This requires an undoing of the self, not only in terms of Eleftherion's declaration that 'we're all becoming animals here' but in Burnett's assemblage of different techniques.[85] The five sections of Burnett's poem 'Sea Holly', co-written with Tony Lopez, combine lists of birds and shells, prose descriptions that anchor the observer in a given time and place (7:45am on a Friday morning near Langstone Rock) and a litany where 'she' becomes both the observer and the land:

> she
>> windblown sand
>> seashell sand
>> shifting sand
> she
>> sea sandwort
>> sea rocket
>> sea holly […]
> she
>> landscape
>> escape
>> seascape
> she half soil
>> she both scape
> she half scape
>> she both soil
> she escapes[86]

In a possible allusion to Eimear McBride's novel *A Girl Is a Half-Formed Thing*, Burnett and Lopez's 'she' is 'a both-formed thing', neither sea nor sand nor human, but all at once.[87] The self is constructed as and through encounter. The sibilance and repetitions here are not a way to privilege discourse over embodiment, but rather to position language as itself a form of embodiment and connection. The poem is where the human and the non-human meet.

Burnett and Eleftherion's poems thus form a response to the anxieties of scale discussed in the Introduction. While both poets frequently reiterate the importance of poetic forms as a way of instigating social change and reflecting Anthropocenic anxieties, they only rarely invoke the planetary scale seen in figures like Kathleen Jamie and Juliana Spahr.[88] Instead, the page itself is the environment for the meeting of human and non-human, and their mutual coming into being. These poems do not privilege human ways of knowing, but invite readers to consider their own framings of the world in new ways and recognize the multiplicity of co-constitutive lifeforms known in and through every encounter.

B. Touch, tradition, and performance: Tanya Tagaq and Karine Polwart

While Burnett's poems are often based in or reflections of performances, the work of Tanya Tagaq and Karine Polwart more directly requires its audience to consider the interplay of performer and environment. Both artists – who might most simply be described as an Inuk throat singer and a Scottish folksinger, respectively, but repeatedly challenge those designations – create assemblages that directly engage their audiences in a variety of ways. For Barad, following Butler, performative understandings of naturalcultural practices take 'account of the fact that knowing does not come from standing at a distance and representing but rather from *a direct material engagement with the world*'.[89] Watching Polwart and Tagaq perform requires the audience members to resituate their understanding of the world, and the use of musical forms, in a material way. Neither the world nor the performer can be seen at a remove: the audience comes into being through this performative encounter. While this section draws mostly on Polwart and Tagaq's published and recorded material, then, I want to begin with two particularly noteworthy performances.

Tagaq's performance of the songs 'Uja' and 'Umingmak' at the Polaris Music Prize ceremony on 22 September 2014 was immediately hailed by the mainstream Canadian press as 'astonishing' and 'unnerving'.[90] The video recording of the performance opens with Tagaq's face in close-up and then reveals a simple stage set where, framed in a circle of light, she moves between multiple registers and vocal styles, gradually joined by drums, violin and choir, while the names of hundreds of missing or murdered Indigenous women scroll continuously on the screen behind her.[91] Tagaq's music employs many elements of Inuit throat singing, or katajjaq, which traditionally is a competition between two women who 'use their voices to imitate landscapes, animals, whatever surrounds them [...]. The sounds and formulas used, generally low and throaty, can be the imitation of animals cries, laughs, rattles, sighs, or grunts.'[92] Tagaq, as a solo performer, takes a more improvisatory approach in her live performances, avoiding some of the rule-based practices of katajjaq, as well as using diverse instrumentation and soundforms. In the Polaris performance what is most striking is how Tagaq uses her body as an intermediary between the scrolling names of the murdered women behind her and the audience. She curls into herself but also continuously reaches out, drawing the audience into a sonic world. Her performance is not reducible to the sounds she makes, or the names she places on screen, or her interactions with audience and other performers, or the movements of her body: it is an assemblage of all these parts that is one of the clearest examples of Deleuzian or Braidottian becoming I know. While, as Alexa Woloshyn notes, mainstream media often frames Tagaq's performances in a way that reinforces a binary between traditional and modern forms, and in doing so 'reinforces stereotypes about Indigenous peoples', Tagaq's work can better be seen as 'a site of agency and autonomy from which to protest against the division of past/present, tradition/modernity'.[93] The use of vocal techniques that mimic environmental and non-human sounds likewise challenges binaries between performer and environment, or nature and culture. Instead, the performance creates a space of transformation and knowing.

Karine Polwart's performance of 'I Burn but I Am Not Consumed' at the Glasgow Royal Concert Hall on 19 January 2017 likewise evokes a sense of political urgency. The song, a special commission for the opening concert of the long-running festival Celtic Connections, was the first performance of the night. Against ambient strings and guitar, Polwart's spoken-word narration tells the story of Mary Anne MacLeod's journey from Lewis to New York in 1930, and of the return to Scotland some years later of MacLeod's initially unnamed middle son, where he transformed the dunes of Balmedie and Aberdeenshire in the name of golf and executive privilege. Polwart contrasts the 'marbled metamorphic rock of Lewis', two-thirds the age of Earth, with the inauguration, 'tomorrow', of MacLeod's son, Donald J. Trump.[94] The remainder of the song, now mostly sung, is the rock's response to these events; Polwart's title takes the MacLeod clan motto as the voice of the stone. As the song grows more impassioned Polwart, like Tagaq, raises her arm to the audience, reaching out for a moment of connection.[95] Polwart's face is transformed in anger and joy as she voices the stone's defiance. While the aesthetics and genres of these performances are markedly different, what unites Polwart and Tagaq is not simply that they use high-profile performances to comment on political issues, as many artists have done, but that they do so by combining multiple vocal styles and types of instrumentation to give voice to both human and more-than-human others who they themselves embody through the promise of touch.[96]

These performances are striking because they combine the aural with the haptic: they present a form of embodied and situated knowing that is transformative. As María Puig de la Bellacasa claims, in reference to Barad among others, 'haptic engagement conveys an encouragement for knowledge and action to be crafted *in touch* with everyday living and practice': focusing on touch presents 'a deepened attention to materiality and embodiment, an invitation to rethink relationality in its corporeal character, as well as a desire for concrete, tangible, engagement with worldly transformation'.[97] Hapticity provides a way of avoiding abstraction and detachment in construction of knowledge systems. In these performances the desire for touch, however, is not fulfilled: while the performer may reach out to the audience they remain, by virtue of appearing on an elevated stage, physically distant. Both performances, however, gesture towards the possibility of an embodied form of knowing, and draw attention to the impossibility of framing any particular concern as solely human. The songs do not equate human and non-human suffering; rather, they suggest that suffering and care must be considered from an entangled, embodied perspective that does not give rise to hierarchies and their concomitant abuses of power.

Tagaq's work can be seen in parallel to other forms of Indigenous knowledge.[98] The Michi Saagiig Nishnaabeg writer and singer Leanne Betasamosake Simpson, for instance, emphasizes the importance of embodiment: 'in order to access knowledge from a Nishnaabeg perspective, we have to engage our entire bodies: our physical beings, emotional self, our spiritual energy and our intellect'.[99] To be Indigenous in the twenty-first century is to be 'bathed in a vat of cognitive imperialism': rather than using Indigenous knowledge and practice to critique this colonialism, Simpson argues, she wants to turn her attention to Indigenous life as it is lived.[100] Following the work of Glen Coulthard, Simpson advocates a form of 'grounded normativity', or ethical frameworks that are generated by place-based practices and recognize that 'our way of life comes from the place or the land through the practice of our modes of intelligence'.[101] Simpson, like Tagaq, is not interested in reviving tradition for its own sake, but rather focuses on Indigenous knowledge as practices and ethical processes: 'how we engage in the world – the process – not only frames the outcome, it is the transformation'.[102] If, as the Métis scholar Zoe Todd has influentially argued, Western and European ontological philosophies – including posthumanism, Actor Network Theory and discourses of the Anthropocene – are 'perpetuating the exploitation of Indigenous people', further attention must be paid to 'the embodied expressions of stories, laws, and songs as bound with Indigenous-Place Thought'.[103]

This focus on embodied practice is visible throughout Tagaq's work, both thematically and performatively. 'Uja' and 'Umingmak' are drawn from Tagaq's third album, *Animism*; in a promotional video, she defines the title as referring to the spiritual entities that inhabit all non-human animals and inanimate objects, and states that it is the closest she can come to Indigenous beliefs.[104] Throughout the album Tagaq's wide range of vocal styles and effects bring to mind a host of non-human creatures. As Kate Galloway clarifies, Tagaq's work 'pluralises how the non-human world is perceived' and invites the audience to 'listen attentively and with care'. This attentive listening ultimately raises the possibility of 'reconnect[ing] human bodies to the land'.[105] Tagaq's combination of katajjaq with both electronic and acoustic instrumentation creates a fundamentally collaborative, multiple sonic landscape. For many listeners, Tagaq's music creates a web of accidental and intentional associations. Listening to Tagaq's music as a non-Indigenous American who is not a musicologist, I hear echoes of everyone from the Bristol trip hop group Massive Attack to the Hungarian violinist Lajkó Félix. Tagaq's music thus simultaneously requires intellectual and embodied engagement: listening is an interactive process. Just as Eleftherion and Burnett present the page as an environment for the meeting and creation of multiple forms of life and knowledge, so Tagaq creates a sonic equivalent.

Although the track 'Cold', from Tagaq's album *Retribution*, is more dependent on English lyrics than the majority of her recordings, it provides an excellent example of her approach.[106] The track opens with a slow, steady, spoken-word discussion of thermodynamics placed against the found sound of ice drilling. Information about melting ice is embedded in the sounds of ice itself, so that it cannot be treated as pure abstraction. More instruments and electronics are added, as well as human vocals from Tagaq, Radik Tyulyush and The Element Choir, over the refrain 'Gaia likes it cold', while Tagaq warns that 'the loss of ice cover will catapult our climate into an uncharted apocalyptic era'; these elements then fade away so that the song ends only with the sound of ice and water.[107] The song combines multiple vocal styles, varieties of instrumentation and musical genres from field recordings to a danceable beat to create a dynamic response to climate change. The combination of these different approaches presents climate change as immanent, and known at the level of individual experience: if climate change is framed through scientific information, it is also felt and heard through the body.

Todd draws on the work of Keavy Martin and the Inuk author Rachel Qitsualik to connect the idea of Gaia, in Bruno Latour's formulation, with the Inuktitut word 'sila', which refers to the environment, in terms of phrases such as 'silaup asijjipallianinga' (climate change), but also ideas of wisdom or intelligence.[108] Tagaq's song, while using English vocabulary, likewise connects images, and sounds, of climate change with embodied knowledge: one cannot think about ice without experiencing it. The transition between the song's different genres and forms likewise forces the reader to reconsider their relation to both art and knowledge: the song repeatedly raises the question of what sort of knowledge we can glean from popular music, and what sort of change it can engender. As much as the lyrics use the voice of scientific wisdom, the temperature variations Tagaq describes are not, in Barad's words, 'laboratory manipulations but causal intra-actions of the world in its differential becoming'.[109] Rather than presenting climate change as a form of received, abstract knowledge, Tagaq's music reveals a continuous, unfinished, interactive (or intra-active) becoming that requires the full participation of the listener.

These questions of embodiment and participation are also prevalent in Polwart's work, particularly in the performance piece *Wind Resistance* and its accompanying recording, co-credited to Polwart and the sound designer Pippa Murphy, *A Pocket of Wind Resistance*. The play, first performed at the Royal Lyceum Theatre in Edinburgh on 4 August 2016, combines, in Polwart's own words, 'elements of writing about landscape and ecology, local history and memoir, traditional storytelling and song. To me, it's more of a poetic essay or musical meditation than it is a play'.[110] Polwart includes her own compositions, traditional ballads and the work of Robert Burns, while the stories she tells are not only autobiographical but include stories of her family and neighbours, alongside reflections on Scottish history and the natural world. The printed version of the play is spatially constructed to represent this multiplicity: Polwart's spoken lines are left-justified and presented in normal type; her songs are indented and italicized; the story of Will and Roberta Sime, a young couple who lived in Polwart's town a century ago, and which in performance is presented in recordings of Polwart's own voice, are doubly-indented and appear in normal type; and a record of Polwart's movements and various sounds played during the production is triply indented and italicized.[111] This textual assemblage is replicated on stage by a set composed of found objects, echoing Jamie's desk as described in the Introduction: '*a Victorian tangle / of roots and gridlines / test tubes and vials / vases and glasses / bog cotton, heather / bracken and bone / a barn owl / a school desk / a Captain's chair*'.[112] Both aurally and visually, on page and on stage, Polwart presents a series of objects, sounds, and actions that gain meaning in their entanglement, and in their personal significance.

The play is not only specific to its performer, but to a place: it is the story of Fala Moor, a peat bog just beyond the village of Fala, itself two miles from Pathhead, Midlothian, where Polwart lives. Early in the play Polwart describes the moor, and the views a visitor can see, and then invites the audience to '[l]isten again' to the sounds underneath their feet, 'the snapping of the muirburn / and the shlooping of the bog'.[113] Polwart highlights the 'magical names' of the bog mosses:

> sphagnum palustre
> with its wee lime green and copper starts
> sphagnum auriculatum
> like clumps of rhubarb and custard.[114]

The Latin names are provided less for classificatory aid than for the sound they make; on the recording they are chanted almost as a mantra. Like Burnett in an excerpt from a project titled *A Poet's Field Guide to Mosses*, Polwart highlights resonances to childhood; Burnett's prose poem describes *sphagnum palustre* as '[b]aby's breath, lamb's bleat, little peach'.[115] In their first appearance in the play, the mosses are framed as a playground for Polwart's children, as well as an ecosystem. This ecosystem is, as the play reveals, textual as well. The names of the mosses reappear several sections later, when Polwart explains the importance of moss bandages in the First World War.[116] The association between moss and medicine is again reiterated in the song, or sequence, 'Sphagnum Moss for a Dead Queen' in the second act, which combines an original ballad, the Latin names of mosses, lists of painkillers and medical tools, and drones and wails to tell the story of the birth of Polwart's son. Moss is known, in each of these songs, through the body, across time and musical genre. Plant life is not there to be witnessed, but to be lived with: the significance of the moss is apparent not in any single discussion, but in the way it appears in different contexts, fully blurring boundaries between human and non-human matter. This sense of life associated with plants is closely connected in *Wind Resistance* with maternity and childbirth: birth is connected to the land, and to the ballad tradition. The rhythms of 'Sphagnum Moss for a Dead Queen' also replicate those of the earlier song 'Labouring and Resting', where Polwart describes the migration of geese, 'stepping up – falling back / labouring – and resting'.[117] Labouring, in the senses of both birth and effort, is the shared activity of all creatures, and can only take place within an environment.

Polwart's use of ballad form links her to a long tradition of Scottish women's art; while many early ballad collectors in the late eighteenth century, including Walter Scott, were men, the ballad tradition 'is one of the most readily identifiable areas of literary performance by women'.[118] Suzanne Gilbert includes Polwart in a discussion of this 'living tradition', arguing that contemporary

Scottish writers 'have been drawn to tradition, appropriating narratives, tropes, and cultural authority for their own, highly original, literary experimentation.'[119] Like Tagaq, Polwart is less interested in tradition for its own sake than as a way of interweaving past and present. Both performers take elements from a communal women's artform and present them as solo performers, combined with aspects of other traditions, in order to suggest ideas of embeddedness and entanglement. Polwart looks to migrating geese, and to modern maternity wards, to suggest a communitarian approach to leave that moves 'beyond our individual selves': 'We are each other's wind resistance, a human skein. / And we're not going to make it on our own. / *A stark wind. A distant keening purl of birds.*'[120] The declaration of connection cannot be made by a human alone, but requires integration with more-than-human others.

Polwart's attention to the living world, filled with moss and geese as well as humans, is echoed in other contemporary Scottish folk performance. The audio-visual production Northern Flyway combines the work of the folksingers Jenny Sturgeon and Inge Thomson (who frequently collaborates with Polwart), the multi-instrumentalist Sarah Hayes and the vocal sculptor/beatboxer Jason Singh. The performance combines human song and bird song, film footage of birds and audio recordings where various children and adults speak about what birds mean to them.[121] While, like Polwart's work, Northern Flyway evokes ideas of mass extinction, environmental devastation and climate change, the tone is often celebratory: in each performance, the performers are able to place themselves in a world that is not reducible to text, image or song, nor to human or non-human elements on their own. As Rowan Bayliss Hawitt notes in an article comparing Northern Flyway and *Wind Resistance*, sound and music offer a way not only of understanding individuals within an environment, but the relation between different geographical and temporal frames.[122] The voices of the living and the dead, and the human and non-human, create an environment where, in Hawitt's words, 'one particular sound is not granted ontological primacy over another.'[123] These performances are as close as theatre can come to a world where, in Donna Haraway's words, 'the partners do not precede the meeting; species of all kinds, living and not, are consequent on a subject- and object-shaping dance of encounter.'[124] The performers resist anthropomorphism: rather than claiming to speak from the perspective of a non-human other, they instead suggest that there is no speech at all without recognizing the entanglement of human and non-human. The work that these performances do is not, then, a description of the relation between human and non-human beings that upholds an anthropocentric perspective. Instead, the complicated relationship between different modes of performance and media is itself an entanglement, or assemblage, that demonstrates the centrality of encounter.

The interconnected stories of birds and birth, moss and memory, indicate an inclusive approach to life that parallels Braidotti's distinction, following thinkers from Aristotle to Giorgio Agamben, between the terms 'zoe' and 'bios'. As she most simply explains, 'bios' refers to human life as it is organized in society, while 'zoe refers to life of all living beings'.[125] While Agamben connects zoe to death, Braidotti stresses ideas of vulnerability and interrelation, calling zoe 'this life in "me" which does not bear my name and does not even fully qualify as human'.[126] Zoe can be seen as the essential generating power of life itself: she defines it elsewhere as 'the raw materiality of life and death', which has 'a monstrously strong capacity for becoming and for upsetting established categorical distinctions of thought'.[127] This idea of a becoming that avoids categorical distinctions is as central to Polwart's play as it is to work of Eleftherion, Burnett and Tagaq. To capture the generating power of life, and avoid an anthropocentric gaze, requires a combination of different forms and perspectives. Such an approach does not lead to abstraction, or a general celebration of life. Instead, Polwart examines various Anthropocenic images, from wildfires to grouse shooting to the prohibition of wind turbines, in relation to Burns's notion of 'tyrannic man's dominion' to indicate how other ways of being have always been possible.[128] Likewise, the use of first-person narration does not reassert the primacy of the self. Rather, framing the self as one being among others allows for new connections between different species to be developed. The central image of wind resistance, where each goose in turn takes the lead and then falls back, is used as a model not only for human communities, but human enmeshment in a more-than-human world. Polwart stresses the idea of cooperation between beings as the only solution to both human cruelty and Anthropocenic devastation.

Tagaq's experimental novel *Split Tooth*, while more pessimistic than Polwart's work, also presents the idea of a life that is not limited to the human. Early in the text the narrator states that 'we are simply an expression of the energy of the sun', asking, 'whoever said only humans can have the universe living in them?'[129] *Split Tooth* combines prose, poetry and illustration to tell a largely autobiographical account of Indigenous life in the last quarter of the twentieth century; while its focus is often on human lives, it also incorporates not only non-human animals but spirit beings, each of which is seen as equal participants in the life of the universe. Like Eleftherion, Tagaq connects the violence visited on children and adolescent girls to that done to the planet; the novel opens with images of assault in each of the three modes before turning to lichen, and the fear that '[g]lobal warming will release the deeper smells and coax stories out of the permafrost. Who knows what memories lie deep in the ice? Who knows what curses?'[130] As in the work discussed above, there is not an equation between different forms of abuse; rather, Tagaq calls for a recognition that, for Indigenous women, Anthropocenic devastation is already endemic. For Heather Davis and Zoe Todd, the 'reassertion of universality' in the very term "Anthropocene" aligns it with the colonial era; they write that 'the ecocidal logics that now govern our world are not inevitable or "human nature", but are the result of a series of decisions that have their origins and reverberations in colonization'.[131] The Anthropocene, and its ideas of environmental devastation, can thus be seen as the reverberations of colonial and capitalist violence on their perpetrators. As Simpson writes, 'Indigenous peoples have lived through environmental collapse on local and regional levels since the beginning of colonialism' and, as such, have more experience in anticapitalist activities than many others.[132] While Polwart responds to ideas of climate change and human frailty with an emphasis on vulnerability and cooperation, then, Tagaq draws attention to much longer-lasting legacies of abuse.

Tagaq's idea of nature is violent and unsentimental: interspecies empathy is useless at best, and only 'for those who can afford it'.[133] At the same time, however, the narrator argues that '[w]e are the land, same molecules, and same atoms. The land is our salvation.'[134] These quotations are taken from prose and poetry selections on facing pages, where the poem reiterates lines from the story. Different genres allow ideas to be reshaped and represented. The adherence to the land without any romanticization of an abstracted nature allows for a combination of Tagaq's human and non-human concerns:

> Land protects and owns me. Land feeds me. My father and mother are the Land. My future children are the Land. You are the Land. We destroy her with the same measured ignorance of a self-harming teenager. That is what I was in my fifteenth year, what is your excuse? I want to save the land as much as my mother wants to save me.[135]

The reverberations of violence must be seen in tandem. Like the Cree-Saulteaux-Métis writer Lindsay Nixon, Tagaq does not shy away from trauma, or placate the reader. As Nixon writes: 'my trauma is not a commodity, but my story doesn't always have to be uplifting, resurgent, or revolutionary to be my truth, either'.[136] Trauma is not an explanatory relationship, but individual trauma still sheds light on larger environmental concerns. Braidotti similarly argues that zoe's traditional association with devalued lives, human and non-human, can be seen in terms of mass colonialism, and capitalist biopower. She argues, however, that because 'zoe exists outside and anterior to sovereign power', it can be seen as an 'inexhaustible generative force that potentially can transmute lives into sites of resistance'.[137] While Braidotti is working within a Western intellectual tradition, her idea of a generative form of life that does not exceed trauma and violence but is not defined by it either has much in common with the Indigenous writings of Simpson, Tagaq and Nixon.

While *Split Tooth* often details a series of horrific events, including rape and infanticide, Tagaq is careful to contextualize them into a much larger picture, writing that 'Time is Matter'.[138] Time, she argues, 'has a way of eternally looping us in the same configurations. [...] We are a product of the immense torque that propels this universe. We are not individuals but a great accumulation of all that lived before'.[139] The echoes of Barad's theory may only be accidental, but equally point to the possibility of using assemblage as a new way of understanding the universe. Time and matter, or time as matter, do not exist outside the human subject to be demarked and observed. Rather, humans are part of a much larger network of beings and spirits. This focus changes the nature of the story that is told. As Simpson writes, Indigenous storytellers are responsive to their audience, such that '[m]eaning is derived from the presence of both the storyteller and the listeners. Storytelling is an emergent practice, and meaning for each individual listener will necessarily be different'.[140] If this responsiveness is key to Tagaq's musical performances, it is also suggested in the mix of forms, genres and themes in *Split Tooth*. The novel intentionally does not cohere, or tell a straightforward story. Instead, it presents an assemblage of forms with which each reader must engage in different ways. Fragmentation here, as in *Wind Resistance*, is a form not of separation, but inclusion. Each reader, or viewer, finds their own resonances in the story. What unites Tagaq's and Polwart's work, despite their origin in different cultural traditions, is the central idea that to tell one story, about one individual, is always insufficient. The text or performance must include the voices of land and spirit, past and present. Reader and performer are united in their act of gleaning. For the Potawatomi writer Robin Wall Kimmerer any 'rebirth' comes from gathering the '[f]ragments of land, tatters of language, bits of songs, stories, sacred teachings – all that was dropped along the way'.[141] The invitation to gather highlights ideas of fragment and assemblage, and in doing so creates the possibility for a new, more-than-human community.

C. Damaged, but not quite over: Burnett's *The Grassling*

The ideas of fragmentation and assemblage discussed above are particularly prominent in Burnett's *The Grassling*, which combines discussions of field guides, maps and embodied experience to discuss the author's relation to her father, before and after his death, and the English countryside. The book is divided into forty-six brief alphabetically ordered sections, from 'Acreage' to 'Zygote', along with three fragmentary 'soil memoirs', while the text as a whole moves between first-person memoir, experimental poetics and the story of the titular 'Grassling'. Burnett explores, in myriad ways, the relations between body, language and land. Partway through, for instance, Burnett considers her own embodiment, asking '[w]hat do I need a body for now', before remembering how her own feet, in swimming, had soaked up water from a brook: 'How water had turned to grass. Euphorbia and forget-me-nots into a floral sea. How each element had worked for another; and how it had all connected.'[142] Embodiment is not a reification of selfhood, but a form of connection with the land. Yet, as she writes on the next page, this does not presume an easy unity. Instead, she argues that 'one of the first seeds for this writing' came from the unexpected appearance of a barn owl: 'It is the unexpectedness – when these birds, these animals appear – that shakes us out of our usual scripts.'[143] Encounters with plantlife and non-human animals are both transformative. As Deborah Bird Rose writes in an account of Indigenous and settler accounts of place, ideas of bodily permeability, as Burnett emphasizes in her stories of swimming, show that '[w]e and other living things are co-participants in earthly reciprocities of being, becoming, and dying. […] A permeable and becoming self is an unfinished project and thus invites considerations of mutual care.'[144] This mutual care is central to Burnett's work: the self fundamentally cannot be known outside of its connection to place, and to the other living beings that inhabit it, as well as to human family ties. In a later passage she lists all the beings that live under a wood: rabbits, badgers, weasels, live bacteria, fungal filaments, sedimentary rocks, gypsum and more.[145] Each animal, bacterium and stone lives in reciprocity and communion: the world Burnett presents is one of complete entanglement.

It is also, however, a highly specific world, experienced by a known individual. Between the two passages quoted at the start of the previous paragraph Burnett includes a rumination on friendship and care in terms of language, wondering why she calls deer and owls by their Swahili names, which she learned while living as a child in Kenya, although her mother's language was Kikuyu. Her father's garden, she reflects, is a place where everyone, human and non-human, is welcome. Her own welcome in the land comes, in part, from contrasting her embodied, poetic understanding with her father's historical, cartographic knowledge. Early in the text she juxtaposes a poetic sunset, where '[s]lices of hot colour peel from the sky, exposing the soft air beneath' with a more prosaic account of 'the soil that my father's fathers farmed' in Devon, as mapped and recorded in her father's book *A History of the People and Parish of Ide*.[146] Burnett does not dismiss these classificatory systems, instead working to understand and replicate them. Walking through the fields, she hears her father's voice in her head, but her own accounts of mapping are initially simplified and reductive: 'Field 1: Blank grass. / Field 2: Rough green.'[147] As she returns to the same ground, she begins to believe that '[t]here is something here', which she realizes is her sense that 'I belong because of my father: tracing his footsteps, his ancestors; following their trail of dusted bone'.[148] The world is known through embodied and sensory perception and through mapping and inventories; it is known through direct encounter with more-than-human others and through maps, field guides, stories and memory. Just as the world she encounters is multiple and entangled, so too are the systems of knowledge used to describe it.

Burnett, like Reddy, writes as someone who both belongs and is removed, as someone whose attachment and detachment must be seen together. She herself becomes an index of the place: 'Since the mapping and drawing, rolling and swimming, I have been feeling, in some way, like a living map.'[149] This mixture of knowledges and experiences can be seen, to a certain extent, as a parallel to Édouard Glissant's formulation of relation, which 'is linked not to a creation of the world but to the conscious and contradictory experience of contacts among cultures'.[150] In a literal sense, this can be tied to Burnett's account of the way her experience of the world is formed by her English and Kenyan heritage. In a more figurative sense, however, *The Grassling* also draws attention to the contact, and contradictions, between ways of knowing. Burnett presents Ide, in Glissant's words, not 'as a territory from which to project toward other territories but as a place where one gives-on-and-with rather than grasps', yet from this interweaving, or interaction, it also becomes possible to understand questions of a planetary scale.[151] As Glissant might also argue, the work of relation reveals not a given people, or even a given person, but 'the fluctuating complexity of the world'.[152] Burnett's Ide is not a microcosm of the world, but a place of contact between different beings and different epistemologies.[153]

Burnett draws particular attention to an ethics of care in her discussions of soil. The chapter 'Nutrients' begins with a conversation with her father, who 'sums up the angst of every environmental writer' when he asks '"But what's your activism? You haven't done anything!'"[154] Burnett flees to the woods and considers the chemical composition of the soil and its micro-organisms, reflecting on her attachment to this particular soil, while her garden in Birmingham goes untended. Understanding and loving the soil is a way to be connected with her father. It is a form, in an admittedly limited sense, of activism, where loving the world is transformative. Her argument in these passages is similar to the work of Anna Krzywoszynska, who argues, following thinkers like Tsing and Puig de la Bellacasa, that '[s]oils as ecosystems trouble these distinctions between "alive" and "lively," and gesture towards the need to integrate thinking about living beings and material flows in more-than-human and materialist ethics'.[155] As Krzywoszynska suggests, an ethics of care is always dependent on attention, because attentiveness is always directed towards an object of care. While Krzywoszynska calls for a systemic approach, in *The Grassling* this form of care is far more individuated: Burnett cares for a particular patch of soil because she cares for her father. Yet this care is not simply anthropocentric, but entangled. As she writes:

> All the skin of me, the pigment, the falling dust, is called to the soil. All the water of me, the churning motion, is called to the fish [...]. All the heart of me, the pulsing inside, is called to the pulsing outside: the grass, the birds, the insects, the worms; and further, to the beating that continues beyond the other, beyond anything tangible: to my father's fathers. And him, on the border; a branch held out to me, as a root slips back to his fathers.[156]

Care, in an entangled sense, is always expansionist. It is a system of relation that recognizes complexity and different modes of contact. It is not an elevation of the self, but a recognition that the self emerges from and within its encounters with the more-than-human world, but not at the expense of its human encounters.

Burnett's ethics of care and assemblage is not only articulated in the prose sections of her memoir, however, but also manifested in the form of the text itself. Thirteen of the chapters open with poetic fragment. Like 'Sea Holly', above, these texts often begin from the word 'she', and expand outwards, each line adding more words. The first appearance, in 'Daffodil', begins '*[s]he cuts*', which five lines later reads in full '*[s]he cuts light speech a pattered petalled reach*'.[157] These texts are not integrated or explained: they are another way of knowing. The epigraphs are often in English, but sometimes include onomatopoeic sounds; like the three 'soil memoirs', they are a mixture of repetition and exploration, of sound and sense: each is complete in itself and gestures towards a new way of knowing. Each of these can, in part, be seen as examples of what Burnett calls 'soil voice':

> 'Soil voice' is a cough. A release. A cough-it-all-up, get-it-all-out, with a widening of the throat, a glottal opening, into chasmic voice: an outburst! An ungovernable quake of a voice; vowels shaped into an eruption of e's and h's, into a stream of 'ehhhh' as in the breath of the earth, as in the coughing up of clumps, of fur balls of blackthorn, of blackbirds, of history, of mourning, of hope, of new mournings; of all this the soil sings – of all that has been held in.[158]

Understanding the world, giving voice to the soil and the non-human animals and the voice of grief and loss, requires a new diction. This is, in part, an answer to her father's question: the ecopoet changes the nature of language in order to reflect a new, more multiple, sense of the world. By the end of the volume, Burnett has trained the reader to listen to grass and birds, to hear differently, and so can begin to combine her techniques:

> I enter the earth and speak with the tongues of birds, of worms, with latticed roots, all along my fibres and fathers and mothers and grasses; I rain speech. Itisoccupiedwithsoundandhowtopressitintosomethingflatitcarrieswithititssound-isallaboutanotheritnamesfatherhetolditaboutthisplaceitsmappedearthedsong-beatshhhhhhhhhhhhhhhhhhhhhhhhhpillowhhhhhhhhhh
> glow,   (gold. willow.)[159]

Like the authors discussed in Chapter 3, particularly Lucy Ellmann, Burnett offers the reader multiple forms of attentiveness, or choice. The reader can dismiss these passages; they can appreciate them aesthetically, as a reshaping of language uncommon in a text presented as nature writing or memoir, but unbounded by generic conventions; they can delve deeply to separate the words out and understand their relation. This is, in part, a glimpse of planetary life, where our understanding of soil, or woods, or family, requires us to know the whole and the component parts at the same time and not privilege either. I want to suggest that this writing is a particularly ethical form of entanglement, because the reader bears a responsibility to the words themselves. Each fragment in the text can only be placed in constellation with the active participation of the reader; Burnett refuses passive reading. As she claims in her monograph, the essay form in particular, and ecocriticism more generally, can benefit from an engagement with indeterminacy, where rather than leading to a synthesis, there is 'increased emphasis on the role of the reader' that moves 'towards the accommodation of doubt'.[160] What this text means to me as a reader, and how it means, may be different than what it means to you. Yet we each bear responsibility for this encounter. As Barad writes, responsibility, in terms of ethics, cannot be restricted to encounters between humans, but must engage with 'an ethics of worlding'.[161] The world, shattered and remade, and always more-than-human, always calls for attention and response, and for resituating the self in a shifting assemblage.

This indeterminacy is particularly highlighted in the chapters that focus on the titular Grassling. The chapters are distinguished by a further set of indentation, but the Grassling is only named at the end. At first, the Grassling seems like a hare or mole. Its first appearance begins: 'One eye first, a half-lid, squint. Both pull fully open. Blue! It had forgotten the breadth of the colour. Sky!'[162] The passage is titled 'Warren', and given Burnett's allusions to Arthur Ransome elsewhere, the easiest connection is to Mole's spring cleaning at the opening of Kenneth Grahame's *The Wind in the Willows*: there is the same thrill of discovery, of emergence into the world. Yet the Grassling is not a recognizable animal. It cannot 'work out' if it is 'a joined-up thing or separate'.[163] The Grassling is a daffodil, a blackbird, a word and Burnett herself: 'I am grass made flesh. Grassling.'[164] It is the voice of the earth, a voice of loss and needing and a voice of integration. And, near the end of the volume, it dies. Just as the second soil memoir focuses on unbearable grief – 'no hope, no body, no love ever as great as this loss' – so too the Grassling becomes the voice of unknowability, of unincorporation.[165] The Grassling is the coming into being of language, the becoming of the more-than-human. The Grassling cannot be enunciated or described. If it is matter, as grass and soil and animal, its story is a repost to the way the 'image of dead or thoroughly instrumentalized matter feeds human hubris and our earth-destroying fantasies of conquest and consumption', in Jane Bennett's words.[166] The Grassling is zoe, in Braidotti's formulations: it is a generative, transversal force of life 'that cuts across and reconnects previously segregated species, categories, and domains'.[167] Yet it is also, reductively but no less honestly, a figure of loss.

As Burnett writes on the penultimate page, her journey in the book records 'a time of becoming, of beginning, of bepersoning, begrassing. Now, it is a letting go. What is it the Grassling leaves here? That awful earthly clinging.'[168] The Grassling is a voice of relinquishment, of the way no human can truly know a place, or call it theirs. This is, in part, why the text can be seen as an example of gleaning, where what is collected is also put aside again. If the fragments of the text can be put together to form an ethics of care, it is still not an explanatory or abstract ethics, but one that pertains to a particular time and place and person.

This may, I think, be the case for all ethics. Burnett closes her text with the same words with which the first chapter end: 'That great continuing. Glow.'[169] The repetition of the phrase creates a sense of cyclicality, of the rhythms of the seasons and of lives. Yet the full stop that separates continuance from light is just as important. What remains remains as it is, separate, and impartial. The world must be experienced in its multiple fullness, and yet as much as Burnett's book moves further past an anthropocentric perspective than any text I know, it also acknowledges that what continues continues without us. This is, in part, a recognition of Anthropocenic devastation, and more simply of human mortality. Yet it is not a voice of desperation, or nihilism. A few pages earlier Burnett ties these ideas together in a passage I want to quote at length, because it moves me:

> But I nudge a plastic bottle, and I stop. I end. How do I go on, when there is nowhere to come back to? No harbour, no shore, as 'all the pores of the rock are filled with water, a dark, sub-surface sea, rising under hills, sinking beneath valleys.' I hear the words of Rachel Carson pass through me as fluidly as my own. 'This groundwater is always on the move,' I say. And I am Rachel Carson. 'It travels by unseen waterways until here and there it comes to the surface… all the running water of the earth's surface was at one time groundwater.' And I am that water.
>
> I hold not only my own fluid but all of the rocks' of all the earth; I float on and in myself. I am zoic: containing fossils, with traces of animal or plant life. 'And so, in a very real and frightening sense, pollution of the groundwater is pollution of water everywhere.' Plastic fossils line my bones. The bottle, adrift in the dour, is the seen pollutant, plastic spectre made manifest, but how many unseen haunt the water; how many chemicals through my pores and in my soil and in my rock and in my leaves and in my sea and will I ever, ever be clean?
>
> I flip. I face the sun. I drift. I am damaged, but it is not quite over. Whatever part of me is here is not over. Whatever part of me is not here is not over. Here is a space for salvaging. I am speaking in a thickened voice now. All the voices of the advocates. All the voices of my family. All the voices of the sea, rising. There is still time. I am still. Here. All of me gathers life.[170]

The quotations from Carson's *Silent Spring* ground the text in an ecofeminist tradition, much as in Andrews's novel in Chapter 1. The scientific information provides a way of knowing that leads to a knowledge of self and integration, and equally leads to a sense of despair and overwhelmedness. And yet the self persists, and that persistence is possible because the self is not known on its own, but as part of a constellation of voices, just as the text is a constellation. The fragmentation of the final lines becomes a way to think through ideas of unity and separation. Burnett's mixture of voices here is similar in many ways to both Polwart and Tagaq: the combination of different voices and different traditions creates a relationality that reshapes discourse. Like each of the other voices in this chapter, Burnett presents embodiment as fundamentally communal: to be a self is to be formed in relation to human and more-than-human others. Likewise, texts are formed in this relationality: these works juxtapose scientific and classificatory models with personal experience not to favour one or the other, but to enlarge the world.

Although the four artists discussed in this chapter work in different genres, and from different traditions, they are united in presenting the assemblage of fragments as a new way of understanding the world. The world is understood in and through interaction. It is understood in processes of becoming. Each of these texts resists ideas of a totalizing knowledge. Instead, experience and information are gleaned, reassembled and in this action made new. This is, in part, why performance is central to these texts: the assemblage is made in the moment, in interaction with audience or reader. It is an act of enunciation and becoming. Entanglement is not simply a way of describing the world, but a way of being in, and caring for, the world. These questions of care and entanglement, of intertextual allusion and personal experience, are also central to the following chapter, alongside the additional concept of the archive.

Notes

1   The *Los Angeles Times*, for instance, called the album 'a rich text to scour in quarantine' while the critics for *The New York Times* juxtaposed 'a feeling of communal excitement around this record's release' with praise for Apple's ability to 'direct a line to my inner self'. Mikael Wood, 'Fiona Apple's Stunningly Intimate New Album Makes a Bold Show of Unprettiness', *Los Angeles Times* (16 April 2020): latimes.com/entertainment-arts/music/story/2020-04-16/fiona-apple-fetch-the-bolt-cutters-review [Accessed 31 August 2020]; Jon Pareles, Jon Caramanica, Wesley Morris and Lindsay Zoladz, 'Fiona Apple Is Back and Unbound: Let's Discuss', *The New York Times* (17 April 2020): nytimes.com/2020/04/17/arts/music/fiona-apple-fetch-the-bolt-cutters.html [Accessed 31 August 2020].

2   Fiona Apple, *Fetch the Bolt Cutters* (New York: Epic Records, 2020).

3   Phoebe Bridgers, *Punisher* (Bloomington, IN: Dead Oceans, 2020).

4   Virtually every review of Swift's album concentrates on its material conditions of making. See, for example, Angela Watercutter, 'Taylor Swift and the Risks and Rewards of the Pandemic Album', *Wired* (7 July 2020): wired.com/story/

taylor-swift-folklore-album-date-release-pandemic/ [Accessed 31 August 2020]. While Swift criticism rests on her album's production during a time of pandemic, discussions of Apple and Bridgers note how the albums seem particularly relevant despite being recorded earlier: the immanent encounter with the albums at a particular moment shapes their reception and interpretation. But anyway, *evermore* is the much stronger of Swift's 2020 albums.

5　Gilles Deleuze and Claire Parnet, *Dialogues II*, trans. Hugh Tomlinson and Barbara Habberjam (London and New York: Continuum, 2006), 38. While Deleuze's name is the only one that appears on the cover of my edition of the book, the volume's origin in interviews with Parnet suggests the importance of a dialogic encounter that echoes the concerns of this chapter.

6　Deleuze and Parnet, *Dialogues II*, 52.

7　Rosi Braidotti, 'A Theoretical Framework for the Critical Posthumanities', *Theory, Culture and Society* 36.6 (2019): 33.

8　Manuel DeLanda, for instance, begins his work on assemblage bemoaning that the English term privileges product rather than process. Manuel DeLanda, *Assemblage Theory* (Edinburgh: Edinburgh University Press, 2016), 1.

9　Braidotti, 'Theoretical Framework', 33.

10　John Law and Marianne Lien, 'Denaturalizing Nature', in *A World of Many Worlds*, ed. Marisol de la Cadena and Mario Blaser (Durham and London: Duke University Press, 2018), 132.

11　Rosi Braidotti, *Posthuman Knowledge* (Cambridge: Polity, 2019), 11. Although I am drawing on European traditions of assemblage, it is important that scholars such as Helen Verran have also argued that assemblage 'is crucial for responsible postcolonial science studies', insofar as it provides a critique of 'foundationist accounts of scientific knowledge' and can be seen in relation to Indigenous knowledges. Helen Verran, 'On Assemblage: Indigenous Knowledge and Digital Media (2003–2006), and *HMS Investigator* (1800–1805)', *Journal of Cultural Economy* 2.1–2 (2009): 171.

12　Anna Lowenhaupt Tsing, *The Mushroom at the End of the World: On the Possibility of Life in Capitalist Ruins* (Princeton and Oxford: Princeton University Press, 2015), 20.

13　Braidotti, *Posthuman Knowledge*, 175.

14　Anna Fisk, *Sex, Sin, and Our Selves: Encounters in Feminist Theology and Contemporary Women's Literature* (Eugene, OR: Pickwick Publications, 2014), xiv.

15　Rosi Braidotti, *Metamorphoses: Towards a Materialist Theory of Becoming* (Cambridge: Polity, 2002), 17.

16　Karen Barad, *Meeting the Universe Halfway: Quantum Physics and the Entanglement of Matter and Meaning* (Durham and London: Duke University Press, 2007), ix.

17　Barad, *Meeting*, 109.

18 Barad, *Meeting*, 90. As Barad clarifies, 'what is at issue is not knowledge *of* the world from above or outside, but *knowing as part of being*' (341, original emphasis).

19 Catherine Keller, *Cloud of the Impossible: Negative Theology and Planetary Entanglement* (New York: Columbia University Press, 2015), 116, 129. Original emphasis. Although I draw more significantly on Barad's work throughout this chapter, Keller's formulations deserve far more attention outside the world of theological studies.

20 Elizabeth Anderson, 'Reading the World's Liveliness: Animist Ecologies in Indigenous Knowledges, New Materialism and Women's Writing', *Feminist Modernist Studies* 3.2 (2020): 207.

21 Barad, *Meeting*, 153.

22 Braidotti's *Posthuman Feminism* has been listed as 'forthcoming' for the entire time I have worked on this volume; by the time you read this, it may be out, but I have not been able to read it.

23 Rosi Braidotti, 'Four Theses on Posthuman Feminism', in *Anthropocene Feminism*, ed. Richard Grusin (Minneapolis and London: University of Minnesota Press, 2017), 41.

24 Jini Reddy, *Wanderland: A Search for Magic in the Landscape* (London: Bloomsbury, 2020), 12. Original emphasis.

25 Reddy, *Wanderland*, 36.

26 Reddy, *Wanderland*, 261.

27 Rosi Braidotti, *Nomadic Subjects: Embodiment and Sexual Difference in Contemporary Feminist Theory*, 2nd ed. (New York: Columbia University Press, 2011), 44.

28 Braidotti, *Nomadic Subjects*, 66.

29 Lisa Kay, 'Research as Bricolage: Navigating in/between the Creative Arts Disciplines', *Music Therapy Perspectives* 34.1 (2016): 26–32.

30 Barad, *Meeting*, 230.

31 Braidotti, *Posthuman Knowledge*, 53.

32 Braidotti, *Posthuman Knowledge*, 45.

33 Braidotti, *Posthuman Knowledge*, 52.

34 Barad, *Meeting*, 376–7. Original emphasis.

35 Barad, *Meeting*, 150.

36 Judith Butler, *Bodies That Matter: On the Discursive Limits of 'Sex'* (London and New York: Routledge Classics, 2011), xii.

37 Barad, *Meeting*, 151. Original emphasis.

38 Butler, *Bodies*, 39.

39 Elizabeth Grosz, *Volatile Bodies: Toward a Corporeal Feminism* (Bloomington and Indianapolis: Indiana University Press, 1994), 117.

40 Rosi Braidotti, *Nomadic Theory: The Portable Rosi Braidotti* (New York: Columbia University Press, 2011), 94. For Deleuze and Guattari's definition see Gilles Deleuze and Félix Guattari, *A Thousand Plateaus*, trans. Brian Massumi (London: Bloomsbury, 2013), 277.

41 Braidotti, *Metamorphoses*, 118.

42 Melissa Eleftherion, *field guide to autobiography* (Brooklyn, NY: The Operating System, 2018), 11. Eleftherion's work is published as an open access text, under a CC BY license, hence my decision to quote some of her poems in full.

43 Eleftherion, *field guide*, 88.

44 Elizabeth-Jane Burnett, *A Social Biography of Contemporary Innovative Poetry Communities: The Gift, the Wager, and Poethics* (Cham: Palgrave Macmillan, 2017), 163–4.

45 The use of diffuse spacing as a way to re-envision the environment can also be found in the work of the Shetland-based poet Jen Hadfield, particularly in poems such as 'Smiles Learnt in the Cockle-beds' and 'The Puffballs'. Jen Hadfield, *Byssus* (London: Picador, 2014).

46 John Law and Michael Lynch, 'Lists, Field Guides, and the Descriptive Organization of Seeing: Birdwatching as an Exemplary Observational Activity', *Human Studies* 11.2–3 (1988): 277–8.

47 Law and Lynch, 'Lists', 293.

48 Michael Lynch and John Law, 'Pictures, Texts, and Objects: The Literary Language Game of Bird-watching', in *The Science Studies Reader*, ed. Mario Biagioli (New York and London: Routledge, 1999), 320.

49 Claire Waterton, 'Performing the Classification of Nature', *The Sociological Review* 51.2 (2003): 125.

50 Eleftherion, *field guide*, 22.

51 Eleftherion, *field guide*, 26. There are over 30,000 different species of scarabaeidae, or scarab beetles, from dung beetles to rose chafers.

52 Eleftherion, *field guide*, 15.

53 Elizabeth-Jane Burnett, *Swims* (London: Penned in the Margins, 2019), 13. As a footnote clarifies, the *Vanity Fair* reference is to Christine Lagard, director of the International Monetary Fund.

54 Louise Green, *Fragments from the History of Loss: The Nature Industry and the Postcolony* (University Park, PA: Pennsylvania State University Press, 2020), 31. Green draws here on Brian O'Connor's reading of Benjamin's *The Origins of German Tragic Drama*, where Benjamin posits that 'the subject mediates phenomena, striving to arrange them in such a way, in "constellations", that they might reveal their idea'. Brian O'Connor, 'Introduction', in *The Adorno Reader*, ed. Brian O'Connor (Oxford and Malden, MA: Blackwell, 2000), 4.

55 Green, *Fragments*, 32.

56 Burnett, *Swims*, 15.

57 Alice Oswald, *Dart* (London: Faber, 2003), n.p.

58 Burnett, *Swims*, 7. An earlier description of the volume has the same emphases, but also includes an attention to 'ritual and bodily practice' and a declaration that the poem 'foreground[s] the importance of pleasure, leisure, and optimism in the

undertaking'. Elizabeth-Jane Burnett, '"Swims": Body, Ritual, and Erasure', *Jacket 2* (5 February 2016): jacket2.org/article/swims [Accessed 5 September 2020]. In the later description, on the contrary, Burnett writes about how the sequence is 'interrupted' by a series of poems for her father, after his death.

59   Burnett, *Social Biography*, 180–1.

60   Burnett, *Swims*, 29.

61   Burnett, *Swims*, 30.

62   Burnett, *Swims*, 35.

63   Burnett, *Social Biography*, 179.

64   Eleftherion, *field guide*, 32.

65   Claire Waterton, 'From Field to Fantasy: Classifying Nature, Construction Europe', *Social Studies of Science* 32.2 (2002): 178.

66   Andrea Blythe, 'Poet Spotlight: Melissa Eleftherion on Survival and How Language Reshapes Our Perception of the World', *Andrea Blythe: Speculative Poetry and Fiction* (8 October 2019): andreablythe.com/2019/10/08/poet-spotlight-melissa-eleftherion-on-survival-and-how-language-reshapes-our-perception-of-the-world/ [Accessed 7 September 2020].

67   Melissa Eleftherion, *little ditch* (Ottawa: Above/Ground Press, 2018), n.p.

68   Eleftherion, *field guide*, 31.

69   Burnett, *Social Biography*, 10.

70   Burnett, *Swims*, 20. Original emphasis.

71   Alexa Weik von Mossner, *Affective Ecologies: Empathy, Emotion, and Environmental Narrative* (Columbus: Ohio State University Press, 2017), 29.

72   Lauren Berlant and Kathleen Stewart, *The Hundreds* (Durham and London: Duke University Press, 2019), 5.

73   Burnett, *Swims*, 19.

74   Burnett, *Swims*, 64.

75   Burnett, *Swims*, 25.

76   Burnett, *Swims*, 37–8.

77   Burnett, *Swims*, 57.

78   Burnett, *Swims*, 58–9.

79   Elizabeth-Jane Burnett, 'Sounding the Non-Human in John Clare and Maggie O'Sullivan', *John Clare Society Journal* 35 (2016): 35.

80   Burnett, *Swims*, 62.

81   Barad, *Meeting*, 106.

82   Barad, *Meeting*, 379.

83   Donna Haraway, *The Companion Species Manifesto: Dogs, People, and Significant Otherness* (Chicago: Prickly Paradigm Press, 2003), 6.

84   Eleftherion, *field guide*, 68.

85   Eleftherion, *field guide*, 75.

86 Elizabeth-Jane Burnett and Tony Lopez, 'Sea Holly', *Poetry* (December 2016): 249–51. In Burnett's subsequent collection, *Of Sea*, five poems from the sequence are interspersed throughout the volume; this passage is presented as 'Sea Anemone'. Elizabeth-Jane Burnett, *Of Sea* (London: Penned in the Margins, 2021), 72–4. This volume incorporates a number of other sea-focused poems, ranging from a 'Seannet' and a 'Sea-olet' to a 'Song of the Sea' complete with sheet music. While Burnett both includes a number of forms and themes present in her earlier work and adds new ones, my reason for not including a longer discussion of the volume as a whole is based on the volume's release late in the composition of this book.

87 Burnett and Lopez, 'Sea Holly', 250. McBride's novel includes, in its depiction of persistent trauma and abuse, a number of poetic observations of the natural world, culminating in the protagonist's suicide by drowning, where 'water take[s] the thing away. Take body.' Eimear McBride, *A Girl Is a Half-Formed Thing* (Norwich: Galley Beggar, 2013), 202. While McBride's text is far more fatalistic and disturbing, the sense of immersion as transformation is shared with Burnett and Lopez's work.

88 Spahr is one of three poets, alongside Bhanu Kapil and Elise Ficarra, who provides a quotation for the back of Eleftherion's collection, arguing that *field guide* 'isn't conventional nature poetry; it's a poetry that helps us understand the future and the world that embeds us'. Kapil's paragraph, much more simply, ends: 'I like that there is a wren in it. I like that there is a whale.' The difference in tone and focus aptly illustrates Eleftherion's appeal.

89 Barad, *Meeting*, 49. Original emphasis.

90 'Tanya Tagaq's Animism Wins the 2014 Polaris Music Prize', *Manitoba Music* (22 September 2014): manitobamusic.com/news/read,article/6177/Tanya-tagaq-s-animism-wins-the-2014-polaris-music-prize [Accessed 13 September 2020]; Kate Robertson, 'Tanya Tagaq Wins the Polaris Prize 2014', *Now Toronto* (22 September 2014): nowtoronto.com/tanya-tagaq-wins-the-polaris-prize-2014 [Accessed 13 September 2020].

91 Tanya Tagaq, '"Uja" and "Umingmak" (live)', *Polaris Music Prize* (2014): polarismusicprize.ca/videos/tanya-tagaq-uja-and-umingmak-live/ [Accessed 13 September 2020]. The studio versions of the song are available on Tanya Tagaq, *Animism* (Toronto: Six Shooter Records, 2014).

92 Sophie Stévance, 'Analysis of the Inuit Katajjaq in Popular Culture: The Canadian Throat-Singer Superstar Tanya Tagaq', *Itamar. Revista de Investigación Musical: Territorios Para El Arte* 3 (2010): 82–9, p. 85. See also Red Bull Music Academy, 'Tanya Tagaq Talks Björk, Throat Singing and the Polaris Prize', *YouTube* (7 October 2016): youtube.com/watch?v=YkD00mGqBxE [Accessed 13 September 2020].

93 Alexa Woloshyn, '"Welcome to the Tundra": Tanya Tagaq's Creative and Communicative Agency as Political Strategy', *Journal of Popular Music Studies* 29.4 (2017): 1–14, p. 4. https://doi.org/10.1111/jpms.12254 [Accessed 13 September 2020].

94 Karine Polwart, 'I Burn but I am Not Consumed', *BBC iPlayer* (20 January 2017): bbc.co.uk/programmes/p04q5cmf [Accessed 13 September 2020].

95 The less formal environment of the NPR Music Tiny Desk Concert series allows Polwart to emphasize these movements in a later performance. NPR Music, 'Karine Polwart Trio: NPR Music Tiny Desk Concert', *NPR Music* (18 April 2019): youtube.com/watch?v=qoyc83-56EY [Accessed 13 September 2020].

96 Tagaq's defence of Indigenous seal-hunting practices received almost as much discussion as her music in 2014, as many of her interviews reveal, but is not the focus of my analysis here. For an overview, see Emiliano Battistini, '"Sealfie", "Phoque You" and "Animism": The Canadian Inuit Answer to the United States Anti-sealing Activism', *International Journal for the Semiotics of Law* 31 (2008): 561–94.

97 María Puig de la Bellacasa, *Matters of Care: Speculative Ethics in More Than Human Worlds* (Minneapolis and London: University of Minnesota Press, 2017), 96. Original emphasis.

98 Kateryna Barnes takes a very different approach, framing Tagaq's work in relation to contemporary eco-horror, where Western settler-colonialism becomes framed as a Gothic monster. Kateryna Barnes, 'Soundtrack to Settler-Colonialism: Tanya Tagaq's Music as Creative Nonfiction Horror', *Gothic Nature* 2 (2021): 62–83. https://gothicnaturejournal.com/ [Accessed 5 July 2021].

99 Leanne Betasamosake Simpson, *Dancing on Our Turtle's Back: Stories of Nishnaabeg Re-Creation, Resurgence and a New Emergence* (Winnipeg: ARP Books, 2011), 42. As noted in the Introduction, Simpson's novel *Noopiming* and the album *Theory of Ice* which sets some of the same texts to music are extremely pertinent to this discussion, and are not engaged with at length here simply for reasons of space.

100 Simpson, *Dancing*, 32. The ethnomusicologist Beverley Diamond uses Simpson's earlier writing as a starting-point for disciplinary critiques: Beverley Diamond, 'The Power of Stories: Canadian Music Scholarship's Narratives and Counter-Narratives', *Intersections* 33.2 (2013): 155–65.

101 Leanne Betasamosake Simpson, *As We Have Always Done: Indigenous Freedom through Radical Resistance* (Minneapolis and London: University of Minnesota Press, 2017), 22.

102 Simpson, *As We*, 19.

103 Zoe Todd, 'An Indigenous Feminist's Take on the Ontological Turn: "Ontology" Is Just Another Word for Colonialism', *Journal of Historical Sociology* 29.1 (2016): 16, 9. See also Zoe Todd, 'Indigenizing the Anthropocene', in *Art in the Anthropocene: Encounters among Aesthetics, Politics, Environments and Epistemologies*, ed. Heather Davis and Etienne Turpin (London: Open Humanities Press, 2015), 241–54.

104   Six Shooter Records, 'Tanya Tagaq Talks Animism (EPK)', *Six Shooter Records* (2 September 2014): youtube.com/watch?v=pFHL341OpHU [Accessed 15 September 2020].

105   Kate Galloway, 'The Aurality of Pipeline Politics and Listening for Nacreous Clouds: Voicing Indigenous Ecological Knowledge in Tanya Tagaq's *Animism* and *Retribution*', *Popular Music* 39.1 (2020): 125.

106   The closing, title track, 'Retribution', also includes spoken lyrics concerning climate change, as well as an excellent dance beat. This combination is reminiscent both of the Icelandic singer Björk, with whom Tagaq has collaborated, and especially the English singer Anohni, whose song '4 Degrees' takes a similar approach. Anohni, *Helplessness* (London: Rough Trade, 2015).

107   Tanya Tagaq, *Retribution* (Toronto: Six Shooter Records, 2016).

108   Keavy Martin, *Stories in a New Skin: Approaches to Inuit Literature* (Winnipeg: University of Manitoba Press, 2012), 5. In Qitsualik's formulation, which is no longer available online, sila is 'a raw life force that lay over the entire Land' (quoted in Todd, 'An Indigenous Feminist's Take', 5).

109   Barad, *Meeting*, 352.

110   Karine Polwart, *Wind Resistance* (London: Faber, 2017), author's note.

111   The CD version compiles most of the songs, and some of the spoken narration (and some of the bird calls), but is not a complete record of the performance. Karine Polwart and Pippa Murphy, *A Pocket of Wind Resistance* (Sheffield: Hudson Records, 2017).

112   Polwart, *Wind*, n.p.

113   Polwart, *Wind*, 7.

114   Polwart, *Wind*, 7.

115   Elizabeth-Jane Burnett, 'Little Peach', *The Willowherb Review* 2 (2019): thewillowherbreview.com/little-peach-elizabeth-jane-burnett [Accessed 19 September 2020]. The importance of sensory perception is also highlighted by Robin Wall Kimmerer, who argues that '[l]earning to see mosses is more like listening than looking'. Robin Wall Kimmerer, *Gathering Moss: A Natural and Cultural History of Mosses* (Corvallis, OR: Oregon State University Press, 2003), 10.

116   See Donald S. Murray, *The Dark Stuff: Stories from the Peatlands* (London: Bloomsbury, 2018).

117   Polwart, *Wind*, 14.

118   Catherine Kerrigan, 'Introduction', in *An Anthology of Scottish Women Poets*, ed. Catherine Kerrigan (Edinburgh: Edinburgh University Press, 1991), 2.

119   Suzanne Gilbert, 'Orality and the Ballad Tradition', in *The Edinburgh Companion to Scottish Women's Writing*, ed. Glenda Norquay (Edinburgh: Edinburgh University Press, 2012), 52.

120   Polwart, *Wind*, 43–4.

121 The performance I witnessed was at the Lemon Tree, Aberdeen, on 27 September 2018. See also Northern Flyway, *Northern Flyway* (Sheffield: Hudson Records, 2018).

122 Rowan Bayliss Hawitt, '"It's a part of me an I'm a part of it": Ecological Thinking in Contemporary Scottish Folk Music', *Ethnomusicology Forum* 29.3 (2020): 339. https://doi.org.10.1080/17411912.2021.1897950 [Accessed 5 July 2021].

123 Hawitt usefully distinguishes between Northern Flyway, where the voices of birds and humans are engaged in 'mutual constitution' and *Wind Resistance*, where 'human lives are sounded out in dialogue with those of more-than-humans'. Hawitt, '"It's a part of me"', 345.

124 Donna J. Haraway, *When Species Meet* (Minneapolis and London: University of Minnesota Press, 2008), 4.

125 Braidotti, *Posthuman Knowledge*, 10.

126 Rosi Braidotti, *Transpositions: On Nomadic Ethics* (Cambridge: Polity, 2006), 123.

127 Braidotti, *Nomadic Theory*, 122–3.

128 Polwart, *Wind*, 16–17.

129 Tanya Tagaq, *Split Tooth* (Toronto: Viking, 2018), 12.

130 Tagaq, *Split Tooth*, 6.

131 Heather Davis and Zoe Todd, 'On the Importance of a Date, or Decolonizing the Anthropocene', *ACME: An International Journal for Critical Geographies* 16.4 (2017): 763.

132 Simpson, *As We*, 73–4.

133 Tagaq, *Split Tooth*, 63

134 Tagaq, *Split Tooth*, 62.

135 Tagaq, *Split Tooth*, 32.

136 Lindsay Nixon, *nîtisânak* (Montreal: Metonymy Press, 2019), 18.

137 Braidotti, *Posthuman Knowledge*, 177.

138 Tagaq, *Split Tooth*, 110.

139 Tagaq, *Split Tooth*, 121.

140 Simpson, *Dancing*, 104.

141 Robin Wall Kimmerer, *Braiding Sweetgrass: Indigenous Wisdom Scientific Knowledge, and the Teachings of Plants* (Minneapolis: Milkweed Editions, 2013), 368.

142 Elizabeth-Jane Burnett, *The Grassling* (London: Penguin, 2019), 46.

143 Burnett, *Grassling*, 47.

144 Deborah Bird Rose, 'Dialogue with Place: Toward an Ecological Body', *Journal of Narrative Theory* 32.3 (2002): 322.

145 Burnett, *Grassling*, 84.

146 Burnett, *Grassling*, 9.

147 Burnett, *Grassling*, 12.

148 Burnett, *Grassling*, 13.

149 Burnett, *Grassling*, 160.

150 Édouard Glissant, *Poetics of Relation*, trans. Betsy Wing (Ann Arbor: University of Michigan Press, 1997), 144.

151 Glissant, *Poetics*, 144.

152 Glissant, *Poetics*, 32.

153 As much as this is a personal account, it is also one that invites dialogue. Burnett's collaboration with Rebecca Thomas draws from both Burnett's book, and its sources, and Thomas's artistic practice in order, in Thomas's words, to create 'a new, third object, one in which text and image play off against one another, operate in a dialogical fashion, multiply possibilities and potential ways of reading'. Elizabeth-Jane Burnett and Rebecca Thomas, 'The Folds of the Fields: A Performative Collaboration in the South of England', *Green Letters* 23.3 (2019): 265.

154 Burnett, *Grassling*, 57.

155 Anna Krzywoszynska, 'Caring for Soil Life in the Anthropocene: The Role of Attentiveness in More-than-Human Ethics', *Transactions of the Institute of British Geographers* 44 (2019): 663. Similar arguments are also found in discussions of human-plant relations; see especially Lesley Head and Jennifer Atchison, 'Cultural Ecology: Emerging Human-Plant Geographies', *Progress in Human Geography* 33.2 (2009): 236–45.

156 Burnett, *Grassling*, 73.

157 Burnett, *Grassling*, 20.

158 Burnett, *Grassling*, 159.

159 Burnett, *Grassling*, 170.

160 Burnett, *Social Biography*, 176.

161 Barad, *Meeting*, 392.

162 Burnett, *Grassling*, 91.

163 Burnett, *Grassling*, 119.

164 Burnett, *Grassling*, 148.

165 Burnett, *Grassling*, 153.

166 Jane Bennett, *Vibrant Matter: A Political Ecology of Things* (Durham and London: Duke University Press, 2010), ix.

167 Braidotti, 'Four Theses', 32.

168 Burnett, *Grassling*, 186.

169 Burnett, *Grassling*, 187.

170 Burnett, *Grassling*, 179–80.

3

Archives of care: Mourning, echoes and the reader as gleaner

Introductory constellation

As I suggested in the Introduction, a focus on storytelling not as a form of human-imposed explanation but as a patterning that indicates the complexity of human entanglements in a more-than-human world is common across the work of many contemporary writers and thinkers. Serenella Iovino and Serpil Oppermann, for instance, highlight the way all bodies, human and non-human, can be seen as 'living texts that recount *naturalcultural* stories'; the narrativity of matter is not, they insist, a metaphor, but illustrates the way humans 'are entangled with [nonhuman] material agency' such that all material forms 'emerge *together* as storied beings'.[1] Jeffrey Jerome Cohen likewise argues that all writing emerges from 'a networked alliance of nonhumans'; while Cohen's examples are more prosaic than Iovino and Oppermann's – he discusses the agency of pens and keyboards and cups of coffee – he likewise insists that thinking of the narrative potential of all matter is a way to undercut fictions of human sovereignty, especially in an environmental context.[2] This impulse to understand the world in terms of the stories matter tells is apparent in a large number of memoirs and poems focused on accounts of gleaning and collection. A. Kendra Greene, in an account of various small museums in Iceland, points to how a collection of stones 'reminds us of what we already suspect: that the world is chockablock with untold wonders', while in her poem 'Museum of Stones' Carolyn Forché writes about the 'hope that this assemblage of rubble, taken together, would become / a shrine or holy place'.[3] While equally celebratory, perhaps, Jean Sprackland's account of beachcombing also recognizes the importance of chance and relinquishment I have argued is central to the process of gleaning: 'Things arrive unannounced, then disappear again under the waves [...]. [T]he real thrill is the chance nature of these encounters.'[4]

Ideas of material agency and chance encounter are central, for instance, to Lisa Woollett's *Rag and Bone*, a family history told through a series of discussions of mudlarking and beachcombing along the Thames and in Cornwall. Woollett's 'growing collection of discarded shore finds', she writes, awakens her interest in a 'branch of [her] family that included dustmen and a scavenger': her acts of collection and relinquishment, of ordering and discarding what she finds, give her insights into her own relations, and previous ways of life.[5] Woollett situates her activities particularly in terms of gleaning, citing an 1883 *Daily Telegraph* article, 'Gleaners of Thames Bank'; while she does not, like the earlier gleaners, search for items that can be resold, she illustrates the book with beautiful photographs of the objects she finds, organized by use, shape or colour. The gleaned object is important not only for itself, but for the way it can be positioned alongside other similar objects in an artistic arrangement, such as a strict line of toothbrushes, a circle formed of the wheels of toy cars, or a resplendent ball of red plastic items ranging from bottle caps and biro lids to artificial flowers.

While none of the photographs clearly indicate the environment in which the objects were found – most employ a blank white background – Woollett frames her journey in terms of a growing awareness of environmental concerns. While on the banks of the Thames she collects detritus that has often been there for centuries, closer to the sea she finds mostly plastic. The older objects allow 'a precious glimpse of things I may otherwise never have known', and prompt conversations with her elderly mother, while her hauls of plastic make her 'suddenly sick': 'There was just too much of it – too much to bear looking through any more.'[6] Woollett continually differentiates between found objects that evoke a history of use and craftsmanship, such as combs and buttons, and the ever-present shards of plastic that have only been used once, and been immediately discarded. These latter items parallel a desire 'not to know the details' of climate change: her stories of found objects indicate a cultural shift from ideas of loss, which imply a previous relation of care, to waste, which implies an intentional comfort with not recognizing the damage humans are doing to the world.[7] Her accounts of Anthropocenic effects on eels, seabirds and humans are often familiar, and parallel Kathleen Jamie's essays discussed above. Gleaning, however, allows her not only the opportunity to reflect on planetary environmental catastrophe, but also on the way material objects not only tell stories, but occasion them: objects are a prelude to conversation, to display and to connection between different people. Telling stories about plastic detritus is as important as any other form of cultural memory, because it indicates the need for systemic change. Woollett's acts of gleaning, much like those of the collectors Greene interviews in her work, are a basis for dialogue and cultural illumination.

The notion that multiple objects, and multiple stories, can be paths to community appears in a wide variety of contemporary texts. The essays collected in Rebecca Solnit's *The Faraway Nearby*, for instance, are less focused on environmental concerns than much of her other recent work. Instead, Solnit emphasizes the overlapping relation between her response to her mother's death, the creation of imagined worlds, the function of storytelling, and the emergence of empathy in a series of pieces constructed like a series of nested Russian dolls. She explains:

> I am, we each are, the inmost of an endless series of Russian dolls; you who read are now encased within a layer I built for you, or perhaps my stories are now inside you. We live as literally as that inside each other's thoughts and work, in this world that is being made all the time, by all of us, out of beliefs and acts, information and materials. Even in the wilderness your ideas of what is beautiful, what matters, and what constitutes pleasure shape your journey there as much as do your shoes and map also made by others.[8]

The stories we tell about each other, and about our relation to the world, are reiterative. Just as the themes and essay titles in Solnit's collection mirror each other – the volume is framed as a nested series beginning and ending with 'Apricots', with 'Ice' as both the second and penultimate chapter, and so on, with 'Wound', 'Knot' and 'Unwound' at the centre – Solnit argues that it is impossible to approach any story, any experience of the world or any empathetic action on its own. Stories have no beginnings or ends, but are 'a cup of water scooped from the sea and poured back into it', such that '[a]ll stories are really fragments of one story'.[9] This nature of storytelling is what permits empathy, which she defines as the dissolution of boundaries and 'imaginative entering' into the life of another.[10] For Solnit as for Donna Haraway, storytelling can be seen as the 'patterning of possible worlds' that can be thought of in terms of 'threading, felting, tangling, tracking, and sorting' as well as 'composting'.[11] As Haraway writes in relation to a discussion of grief, penguins and Ursula K. Le Guin, it 'matters what stories tell stories': stories provide a way to understand entanglement precisely because, as in Solnit's account of her mother's death, they allow us to 'grieve *with*' in a 'fabric of undoing' that curtails any notion of human, or individual, exceptionalism.[12] Solnit's stories range from accounts of preserving apricots to reading *Frankenstein*: each encounter with the world is an encounter with human and non-human others that is ultimately expansive and potentially transformative. If, as Judith Schalansky writes in her own collection of stories about collections, the world 'grieves only for what it knows', the processes of collection and juxtaposition can bring people, objects and non-human lives into relation, and occasion new stories, forms of memory and grief.[13]

Solnit's text is particularly interesting, however, not only for the stories it tells, but also for the one it leaves behind. Alongside the thirteen titled chapters there is another text included in the book but not listed in the table of contents, an untitled essay that appears in a single line on the bottom of each page of text, presented in italics and separated from the body of the page by a continuous border. The text begins with a phrase it will repeat often, '[m]oths drink the tears of sleeping birds', which Solnit argues is 'a template for many things; it is a container of the familiar made strange, of sorrow turned into sustenance, of the myriad stories the natural world provides that are as uncannily resonant as any myth'.[14] The essay, if it is an essay, reflects on moths and story of Cupid and Psyche, on the work of Rainer Maria Rilke and on Solnit's own life. At times it mirrors the text above, so that the first appearance in the bottom line of the word 'empathy' echoes the content of the paragraph immediately above; at other times it provides a self-reflective gaze, asking: 'And this book, is it tears?'[15] Thematically the text clearly echoes the rest of the volume and yet, by being placed on the periphery, it suggests the uncertainty that must face any claim for an integrated or entangled form of storytelling. If, as Caroline Levine has argued, literary, aesthetic and social forms can be seen in terms of 'all ordering principles, all patterns of repetition and difference', Solnit asks the reader to consider what to do with the material that is left out.[16] For Levine forms are useful in thinking of political power and the creation of hierarchy, which always includes inequality; in her attention to form, and storytelling as patterning, Solnit implies a similar point, in that even the material revealed in repetition and difference, which initially seems to be ordered, is a product of a model of hierarchies and selection. The reader of *The Faraway Nearby* must choose whether to read this piece as it appears, at the bottom of the page, in which case its resonances with the text above will become apparent, or separately, in which case its placement becomes more arbitrary but it maintains its own internal coherence. The text forces us to ask why some material is included in a story, and other material is abandoned; it forces us to accept our own processes of judgement in deciding what is worth attending to; it highlights the physical page as a material environment over which humans exert control.

As Jenn Ashworth writes in her own nested, fragmentary work of lifewriting, while it may be impossible to 'make something better – more coherent – than the world that makes us', or 'to be something other than embodied and enworlded', we are still 'supposed to take the parts inside somehow'.[17] Ashworth laments that it 'is impossible to write a memoir when pieces of the story are missing'.[18] *Notes Made while Falling* nevertheless, in the interaction between its component essays, which fold into each other in a variety of ways, showcases the way any individual life cannot be known as complete, but always must be seen in relation not only to a more-than-human world, but also to all the stories that cannot be told. A similar tension appears in Sarah Manguso's *Ongoingness* which tells, in enigmatic fragments, the story of a twenty-five-year diary, totalling eight hundred thousand words, that Manguso finds herself unable either to excerpt or present in full. As she writes in an afterword, to provide excerpts would be 'troublingly arbitrary'; instead, she decides only to refer to the diary, while the reader must '[i]magine it as dark matter or as one of the sixty-seven confirmed moons of Jupiter or whatever real thing you must nonetheless take on faith'.[19] Sprackland, in her volume on graveyards, uses the same image, writing that '[g]aps and absences are everywhere: in the writing of history, the telling of a story, the drawing of a family tree. Like dark matter, they make up most of the human cosmos.'[20] Graveyards, she writes, provide 'a few fragments of story' that must be pieced together into 'threads of meaning'.[21] For each author stories are not, and cannot be, presented whole and complete, but are the interweaving of what has left behind. Ashworth's text is often full and dense, while Manguso's emphasizes blank space, yet both writers present their memoirs not as a story of a life, but as a series of fragments that, in constellation, reveal something of that life when narrative has failed.

Ashworth explains that *Notes Made by Falling* was written over eight years, while she was also writing novels, and constructed from individual pieces that somehow did not work on their own, instead being relegated to a 'compost of failure'.[22] The construction of the book was an act of 'salvaging', making a whole of texts of which she was unsure. Likewise, Schalansky notes in the preface to *An Inventory of Losses*, which combines fiction and memoir to approach ideas of collection, loss and extinction, that it was only after finishing the book that she realized how studying 'the diverse phenomena of decomposition and destruction [...] is just one of the myriad ways of dealing with death'.[23] The losses that Ashworth, Solnit, Manguso and Schalansky describe are very different, and range in scale from the personal to the planetary, yet each of these texts gestures to the necessity of telling stories that incorporate what stories cannot tell. This is, in part, the purpose of the fragment, which holds, in the blank space that surrounds it, a potentially infinite set of tales and associations that cannot be fixed in print. The literary fragment is not only the text, but the absence it highlights. As Schalansky writes in a discussion of Sapphic fragments, as translated by Anne Carson, 'these mutilated poems demand to be completed'.[24] Yet the beauty of the fragment is that it resists that completion: even when organized or rearranged, as in Woollett's work, the fragment remains stubbornly itself.

In combining these different texts, I want to suggest that the gleaning of material fragments, in terms of beachcombing, for instance, and the gleaning of literary fragments, in terms of storytelling and lifewriting, are fundamentally similar acts. Gleaning, in both cases, requires knowing when to let go. It requires an acknowledgement of absence and incompleteness and a recognition of the fallible role of the gleaner in attempting to assign meaning or pattern. At the same time, gleaning creates a central responsiveness. Reading these works requires you to see yourself as entangled and co-constituted. The material form of the literary fragment is inseparable from the gleaned object. Indeed, as I pile these books around me I use conkers, seaglass, small rocks that shone when wet and have since dulled, and all manner of other found objects as bookmarks. The text, the reader and the material world work in connection with each other. Kate Zambreno, in her discussion of Bhanu Kapil's *Ban en Banlieue*, discussed below, alongside other texts, refers to an interview with Carson in which she says that to write an essay, an author simply needs to set a pile of books in front of them and 'write about how they connect with each other'.[25] The books on her desk, Zambreno notes, are used both for her inspiration and toys for her baby, while one of her books must be retrieved from beneath a garbage bag of outgrown baby clothes. Certainly not only fragmentary texts remind readers of their material form, and yet the fragment, in its continual openness to the material world, creates a dialogue with its surroundings that more conventional narrative can elide.

Zambreno's work is, in part, focused on archives, while as quoted above, Ashworth, like Haraway, uses the metaphor of compost. These two images govern the discussion that follows. While both may be sharply differentiated from my account of gleaning, all three notions emphasize the interplay of fragments, and the need for new forms of storytelling. Composting, as Jennifer Mae Hamilton and Astrida Neimanis explain, is a way of understanding how 'environmental humanities scholarship emerges from and contours the world around us. This is because how we *think, speak, and write* the world can shape how we *act* in it and *make* it'.[26] Composting, as metaphor and as practice, reminds us of the material significance of our thinking of environmental concerns, as well as the way contemporary approaches to environmental thought derive from previous ideas. In Haraway's work, composting is a way to move past 'the trash of the Anthropocene [and] the exterminism of the Capitalocene' and, by 'chipping and shredding and layering like a mad gardener', make way for new possible pasts, presents and futures.[27] Composting, as one of the central approaches to what she calls the Chthulucene, is a way of recognizing 'ongoing multispecies stories and practices of becoming-with' that emphasizes the way humans must care for and with other species.[28] She illustrates this with reference to a series of co-authored speculative fictions surrounding the figure of Camille, as created by and through the Children of Compost; the stories suggest, as Haraway puts it in relation to Tsing's work, the need 'to write stories and live lives for flourishing and for abundance', which she argues can be done through linking and layering, through combination and curiosity.[29] Composting in this sense is a figure for the creation of narratives that take the detritus of other ways of imagining and layer them to be something new, but without specific human agency. Rather, the compost pile, in this central image, becomes an image of being-with. This approach can be seen not only in Ashworth's text, but in Solnit's and Woollett's as well: understanding stories in their relation, or in the way they come into being with other stories and in so doing generate new ones, allows for a new approach to narrative that does not depend on cause and effect, or on linear chronology, but rather illustrates entanglement at the level of the page.

If composting carries with it connotations of amalgamation and generation, as well as decay, archives are more often thought of in terms of what is left behind. Carolyn Steedman calls attention to the tension between Dust, or the recirculation of ideas, and Waste, or their abandonment. She argues that our understanding of narrative, whether fictional or social, is caught up in the story that emerges from the understanding that there is 'sequence, event, movement' at the same time that 'things fall away, are abandoned, get lost'.[30] Sonja Boon likewise proposes speculation and magic realism as 'a radical approach that challenges us to think not only about archival silencing and erasure, but also, about archival violence'.[31] Boon's memoir *What the Oceans Remember* highlights the seductiveness and comfort of archival spaces, and their limitations. Archival researchers, she cautions, can often fill in the gaps in an archive with what they want to see: 'They'll look into the gaps and the silences, and they'll imagine all the possible riches there, because that's where the story lives.'[32] Yet the archival process of 'hold[ing] the fragments to the light', Boon notes, can ultimately give rise to pattern and meaning: she compares archival work to music-making, where 'each fragment is like a musical note, a phrase, a score marking. Each one is a window into the intentions of the past.'[33] In this sense, composting and archives both highlight the role of creativity in any assemblage. Archives and compost piles both reveal the tension between decay and rebirth, between assemblage and individuation. Both practices suggest the need to reconceptualize narrative in terms of what has been collected, and what has been left out.

While these practices can be explored in a variety of traditions, they have particular resonance in relation to the work of marginalized writers. Zambreno, in a recent volume, recounts a conversation with Kapil where she describes 'making a study of coherence', differentiating herself from writers who are secure 'in the status of their art form', perhaps for cultural reasons.[34] Dionne Brand explores these ideas at length. In *A Map to the Door of No Return* she describes

> collect[ing] these fragments [...] – disparate and sometimes only related by sound or intuition, vision or aesthetic. [...] [B]y relying on random shards of history and unwritten memoir of descendants of those who passed through it, including me, I am constructing a map of the region, paying attention to faces, to the unknowable, to unintended acts of returning, to impressions of doorways.[35]

Gleaning, in this case, is necessitated when official stories are withheld or irretrievable. For writers such as Boon and Brand, living in what Christina Sharpe calls the wake of slavery allows 'particular ways of re/seeing, re/inhabiting, and re/imagining the world'.[36] Collecting fragments is a way of creating an environment, a map, that acknowledges gaps. It is a way of 'invent[ing] in absence', in Brand's words.[37] The archive, in this sense, is not a record of what has happened, but a collection of fragments that is brought to life in the interplay between gleaner and material. These contemporary formulations of both composting and archive are ways to avoid easy assumptions of authority and even, in Kapil's terms, of coherence. Fragmentary form becomes a way of creating the world that simultaneously refuses any preordained sense of wholeness or order.

Such ideas are central to the work discussed below. Valeria Luiselli's novel *Lost Children Archive* is explicitly an attempt to tell the stories of migrant children whose stories have been lost, with specific reference to archival practice. Bhanu Kapil's and Poupeh Missaghi's texts, which float in fragmented form between memoir, fiction and history, go further in illustrating the impossibility of telling a linear story, and the possibility of a text made of gaps and fissures. None of these authors are focused primarily on environmental themes, but their focus on what Deborah Bird Rose and Thom van Dooren call 'the death of the disregarded' aligns them with many of the concerns discussed throughout this volume.[38] The fragmentary form allows for new attention not just to the entanglement between humans and non-humans, but between different humans; each of these three writers is interested in the tension between state power and individual lives, and how fragmentation can give voice to absence and loss.

The two novels discussed in the final section, Lucy Ellmann's *Ducks, Newburyport* and Jenny Offill's *Weather*, similarly use fragmentary form to illustrate the complexity of telling any story of modern life. Each text is grounded in absence as much as presence: in each, the fragment is used to highlight all the material that has been left behind. Like the texts discussed in Chapter 2, the work of all five writers illustrates and instantiates ideas of entanglement and co-constitution. More than the writers discussed above, however, they also use fragmentary form to highlight gaps and disfluencies. As much as, by their very existence, they demonstrate the power of texts to generate new ways of thinking, and new forms of representation, they simultaneously foreground loss and incompletion. They are united in focusing on ideas of loss, grief and care.[39]

Each of these texts, in different ways, highlights the importance of care and relation in telling a story of the world. As María Puig de la Bellacasa has argued, at the present moment, '[e]ven more than before, knowledge as relating – while thinking, researching, storytelling, wording, accounting – matters in the mattering of worlds'.[40] Puig de la Bellacasa draws on a definition of care devised by Joan Tronto and Berenice Fisher, who argue that care is neither dyadic nor individualistic, but 'a practice and a disposition' that is not limited to the human.[41] Puig de la Bellacasa emphasizes that this definition moves ideas of care from what a straightforward account of 'we' do to more disruptive ideas of subject-object relations and human supremacy, so that 'what counts is the "interweaving" of living things that holds together words as we know them, that allows their perpetuation and renewal – and even that which helps to their decay as we have seen with the example of worms' labor of composting'.[42] Care is not a dyadic or binary relation, but creates relationality; while it is predicated on multispecies flourishing, it also acknowledges, as the mention of composting suggests, the importance of composting and relinquishing.

Eva Haifa Giraud cautions that accounts such as Puig de la Bellacasa's can reinforce 'normative sociotechnical arrangements' rather than unsettling them; she argues that accounts of relationality and entanglement often ignore the productive force and necessity of exclusion, as well as recentring the politics and practice of care on human behaviours.[43] Embodied care, Giraud claims, is not a way of 'staying with the trouble' so much as it is 'fundamentally *untroubling*' and ignores the longer histories of relations between species and narratives of suffering.[44] Particularly in her account of human-soil relations, however, Puig de la Bellacasa is careful to avoid the charge of imposing a human ethics onto a more-than-human world. Instead, she argues that care for and with the world requires a sense of immersion and recognition of multiplicity, as well as a new sense of time. Ecological care does not only require attention to cycles of living and dying, but acknowledge that 'the time of soil is not "one"; it exposes multifarious speeds of growth becoming ecologically significant to each other'.[45] Care calls attention not only to the way multispecies cooperation can lead to flourishing and renewal, but to the fact that this flourishing is experienced differently by different species. Rather than proposing a blanket, anthropocentric solution, Puig de la Bellacasa's account of care privileges difference.

These ideas of gleaning, composting, archiving and care are, in many respects, very different, as are the rhetorical strategies their authors use. Yet each proposes a potential solution to the problem that underpins this chapter, and the volume as a whole. Being attentive to the world is simultaneously a question of recognizing one's entanglement and singling out individual elements. Every act of collection or attention excludes as much as it includes; every story, every archive, is necessarily partial. Yet, as I have argued throughout this book, this partiality is itself productive. Attention to entanglement and assemblage does not require a sudden shift to planetary scale. Rather, every act of attention allows for a further understanding of what is left out. As Boon writes in an account of ruins:

> Decay is a site of growth. It is ripe, generative. Ruin is about potential, about the promise of the past embedded in an unknown future. [...] Decay is living essence of the past. It's alive. It's uncomfortable. It's ugly. It hurts. But it's also deeply moving and very beautiful. Ruin is about strength in the face of destruction.[46]

The fragment, as I argue in the Introduction, should be thought of not only in terms of ruin or decay: the fragment is not only what is left, but is also whole in itself. Yet the fundamental appeal of the fragment is the way it balances generation and decay, incorporation and exclusion. As much as this is a question of responsibility for the world, it is also a question of storytelling. Fragmentary stories, such as those discussed in this chapter, are able to give voice to those who are marginalized or overlooked precisely by highlighting absence and aporia. These stories illustrate not only the failures of archives and explanatory narratives, but their potential. Emerging from the ruins of narrative, they illustrate the generative power of storytelling to generate new ways of knowing. If, as I suggested in the Introduction, stories of climate change often end with the comfort of cataclysm or propose overly easy solutions, the texts discussed below do stay with the trouble. These texts are not limited to explicitly environmental concerns, but in their emphasis on accident and contingency illustrate how fragmentary narratives create the possibility of new syntheses and ways of thinking. These texts trouble ideas of individual and collective responsibility and forms of knowledge; they ask who has the right to tell a story; they ask what potential futures remain when the present seems predicated on rubble.

A. Echoes of other children: Valeria Luiselli

Valeria Luiselli's *Lost Children Archive* begins with the difficulty of story. The initial first-person narrator, an unnamed woman who is mostly referred to as 'Ma', ponders how she and her husband will tell the story that follows to her children in later years: 'I'm not sure which parts of our story we might each choose to pluck and edit out for them, and which ones we'll shuffle around and insert back in.'[47] Her children relish hearing their own stories, and seek stories that explain their lives back to them, with a beginning, middle and end, and yet the narrator worries that this coherence may not be possible. Her concern is made evident in the novel's structure. The novel is organized into a series of titled fragments, for the first half of the novel narrated by the mother, that describe the family's journey from New York to the American Southwest. The family travels in search of both two specific child refugees and the stories of the thousands more unnamed and unrecorded child refugees who have crossed the United States-Mexico border, as well as for the father's work on a sound documentary about Apaches. These fragments are interrupted or contextualized by catalogues of boxed archives that contain notebooks on the themes of the preceding passages, lists of intertexts both explicit and less overt, and assorted other elements including compact discs, fragments of poems, photographs and government documents. As Luiselli explains at the start of a list of works cited at the novel's end:

> The archive that sustains this novel is both an inherent and a visible part of the
> central narrative. In other words, references to sources – textual, musical, visual,
> or audio-visual – are not meant as side notes, or ornaments that decorate the
> story, but function as intralinear markers that point to the many voices in the
> conversation that the book sustains with the past.[48]

In the first part of the book, these references are often explicit: the narrator discusses reading Susan Sontag, and Sontag's work is listed in one of the boxes. The second half of the novel introduces a second first-person narrator, the family's son, who often refers to similar material, but more allusively. Both of these sections are interwoven with excerpts from a text by the fictional Italian author, Ella Camposanto's *Elegies for Lost Children*, which is, as the first narrator explains, 'loosely based on the historical Children's Crusade' of 1212, but in this version is set 'in what seems like a not-so-distant future in a region that can possibly be mapped back to North Africa, the Middle East, and southern Europe, or to Central and North America'.[49] While the initial excerpts from Camposanto's text are often brief, as the novel proceeds they get much longer, and begin to overlap with the central narrative. This book itself is filled with Polaroid pictures the boy takes over the course of the family's journey, which are themselves provided at the end of *Lost Children Archive*. Thus, there are at least three narrative strands – the mother's, the boy's and Camposanto's – which each are presented, for the most part, in fragments, and each of which makes allusion to and draws from many other sources.[50] As Luiselli explains in an interview describing her own archival process, *Lost Children Archive* is both 'the book and an archive of the book', while also written 'in a very intense dialogue with books'.[51]

The density of the novel's intertextuality is unmistakeable. As with *Ducks, Newburyport*, individual readers will seize on different allusions. Reading the narrator's early account, in one of several fragments simply titled 'Archive', of how she spends 'long sleepless nights reading about archive fevers', as she collects 'loose notes, scraps, cutouts, quotes copied down on cards, letters, maps, photographs, lists of words, clippings, [and] tape-recorded testimonies', I was delighted to recognize the reference to Jacques Derrida, although for another reader such an allusion may seem less meaningful. The story that I, as a reader, tell of this novel is partial and incomplete, as is the story that the narrator tells. Indeed, there is another central intertext to the novel, Luiselli's own non-fiction volume *Tell Me How It Ends*, which tells a very similar story of a family, Luiselli's own, making a similar trip, for roughly similar purposes.[52] While the protagonist of Luiselli's novel is a 'documentarist', working in a sound-recording tradition that is based on journalism and narrative – in opposition to her husband, a 'documentarian', who samples sounds at random – Luiselli herself was working as a translator, interceding between child refugees and government officials.[53] On the first page of the nonfiction work, she raises the problem that governs the novel as well:

> I hear words, spoken in the mouths of children, threaded in complex narratives. They are delivered with hesitance, sometimes distrust, always with fear. I have to transform them into written words, succinct sentences, and barren terms.

The children's stories are always shuffled, stuttered, always shattered beyond the repair of a narrative order. The problem with trying to tell their story is that it has no beginning, no middle, and no end.[54]

The two volumes thus open with the same set of questions, but voiced in different ways: the memoir highlights the traumatic speech of child refugees, and the need for the translator to piece these fragments back into a story, while the novel frames this as a common experience of all children and parents. While the novel's first narrator laments that she had assembled 'an archive full of fragments of strangers' lives but had close to nothing of our own lives together', the novel as a whole challenges any such distinction.[55] Fragments and archives are the only way to understand the world, but they do not combine to produce an external reality; rather, these fissures and gaps, and the constant appeals to a larger, intertextual world, are all that remain. Writing is simply 'a kind of scaffolding holding all of those broken stories together'.[56] The central difference between the two texts is not so much one of style, although *Tell Me How It Ends* is ultimately more linear, but of which fragments each includes. The memoir draws on government documents and forms, while the bibliography lists documentaries, newspaper articles and other factual material; the novel does not exclusively draw on works of fiction, philosophy and literary theory, but certainly privileges them. The combined fragments are simply those most appropriate to the given form a single telling of the story takes, yet in their combination Luiselli demonstrates that no single telling is ever sufficient.

In this sense, Luiselli's work can certainly be thought of in terms of the ideas of assemblage discussed in Chapter 2. Elizabeth Grosz clarifies, in relation to Deleuze and Guattari, that

Assemblages are the provisional linkages of elements, fragments, flows, of disparate status and substance: ideas, things – human, animate, and inanimate – all have the same ontological status. There is no hierarchy of being, no preordained order to the collection and conjunction of these various fragments, no central organization or plan to which they must conform. Their 'law' is rather the imperative of endless experimentation, metamorphosis, or transmutation, alignment and realignment.[57]

At a simple level, this suggests that Virginia Woolf and Jacques Derrida are no more, or less, useful as insights than the Comisión Nacional de Derechos Humanos or the U.S. Accountability Office's report on 'Unaccompanied Alien Children: Actions Needed to Ensure Children Receive Required Care in DHS Custody'. If the act of reading, in *Lost Children Archive*, 'highlights the nature of the narrator's own expressive problems', it also suggests the potential paths available to the book's own readers.[58] The reader, like the narrator, must select from this diverse set of materials, collecting and relinquishing, to create a narrative that is itself predicated on absence and impossibility. There is, Luiselli suggests, no other way to tell the story: it is known only in echoes and reverberations. As the mother reflects in a passage that summarizes the novel itself:

> What ties me to where? There's the story about the lost children on their crusade, and their march across jungles and barrenlands, which I read and reread, sometimes absentmindedly, other times in a kind of rapture, recording it; and now I am reading parts to the boy. And then there's also the story of the real lost children, some of whom are about to board a plane. There are many other children, too, crossing the border or still on their way here, riding trains, hiding from dangers. There are Manuela's two girls, lost somewhere, waiting to be found. And of course, finally, there are my own children, one of whom I might soon lose, and both of whom are now always pretending to be lost children.[59]

To distinguish between these stories, ultimately, would be to replicate the power hierarchies of the U.S. government, which decides which stories, and which people, are more valuable. To tell only the story of the child refugees might potentially be voyeuristic or appropriative, while to tell only the stories that are already upheld in textual form would replicate a different sort of hierarchical knowledge.[60]

As the family travels West, the stories they tell, and the stories they listen to as audiobooks, are stories of the end. Early in the trip, the mother expresses her desire to go to Texas, 'the state with the largest number of immigration detention centers for children', while the father wants to go to the Chiricahua Mountains in Arizona, 'the heart of Apacheria [...] where the last free peoples on the entire American continent lived before they had to surrender to the white-eyes'.[61] This juxtaposition does not simply highlight ongoing colonial oppression, racism and genocide, but can be seen in terms of the long Anthropocene. As Kathryn Yusoff argues, in relation to Aimé Césaire's equation 'colonization = "thingification"', where colonization is described as 'a principle of ruin', the notion of the Anthropocene cannot be separated from enslavement and systematic violence.[62] The Anthropocene, mostly simply, 'began with the annihilation of the Colonial Other'.[63] The 'predictable, fucked-up plot' of the child refugees reiterates this pattern.[64] As Luiselli explains in an interview, *Lost Children Archive* is not 'a novel about the immigration crisis', but a novel that grapples with political violence more generally.[65]

The Anthropocene is not reducible, as the mother thinks in relation to oceanic waste and Ezra Pound, to 'ships cutting through centuries of rubbish', but rather must be considered as the inability of humans to 'free themselves from destructive patterns'.[66] The barrenness of the land is explained both by the forest fires that are an increasingly a symbol of climate devastation, and by a longer history of '[g]enocide, exodus, diaspora, [and] ethnic cleansing'.[67] While the narrator believes that '[s]omething changed in the world', quite recently, that makes it impossible to imagine the future, since the present is overwhelming, the larger narrative strands situate the text in a world of constant atrocities.[68] The world can only be known in fragments, and as ruin. Yet, as Lauret Savoy cautions, '[f]ragmented needn't mean gone'.[69] Savoy's work traces the same landscape as Luiselli, 'assembling fragments of this land's past' and its '[p]hantom histories' as part of a collective enterprise to assemble a new idea of home: 'Home indeed lies among the ruins and shards that surround us all'.[70] Attending to fragments, Savoy argues, is a form of memory that can shape the present; by paying attention to the land itself, the realities of loss and displacement, and the legacies of violence, can be given new voice. This, too, is the focus of the parent figures in the novel, who in documenting the voices of the erased and the displaced hope to integrate past and present, in full recognition of the continuing cycles of human and material devastation.

This aim, however, is rendered difficult by its very narrative form. The husband brings along an 'all-male compendium of "going a journey," conquering and colonizing', from Joseph Conrad to the Bible.[71] On their own journey the family listens to familiar narratives of decay, particularly Cormac McCarthy's *The Road* and William Golding's *Lord of the Flies*, to the extent that the narrator begins to wonder how any form of storytelling can 'be a means to a specific end'.[72] Children, and media conglomerates, look to stories for resolution or clarity, yet the only potential endings she sees are apocalyptic. As Luiselli writes in her essay, when she describes the plight of child refugees to her own daughter, she can only conclude 'I don't know how it ends yet'.[73] If, as discussed in the Introduction, this problem is endemic to climate change narratives, which too often end either in praise of individual agency or in catastrophe, both of which produce their own comforts, Luiselli's protagonist attempts to find ways to incorporate the echoes of the past without explaining them, or reducing them to a straightforward story.

The focus on echoes here is surprisingly literal. When the family first reaches Echo Canyon in New Mexico, they play a simple game, shouting nonsense words into the mountains and hearing them refracted. The same pattern takes place in the book as a whole, as reflected in the shift in narrators midway through.

The stories repeat, often in a refracted way. The mother, in her narration, takes comfort in the boy's storytelling: 'as I listen to the boy telling the story of what we are seeing and the story of how we are seeing it, through him, a slow but solid certainty finally settles in me. It's his version of the story that will outlive us.'[74] While the boy's initial narration follows the same model as his mother's, later in the novel there is a sudden turn, where the two children set out on their own, and the boy's narration becomes a continuous sentence. He describes

> four lost children [who] know they are still alive, although they walk among the echoes of other children, past and future, who kneeled, laid down, coiled into a fetal position, fell, got lost, did now know if they were alive or dead inside that vast hungry desert where only the four of them now keep walking in silence, knowing they might also soon be lost.[75]

The children make their way back to Echo Canyon, where they are eventually reunited with their parents. This narrative structure does more than merely suggest that all children may be lost, however. The archive box following the boy's narration is filled not with texts, but with echoes. There are 'Echo Echoes', 'Mem mem mem mem' and 'Wa wa wa wa wa', but also 'Car Echoes' that replay, in distorted form, earlier scenes – 'Stop, go, no, more, less, Jesus Fucking Christ, ist, ist, Ma and Pa talking, arguing, whooooo, hhhhh, hhhhh, all of us breathing, silence' – and 'Stranger Echoes': 'Papers, passports, where are you from, why are you here, ere, Border Patrol conversations.'[76] The combination of acoustic and narrative echoes points not only to the ubiquity of these narratives of trauma, and to the distortion that every such narrative undergoes, but to the way storytelling is always tied to space. Sound is a way of understanding space and history without imposing a linear or explanatory story upon it. As Grosz writes, refrains 'shape the vibrations of milieus into the harmonics of territories', while music, conversely, moves 'beyond territories'.[77] For the mother, likewise, '[s]ound and space are connected in a way much deeper than we usually acknowledge. [...] [W]e experience space through the sounds overlaid upon it.'[78] The echoes of the children's shouts create a refrain that situates them in a particular place – a place where they can be found – at the same time that it demonstrates the continuity of experiences. Echoes and archives distort the past, but also, in their gaps and repetitions, provide a form of access. Luiselli's double paralleling of the boy's narration with his mother's and of the family's lost children with all other lost children is a way to indicate that even when it is impossible to tell a new story, the story of gaps and erasures, and of the repeated systems of erasure that govern experience, can still be told.

While the multiple doublings and allusions within the text are used to illustrate the pervasiveness of Anthropocenic and genocidal violence, they are also used to suggest the possibility of storytelling, in its most fragmented form, as a form of care. The boy's stories are told to his sister, and in his descriptions of the journey he creates a space for empathy and compassion. Like the mother, the boy frames his stories as a form of comfort, granting stability to experiences that themselves might some overwhelmingly chaotic. When the children venture into the wilderness he says:

> You gave me your hand, and I held it tight. We walked into the unreal desert, like the lost children's desert, and under their blazing sun, you and me, over the tracks, and into the heart of light, like lost children, walking alone together, but you and me holding hands, because I was never going to let go of your hand now.[79]

Both the mother and the boy tell their stories not in order to make sense of the world as such, but to demonstrate their care for both the subjects of the stories and their potential listeners. Storytelling is a form of communion, here rendered in specifically tactile terms. Puig de la Bellacasa frames her discussion of posthuman care precisely in relation to Césaire's idea of 'thingification', imagining a form of reclamation that 'doesn't expurgate the stories of minoritarian struggles against thingification but thinks with them in order to problematize the oppressive dynamics involved in bringing a being to qualify as a matter of concern and therefore to deserve (research) attention and care'.[80] Both the mother's and son's stories are not told in order to speak for the minoritarian voices that have been erased by government discourse and public disinterest, but to speak alongside them. The stories that can be told in *Lost Children Archive* do not supersede or erase the myriad stories of immigrant life, but instead, in presenting storytelling as a form of connection and thinking-with, demonstrate the need to pay attention to all of those stories that cannot be fully incorporated within the narrative.

Marianne Hirsch cautions that while the individual stories of underrepresented and oppressed people can function as 'a form of counter-history' that provides 'a means to account for the power structures animating forgetting, oblivion, and erasure and thus to engage in acts of repair and redress', communal narratives can often erase individual memory.[81] Hirsch draws particular attention to 'the sentimentality attached to the figure of the lost child', the very image that underpins both *Lost Children Archive* and its fictional intertext *Elegies for Lost Children*.[82] Luiselli avoids this sentimentality, and the temptation towards 'politicized forms of remembering' that Jan Assmann sees as a particular danger of collective memory, however, by focusing on the way such texts are interpreted by individuals.[83] While the stories presented in *Elegies*, in particular, are communal in a way that arguably erases individual voices, and while *Lost Children Archive*, likewise, elides the voices of the immigrant children at its centre, this is not a violent or sentimental erasure, but one that is seen as a problem inherent in texts.

The mother begins reading *Elegies for Lost Children* halfway through *Lost Children Archive*. 'The First Elegy' is presented as a fragment on its own, and opens abruptly: 'Mouths open to the sky, they sleep'.[84] The children in Camposanto's novel are undifferentiated: they have no names, ethnicity or origins: they are simply six children travelling on a train. The mother finds herself baffled, 'getting a little lost in the words and syntax' and reads the explanatory foreword to understand the relation between these 'numbered fragments', and re-reads the text again.[85] The same fragment reappears sixty pages later, in the boy's narration, where he too 'read[s] the lines over and over, and trie[s] to memorize them, until I thought I understood them'.[86] This idea of attention and incorporation is central to the novel's representation of care: the reader must necessarily read the fragment twice, from both narrators' perspectives, and seek to understand it in these contexts, as well as potentially looking at Luiselli's notes to discover that it incorporates allusions to Ezra Pound. While the text appears to present a universal, collective experience that might erase individual voices, the act of attentive, engaged reading re-individualizes it.

These acts of reading and gleaning, I want to argue, are central to Luiselli's presentation of care. Sherilyn MacGregor summarizes a range of ecofeminist perspectives to highlight the relation between care as a set of material practices – to take care of something – and caring as a disposition – to care for something. In the often-essentialist binary that underlies some ecofeminist approaches, as discussed in Chapter 1, '[m]en may *care about* their children and environments but may not be required [...] to do much work to *care for* them'.[87] Concern for both children and environments is, in this context, often tied to a maternal instinct that is not simply different from masculine ways of knowing, but superior to them.[88] Luiselli's novel initially appears to represent such a binary: while the mother is shown both caring for her own children and child immigrants, the father is far more interested in caring about the Apaches. Yet the dual focus on the boy and mother as readers, and as figures who tell their stories precisely as a form of caring, begins to destabilize this relationship. Like Alexis Wright's more dystopian *The Swan Book*, which combines Indigenous and Western perspectives, often in intertextual fragments, to show that no single story can encompass the end of the world, Luiselli suggests that discourses of the Anthropocene, genocide and political violence are made more, rather than less, urgent by being framed as stories.[89] Storytelling, the mother reflects, is a way to avoid being lost in 'the chaos of history repeated', which leads to 'tribes, families, people, all beautiful things falling apart, debris, dust, erasure'.[90] The stories of children who arrive, who survive, have been told; what she must do is tell the stories that are permanently lost.

These lost stories are most effectively presented when explanatory narrative is left behind. Archival Box V presents maps drawn by the children and provided by the government, photographs of objects recovered on migrant trails, historical notes on homeless and abandoned children earlier in American history, scholarly and literary sources, and a photograph of a poem by Anne Carson. It also includes six 'migrant mortality reports', which list the name, sex, age, location, cause of death and geographic coordinates of the recovered bodies of children, who have mostly died of hypothermia, although in one case of 'multiple blunt force injuries'.[91] These various lists and images might be seen as a re-emersion of the real; they are not integrated into the narrative, and yet are at its heart. In one sense the work is collaborative, or what Puig de la Bellacasa calls writing-with, with 'its acknowledgement of always more-than-one interdependencies'.[92] No one discipline or approach can encompass these stories, and in presenting them in an apparently unmediated manner, Luiselli potentially invites the reader's own care, or lack thereof. The material in the archive is doubly gleaned: the images and texts are selected by Luiselli as particularly meaningful to the story she tells, while the reader too must select particular elements themselves.

The involvement of the reader in this process of care and interpretation might open Luiselli's novel to charges of sentimentalism or solipsism. In her linking of ideas of archives, the Anthropocene and auto-affection, Claire Colebrook argues that

> We now, narcissistically, imagine the tragedy of the post-human future as one in which death and absence will be figured through the unreadability of our own fragments, as though our self-alienation through archive and monument yields some sentiment that we ought to remain as readers of ourselves.[93]

That is, discourses of the Anthropocene, and especially fictional disaster scenarios, often imagine a world in which humans may have disappeared, but in which their archives remain. The archive does not preserve, but replaces, and serves as a monument to human achievement. If not presented in triumphant terms, this approach is arguably evident in Luiselli's novel, where archival remains outlast the humans who left them, and gain value in their use and interpretation. Colebrook argues against a sentimental or anthropocentric perspective that insists that humans must survive in order to read and interpret their own archives. Instead, she argues that a world without humans '*would not be a world without reading*', but one in which reading 'would take a radically different form'.[94] At first glance, Luiselli's focus on the survival of text and image suggests some of this material emphasis that Colebrook repudiates. The final textual passage of the novel is titled simply 'Document', and is a recording the boy provides for his sister, before she and the mother fly back to New York. He explains that '[w]hen you look at all the pictures and listen to this recording you'll understand many things, and eventually maybe you'll even understand everything'.[95] The archive is a form of explanation, as well as care: the boy insists that the recording shows that he and his sister will always be able to find each other again, whenever they might feel lost. The narrative thus has an end, and a relatively happy one: while the lost children will never be found, the children at this story's heart will. The final document is valuable as it will be read (or heard) in the future, and demonstrates a commitment to the ongoingness of human life.

Yet this reading is complicated by the following archival box, which consists of a series of polaroids. Like the illustrations in Baume's novel in Chapter 1, they are often slightly indistinct, distorted by patterns of light. Each maps on to a scene earlier in the text where the boy is described taking photographs; the final image is of a young girl in a cave, her face washed out by the sun, wearing a large hat. The reader cannot help but interpret this image as showing the girl in the story, at the end of her journey. There is, however, no textual attribution, and no textual response. Luiselli suggests, in including these images, both that there is a real world to which all of these stories refer, and that the reader's response to the images, and to all of the previous archives, is only made possible by their desire to incorporate disparate elements into a story. As in Boon's account, looking into gaps and silences opens the space for imagination and storytelling. Use of visual media is particularly important in this instance. As Ella Mudie notes, in response to Colebrook's argument, the photograph has often been seen as 'a trace, a document, and an index of the real' that can memorialize, or serve as an act of mourning for, vanished species, places and implicitly vanished peoples.[96] She argues, however, that photography can go 'beyond mourning' to register 'the inherent fragility and precariousness of our entangled relationship[s]' and serve as a call to responsibility.[97] The closing photographs, like the archival boxes, the intertextual allusions and the stories themselves, are not, or not simply, representations of suffering, or acts of memorialization. They do not stand in place of the 'lost' stories that cannot be told. Instead, the novel's urgency comes from the way each of these fragmentary elements must be combined by the reader that foregrounds responsibility and care.

Lost Children Archive thus fundamentally works in two opposing directions. In telling the stories of lost children who are not voiced or depicted in the novel, Luiselli establishes a sense of communal memory, where patterns and echoes can elide individual experience. While Luiselli does not suggest that all experiences of being lost are the same, she certainly suggests their commonality. Memory, in this sense, becomes of means of 'impos[ing] a meaningful order upon reality', in Barbara A. Misztal's words, that relies on 'symbolic representations and frames'.[98] At the same time, however, the fragmentary presentation of these stories and memories requires the reader to join with the character in acts of gleaning and selection, reconstructing myriad episodes and events into a story that will always remain partial and incomplete. The novel creates empathy by having the reader join the narrators as excavators of personal and collective archives, and draws awareness to their limitations. The archive, in this sense, is not a record of history, but a means to understand what history has failed to record. As Paul Connerton argues, the 'legitimation thesis' can be read positively or negatively, arguing either that 'to speak of historical narratives as justifications of a current political order is to point to a cultural universal' or that in seeking to justify that political order, such narratives exclude everything that does not fit.[99] Yet, he argues, these theories must always bear in mind that these historical narratives are just as often 'generated also by a sense of loss, grief and mourning'.[100] Luiselli goes further to suggest that loss, grief and mourning do not only co-exist with dominant historical narratives, nor do they supplant them: rather, attending to the fissures in dominant narratives provides a new understanding of history. The stories in Luiselli's novel matter precisely because they cannot be clearly told: rather, author, narrators and reader are united in an act of gleaning that focuses on the stories constructed from remnants. The voices of the lost are heard in their echoes; their archives are marked by both inclusion and exclusion. There can be, then, no end to this story, and no resolution, but the constellation of fragments does, in requiring the active participation of the reader as gleaner, allow attention to the entanglement of stories and lives that haunts the present.

B. Bodies and archives: Poupeh Missaghi and Bhanu Kapil

The use of fragmentation as a way of highlighting themes of mourning and absence is not restricted to Luiselli's texts, but is evident in work from many different literary traditions. Han Kang's impressionistic work of mourning *The White Book*, for instance, begins with a list of white objects; even as the narrator wonders 'what meaning might lie in this task' of list-making, she highlights the necessity of 'sift[ing] those words through myself'.[101] Turning attention to the material world becomes a way of processing grief, and accessing lives that have been lost. If Han's book is introspective, its fragments largely illuminating one life, Poupeh Missaghi's *trans(re)lating house one* is far more expansive. Like Luiselli, and like Kapil's texts discussed below, Missaghi combines theoretical references, government descriptions of corpses, and ruminations on memory to create a new form of archive. As the first-person narrator asks:

> In the absence of official archives, in the presence, even, of systematized erasure of the past, the body and the unconscious become depositories for archives, hidden, dormant, lying in wait. But what about archiving systematically, consciously? How to move toward it? How to encompass a time and a place in an archive that extends beyond the bodies of its people?
>
> How to encompass the infinite on the page, between the covers of a book?
>
> Will the archive ever be whole when we do not have access to the voices of the dead?[102]

Both Han and Missaghi use fragmentary forms to write about histories of loss that are excised from the public record, while acknowledging that the material record is all that survives. Both texts focus on the interplay between presence and absence, whether the search for missing public statues in the aftermath of Iranian elections in 2009 that motivates Missaghi's novel or the foregrounding of small domestic objects that fill Han's text. Fragmentary form, in this way, becomes a method of acknowledging not only the gaps left in official records, but the role of the writer or researcher in filling them. Boon writes of her own archival research, for instance, that while her time in the archive 'was supposed to build a firm foundation', her own process of research left her 'scrabbl[ing] for fragments and hints left by others, filling in the gaps – there were so many gaps – with speculation and my own desires'.[103] Rather than upholding an idea of sure, sanctioned or legitimate knowledge, engaging with the archive foregrounds the role of the researcher: reading the archive is a fundamentally imaginative act. As Verne Harris similarly notes, while the lure of the archive is its possibility of capturing state or collective memory, at best they can offer a 'sliver of a window', or a 'fractured, shifting play of light' into social memory.[104] The way archives both shape social memory and are known in their partiality is reflected in a number of texts; Missaghi's work is particularly noteworthy not only for its emphasis on the writer's own role in the creation or dissemination of knowledge, but also for its focus on the body.

Missaghi presents the body in multiple ways, including drawing attention to the physical layout of the text as itself a form of embodiment. The central narrative of the novel is presented in third-person narration, double-spaced and right-justified. Associated commentary, and quotations from theorists and writers ranging from Theodor Adorno and Hélène Cixous to Anne Carson and Maggie Nelson, is presented in first-person, single-spaced, left-justified paragraphs. Descriptions of statues and corpses are single-spaced and justified on both sides, with wide margins. Each of the three textual strands thus has its own way of inhabiting the environment of the page. As Missaghi, or her first-person narrator, comments, the right-justification of the central narrative is a 'ghost' of Persian, her first language: aligning the text in this way forces the reader to 'acknowledge the Otherness of both the territory and the language', even though the work appears in English.[105] She asks, later: 'How can [these stories] be "originally" written in English when their sources were in Persian, when I experienced them in Persian, when their reality was Persian?'[106] Like earlier texts such as Theresa Hak Kyung Cha's *Dictee*, the combination of different formal styles, intertextual allusions and modes of storytelling becomes a way of creating new connections between writer and reader. The writing self is revealed in both their individuality and their relation. Missaghi's blend of fiction, reportage and presumably autobiographical meditations is a way to speak both for herself and for a particular culture without evoking simplistic definitions of either.

If, as Missaghi says in an interview, her novel is an attempt to record the '[f]ragments' of the lives of those who have been killed by the government, it can only take a fragmented form, much like Luiselli's book.[107] Here, however, as much as the citations from North American and European writers often speak to a potentially international – if educated and Anglophone – audience, Missaghi calls attention to a particularly Iranian context. As she says in a discussion of archives:

> I'm obsessed with the archive and lack thereof. What does it mean to document and archive? What are the approaches to archiving, its purpose, and audience? I am invested in the paradox between the lack of archives and documentation in many spheres of Iranian life and the widespread obsession Iranians have with the past. Perhaps this obsession is the very result of this lack.[108]

This mix of cultural specificity and more abstract rumination, often framed in rhetorical questions, dominates the novel itself. Early in the novel, for instance, the narrator asks, in a long sequence of questions: 'What is in the body that offers closure? / [...] Can narratives tell stories the way bodies do? / What is in a story that makes it like a body?'[109] These unanswerable questions are immediately followed by the first description of a corpse, a 23-year-old male who was shot in Tehran in 2009, died of shrapnel residue in his brain in Boston in 2011 and was buried in Berlin in 2012. In a long series of fragments Missaghi tells the story of the unnamed man's struggle for medical care and for immigration status, and his family's struggle for the timely transfer of his body, none of which are reflected in the official record. While the man is unnamed, his story clearly refers to a real, mourned individual. The storyteller must bear witness to these deaths, must add narratives of care and mourning to the dry language of the archive. The archive is insufficient, and yet it holds within it stories which must still be told.

While Luiselli tells imaginative stories that illuminate the lives of the dead, then, Missaghi personalizes these archives. While the novel gives voice to thirteen of these known individuals, however, these stories are juxtaposed with accounts of myriad other corpses who cannot be integrated into the narrative. The first fifty-seven examples of the latter are presented with the word 'corpse' and a number in brackets, often alongside a line or two indicating the cause of death. As the novel proceeds, however, it becomes impossible to incorporate even these fleeting references. Before 'corpse (58)' a page reads 'one body / one body / two bodies'; the next two pages begin to skip in sequence, from 'corpse (72)' to 'corpse (80)', and the passage ends with three pages reading 'corpse ()', 'corpse / corpse / corpses' and 'corpses / corpses / corpses'.[110] The individual body cannot even be assigned a number, but is part of an indefinable multitude. The narrator asks earlier how these stories might 'restore our faith in our ability to rise beyond the oppressor' and 'restore our faith in our imaginations', wondering if 'the storyteller want[s] to remember or forget'.[111] At the end of the novel, the magnitude of state violence appears to take over: there are more stories than can ever be told. Yet the novel is not despairing, precisely because of its focus on embodiment. Loss, Missaghi writes, is initially born at the level of the body, '[o]n one's skin, on one's hair, on one's lashes, on one's nails, on one's nerves, on one's cells, in one's heart, on one's tongue'; only once loss has been experienced in the body can it be translated into language.[112] This is specifically a 'woman's language, like a woman's body', defined by its openness; Missaghi here cites Lyn Hejinian's differentiation between a 'closed text', where all of the elements are directed towards a single reading, and an 'open text', which 'invites participation, rejects the authority of the writer over the reader', and is generative rather than directive'.[113] Hejinian emphasizes 'the gap between what one wants to say (or what one perceives there is to say) and what one can say (what is sayable)' to argue that the longing 'to join words to world – to close the gap between ourselves and things' is a source of both sensuous pleasure and anxiety.[114] This delight and anxiety are central to Missaghi's text, and to all the work covered in this chapter. Fragmentation creates an openness to language and the world, and a relation between text and body, that is often insufficient, even as it remains desired. Writing these stories of lost bodies is a way to explore the tensions not only between language and world, or official records and intimate testimonies, but also between text and body.

The concerns Missaghi raises are endemic to discussions of the archive.[115] As the Classical scholar Page duBois puts it, '[w]hat remains to us of the past, what we know of the present, of the consciousness of others, for example, is fragmentary. One way of responding to this recognition is to pursue a dream of wholeness, transparency, perfect access to what we desire to know. Another is to accept the partiality of our experience.'[116] The 'patterns of knowing and not knowing' that come from any archival research highlight this tension between the dream of a comprehensive account of the past and a reliance on material that is fragmented, incomplete and partial.[117] Harris similarly writes that the archival record 'is a fragile thing, an enchanted thing, defined not by its connections to "reality," but by its open-ended layerings of construction and reconstruction'.[118] In these accounts, archives are simultaneously repositories of the past, or social memory, but are also known as partial, so that the archival researcher's own prism shapes the fragments into new forms of knowledge and understanding. Archival research is a process of sifting through fragments and reconstructing them in ways that might offer the promise of wholeness, but also emphasize partiality and fragmentation. Yet the mode of storytelling this activity occasions is still distinct. The archive, as Ernst van Alphen notes, is 'responsible for significations that differ fundamentally from meaning produced by narratives'.[119] Archival narration always emphasizes gaps and absence and the impossibility of linear or causal narrative.

The same questions can be thought of in terms of corporeal inscription, following Elizabeth Grosz, where, as discussed above, the body can be seen both as and in relation to textuality. Grosz examines the way '[c]orporeal fragmentation' can be seen in terms of discourses of civilization, reason and knowledge.[120] The body, like the archive, is not knowable in wholeness or independence, but in fragmentation and relation. It is 'transcribed and marked by culture', and can be seen as a network 'of meaning and social significance', rather than a complete entity in itself.[121] Throughout Missaghi's text, she emphasizes how both bodies and archives are incomplete, and resist narrative incorporation. Language is tied to the body, and yet language is never sufficient. Missaghi's novel ends with a brief, suggestive fragment in the third-person narration:

> She pulls the newspapers toward her. There's something hard
> between the pages. She leafs through them and comes to a dossier
> hidden inside. There is a note on the cover in a handwriting
> that she's come to know. It reads,
> 'You've been following the wrong bodies.
> The bodies you want are in here.'[122]

Bodies and archives are both out of reach, figures of promise and a completion that is yet to come. The explanatory dossier is not opened: it remains a figure of anticipatory fulfilment that cannot be included within a narrative. *trans(re)lating house one* is both an act of recovery and a refusal of the same: as much as it brings untold stories to light, it recognizes that these stories, and these bodies, will never be enough. The only possible response is one of questioning.

The tensions explored in Missaghi's text are equally apparent in the work of Bhanu Kapil. Her texts combine poetry and prose, memoir and fiction, performance notes and scholarly citations, in a series of displaced fragments that often explicitly gesture to the narratives they cannot encompass. *Ban en Banlieue* tells the stories – or more particularly, is unable to tell the stories – of Jyoti Singh Pandey, a young woman raped and beaten to death in New Delhi in 2012, and of Blair Peach, a teacher from New Zealand who was knocked unconscious while protesting a gathering of the National Front in Southall, Middlesex on 23 April 1979, the *banlieue* of the title, and subsequently died, although his cause of death was not released until 2010.[123] It is just as much the story of Ban, 'the parts of something re-mixed as air', or a 'black (brown) girl' in the late 1970s, encountered just before the riots and a witness to the events; Ban is 'a warp of smoke', 'unreal', '[p]ychotic, fecal, neural, wild'.[124] Ban is an autobiographical figure and a 'vector of refusal', a monster and a 'blob of meat on the sidewalk', an immigrant and 'not an immigrant [...] but a shape or bodily outline that's familiar'.[125] She is at various points a figure of Kapil's childhood and of her adult performances; she is a symbol of Asian girls in Britain at a time when 'Caribbean and Asian Brits self-defined as black'; she is both body and spirit.[126] Ban is repeatedly defined and identified in relation to boundaries and categories, but is also representative of the refusal of such boundaries, and is broken by them. Ban is a 'dessicating form on the sidewalk'; Kapil laments that she 'should have written the alien body as a set of fragments', rather than historical fiction, although the book itself is certainly both alien and fragmented.[127]

Ban is also, in a way, the book itself, for reducing a discussion of *Ban en Banlieue* to its themes or potential narrative or points of focus is deeply misleading. The text is a series of performance notes and testimonies, of quotations and ruminations, and above all of fragments. While Luiselli and Missaghi's fragmentary stories still hold to some promise of linear narrative or development, even as they contest it, Kapil's fragmentation is far more violent and disruptive. This is not simply the story of gaps and absences but of the rupturing of textual form. The published text is composed of excerpts from thirty-three notebooks: like Manguso's *Ongoingness*, the remaining fragments speak as much to deletion as incorporation. The book comprises a list of 'Contents', which is not a list of contents but a series of refusals, end-notes, dedications and epigraphs, each of which approaches the material and examines its own inability to approach it; '13 Errors for Ban', which among other things details the performance history underlying the text; the lengthy sequence 'Auto-Sacrifice (Notes)', twenty-three numbered sections which comprise the majority of the text; 'End-Notes', a list of acknowledgements and explanations which is over 10 per cent of the total text, and offers a great deal of explanatory material; and 'Butcher's Block Appendix', comprising fragments from Kapil's notebooks. Even this description fails to convey the nature of the text. The relation between any two lines, or two fragments, is sometimes unclear. There are references to the various writers and thinkers discussed throughout this chapter, and this monograph: Grosz's work is central, but Agamben and Adorno also appear, while the text opens with a discussion of *Dictee*. As Kapil writes at the end of the 'End-Notes', in a discussion of hybridity: 'You can be hybrid and not share a body with anything else. Thus, the different parts of "Ban" do not touch. They never touch at all.'[128] The text neither starts nor ends, but constantly refracts itself: if it is a constellation of fragments, it is one that is particularly unstable, changing with every page.

Like Eleftherion and Burnett, and indeed like Barad, as discussed in Chapter 2, one of the central features of Kapil's text is the emphasis placed on the acknowledgements, which not only bridge the gap between text and reader, or text and world, but illustrate how the text emerges from entanglement. The text, Kapil explains, emerges from an interest in 'vibration' and 'what happens when you don't say anything at all'.[129] In this sense, the text mirrors Luiselli's and Missaghi's work: it is predicated not only on absence, but on echoes, and by the way trauma and death reverberate in the present. This reverberation, or what

Kapil calls 'attraction', is central to her fragmented approach. She writes in a fragment from her notebooks:

> 'I think, too, of Elizabeth Grosz's formulation of the fragment as "rough" – where the edge of it is, like glass or fur or light, so that it adheres to other fragments, not through historical or phatic means: but through the force of attraction. I place the fragments in a chrysalis: to recombine.'[130]

This fragment is doubly displaced: it appears in quotation marks, after the main body of the text – if the text can be said to have a 'main body' at all – and seems to contradict the statement three pages earlier that the parts of the novel do not touch at all. Kapil's approach closely resembles the ideas of assemblage and constellation discussed throughout this book, but slightly shifts the emphasis. In the acknowledgements to her earlier work *Schizophrene*, Kapil explains, in part, the relation between fragments and touch, again in relation to Grosz, as well as to her discoveries about the importance of impersonal light touch for 'non-white subjects (schizophrenics)': 'In making a book that barely said anything, I hoped to offer: this quality of touch. [...] I also wanted to think about [... the] capacity of fragments to attract, occur, re-circulate or shake (descend): in play.'[131] Kapil again places these ideas in terms of vibration. Fragments, in this sense, attract and touch, they recombine, but they do not form a whole. Fragments are not only what is left behind, but what can only, as in Barad's work, be seen in relation to their material becoming. As Grosz herself writes, some years after Kapil's text:

> being is, at best, a stage of becoming, [...] a momentary and abstract fixing of what is always changing. [...] At their most consistent and unchanging, beings are nevertheless points of convergence for an infinity of relations that ensure the entire system of things, the universe, is always changing. Any stability or foundation is itself only relative to the instability and interactivity that mark the broader and further-reaching environment, the infinite connections between all things and processes.[132]

Becoming, as Grosz explains elsewhere, is movement: movement is not attached 'to a stable thing, putting it in motion', but rather 'preexists the thing and is the process of differentiation that distinguishes one object from another'.[133] That is, it is not things, whether subject or object, that become, but rather 'something in objects and subjects that transforms them'.[134] This idea of transformation is central both to *Ban en Banlieue* and to Ban: neither text nor body is given in wholeness, but only in the movement, or the promise of touch, between often contradictory modes of existence. The fragments of the text are not stable, but known in their movement and their potential.

Ban en Banlieue gestures throughout to ideas of becoming and entanglement or enmeshment, particularly in relation to death and non-human animals. Ban's movements in death 'are transforming her forever into something new', while she is preceded by 'the strangely intrusive image of a drowned woman' carried by dolphins into the Bay of Bengal, and nibbled at by aquatic sea creatures.[135] A few pages later, now in the first person, Kapil writes that 'I am a mixture of dead and living things – all the creatures of the sea are breathing with me and for me.[136] Death is beginning and ending, becoming and stasis. Kapil explains her idea of 'worlding', and the relation between body, text and landscape, in a lengthy interview where she asks:

> How can we attend to the earth memory, the body of the witness – the body of the reader, perhaps – as much as our own bodies or the bodies that appear in our writing? What are the ethics of asking a reader to discharge the 'event' – the materials and matter of a violent event, in particular – through what the reading will be itself? I think this is where syntax – in its capacity to repattern the eye movements of the reader [...] helps. [...] So that a part of writing the character is to look away, to glance into the environment that surrounds her – or deflects her, I suppose, then return. This makes for a wet book, a book that opens and closes – fluttering – all the time.[137]

The relation between the body, especially the material body on which violence has been perpetrated, and the text is one that necessitates a complicated, nuanced understanding of environment, and the 'beings – seen and unseen – who arrive at the edges of the work'.[138] To firmly separate body from environment, or death from life, would be, ultimately, a way of occluding the body of the witness. Instead, each element in the text, and the continually developing relation between text and reader, must continually be resituated, without privileging any single reading or interpretation.

Kapil's work here echoes Braidotti's ideas of zoe, as discussed in Chapter 2, where 'life as zoë [...] lives independently of the gaze or even the existence of the human beholder'.[139] Zoe, as animal life, is not tied to the subject, but preexists and transforms it. Braidotti is careful to distinguish her account of 'a bios-zoe ethics of sustainable transformations' from Agamben's 'overemphasis on the horizons of mortality and perishability'.[140] While Agamben associates zoe with 'bare life', or life as disposable matter, Braidotti argues that the focusing on finitude ignores the way that death itself is only another stage in the generative process; for Braidotti, like Colebrook, thinking of life as something that does not have the human at its centre raises new possibilities for thinking of sustainability and futurity.[141] In the section 'Inversions for Ban' Kapil first frames Ban in terms of Agamben's concept of bare life, figuring both Ban and herself as figures placed on the perimeter, not associated with the bios of politics and language. Ban is framed as human and animal, text and body, inside and outside political communion:

> Here, extreme snow. I mean fire. The extreme snow makes me neutral about this first intact fragment. Of Ban. A novel of the race riot, 'Ban.' Nude studies/ charcoal marks: wired to the mouth of a pig. A boar. Some of the work is set in the outlying, wooded regions of Greater London.[142]

Ban is always simultaneously inside and outside the city, and inside and outside the narrative. Ban is the material left over, and the promise of transformation. Ban is known in death, but not defined by that death. Rather, Ban is a figure for the dissolution of boundaries: she cannot be contained by the narrative, but is always fragment, always becoming. As Kapil ends the novel, echoing Luiselli: 'Write: the findings. Write what never ends.'[143]

For all of *Ban en Banlieue*'s admitted complexity, as Zambreno argues, the book can be seen as an act of resistance, marking the 'beautiful, ravaging impossibility' of '[n]arrative's urges'.[144] Kapil's work asks what books can do, what bodies can do and how a work can encompass all the stages of its own becoming: it is the tracing of 'disappearance and documentation'.[145] Kapil's work, by engaging so closely with the limitations of the fragment, the way fragmentation often revolves around ruination and failure, finds a way to suggest its generative possibility. This approach can also be seen in her earlier work. *Schizophrene* is, in part, the story of a text as object, and its own eternal return. Kapil begins the book with an account of how she tried to write an epic on Partition, and 'the high incidence of *schizophrenia* in diasporic Indian and Pakistani *communities*', among much else, and failed: she throws her notebooks into the garden of her house in Colorado and in the spring retrieves them and begins 'to write again, from the *fragments, the phrases and lines* still legible on the warped, *decayed* but curiously rigid *pages*'.[146] The book is literally composted, 'rotted to the bone', and also a revenant.[147] Throughout the text the physical book, the book that *Schizophrene* is emphatically not, but is constituted in relation to, and is in part a rewriting of, or a writing over, continues to reappear; like Ban's body, it is known in presence and absence.

Far more than in *Ban en Banlieue*, Kapil situates the text in *Schizophrene* within a natural environment; much of the text concerns a form of nature healing, while the original notebook itself is at the same time 'damaged' or 'dead' and 'a vegetal structure bulky with dried marigolds and tiny pink roses, knotted with red cotton thread'.[148] While London, in *Ban en Banlieue*, is 'packed inside the remnants of [a] forest', *Schizophrene* offers opportunity of direct access to vegetal life, particularly in the recurring imagery of a lemon tree.[149] Both texts echo the assertion in Kapil's *Humanimal* that the physical world is known in vibration and in its fragility:

> The tropical modern is breakable, a fragile globe enclosing the jungle. When it breaks, the green is, thus, muted, intensifying the pink of feathers, eyes, clothing and flowers. Heat doesn't break it. The sky does. No. I don't know what perturbs then banishes environment forever, but it does.[150]

The three books are set in very different environments – city, garden, jungle – and have very different focuses, although each coalesces around a set of traumatic narratives. In each, the body and the text are equally entangled with the world: Kapil breaks down divisions between human and animal, between self and other, between making and unmaking. Each employs a different ordering principle. Kapil does, however, frame the relation between humans and environment through a similar approach to the ideas of gleaning discussed above. *Humanimal* combines, among other elements, the story of Kamala and Amala, two girls found in Bengal, India, in 1920, apparently raised by wolves, the diary of the missionary Joseph Singh recounting these stories, and Kapil's own expedition with a film crew to the area in 2004. In one of the fragments detailing Kapil's journey she finds herself in a forest, but recognizes that the plantings are too recent to be the same trees that the humanimal children would have seen:

> In this third space, the trees make a sort of heart, a red space filtered loosely – pink light – to the rim. Gleaners – nomads, from Bhutan and present-day Orissa – are pushed back each year into the darker, more rigid sections of the jungle. Behind the film-makers, I walk through alternating bars of sunlight and shadow, luxuriating, nowhere.[151]

Gleaning is an activity consigned to the past, or at least seen as difficult to integrate in the modern world; as in Tsing's formulation, it exemplifies a friction between cultures. Yet, while Kapil does not make the connection explicit, these gleaners also exemplify the project of each of the three books. In *Humanimal* Kapil describes the origin of the text, as she stands in a library stack, closing her eyes and letting her hand drift until she seizes upon Singh's text, which in this fragment is quoted at length but not named. The archive is a catalyst for discovery, but limited. So too is experience: while Kapil 'want[s] to write until [the girls] were real', placing them as 'part of the monsoon wind, the molecules of rain circulating from ocean to land and back again', she finds she cannot see the girls 'to completion': they are lost between myth and history.[152] Like Missaghi, she can only ask questions. This is the task of gleaning: to look at the archive and the world, to retrieve and discard, and in the recording of that activity to give voice to the lost only in recognition that their voices will never be heard.

Missaghi's and Kapil's works are as different from each other as they are from Luiselli's.[153] Yet each points to the complicate use of the fragment as a textual figuration that highlights not only separation, but touch. In her philosophy of the incorporeal, Grosz argues that she is not proposing a new dualism between ideality and materialism, nor privileging the former, but rather approaching them as 'fundamentally connected and incapable of each being what it is without the other to direct and support it'.[154] Thinking through materiality without ignoring its ideal dimension, and recognizing the material basis of the ideal, allows for new forms of ethics and relation. This is a similar approach to the one taken by the authors discussed here. The fragment is material, and points to the material world, human and non-human, body and environment. That materiality, however, cannot be thought of without relation to ideality. Missaghi and Kapil both suggest that the connection between presence and absence, or even between body and spirit, is not known in things themselves, in the archives or the texts that remain, but in movement and vibration. That is, fragmentation in these texts does not signify that the fragments that remain are important in and for themselves. Rather, their importance lies in the way they can gesture to everything they are not, and in so doing exceed themselves. This is not, however, a utopian or all-encompassing vision. Rather, in highlighting the role of both author and reader in selecting these fragments, and the implicit partiality of such a project, they show how texts can reflect a world that is broken, thriving, incomplete, and always in motion.

C. The Fragmentary Present: Jenny Offill and Lucy Ellmann

In a lengthy and often scathing review of Offill's *Weather*, Adam Mars-Jones disparages not only Offill's novel, but the entire fragmentary approach I have been describing here. While literature has often privileged microcosmic over macrocosmic approaches, he writes, in the present moment 'this is not just an inadequate response but an indefensible one'.[155] Fragmentary narrative is not only inappropriate for discussing questions of climate change or the election of Donald Trump, two of *Weather*'s central themes, but for discussing the family life that is equally foundational to the text. Mars-Jones finds the novel 'baffling', lamenting 'the excision of connective tissue from a novel dedicated to the importance of linking things up', and questioning how 'an aesthetic that exalts the fragment' can 'serve the human agenda of reconnecting us with the terrible things we would rather not think about'.[156] Parul Sehgal, in a far more positive response, argues that *Weather* shows how the climate crisis 'is reshaping not just our world but also our minds'.[157] For Sehgal, while the fragment is 'an old form, perhaps even our native form', Offill makes it 'something new, [...] a method of distilling experience into its brightest, most blazing forms – atoms of intense feeling'.[158]

For both critics, and many others, Offill's novel asks two of the central questions at the heart of this monograph: what is the proper form to discuss issues of planetary devastation and transformation, not least climate change, and what, more broadly, is the role of form in contemporary literature? These considerations are just as common in discussions of Ellmann's *Ducks, Newburyport*. The novel, often described as consisting of a single sentence over its more than a thousand pages of densely-set type, includes, in Katy Waldman's summary, considerations of 'school shootings; the collapsing climate; Flint, Michigan; types of cakes; types of sandwiches; taxes; necrotizing fasciitis' and so endlessly on. As Waldman writes, '[i]nstead of evoking the felt experience of inner life, Ellmann seems to be creating a stylized braid of conscious and unconscious thought – an artifice that's aware of its own construction'.[159] Both novels, the apparently macrocosmic and the apparently microcosmic, the fragmentary and the encyclopaedic, draw attention, more than the vast majority of contemporary novels but as much as the works by Luiselli, Missaghi and Kapil discussed above, to their construction: whether in praise or bafflement, critics and readers wrestled with the relation with form and theme.

Both Offill's and Ellmann's novels are, in many ways, rooted in the traditions of American realist fiction. The focus on quotidian American domestic life and family structures, coupled with relatively linear, if not particularly plot-driven, narratives makes them far more straightforward than Kapil's work. *Weather* suggests, often in single lines, many of the ideas discussed above – there are ruminations on the relation between the Holocene and Indigenous thought, on the fragments of Democritus and the dreariness of environmentalists, on technology and late capitalism; family members are described as 'enmeshed', rather than close.[160] The protagonist, Lizzie Benson, is torn between wanting to appreciate or understand these theories and ideas, these fragments of the modern world, and being able only to focus on their local effects. Early in the novel she listens to a podcast, 'The Center Cannot Hold', and while she finds the 'soothing' narration 'almost worth the uptick in dread', she distracts herself from the news of societal collapse by simply looking out the window.[161] Later, she responds to the news that '[a]ccording to the current trajectory, New York City will begin to experience dramatic, life-altering temperatures by 2047' by lamenting the potential loss of apple-picking escapades.[162] If the novel is about climate change in any real way, it is about the failure of the individual to place themselves within such a narrative.

While the novel includes plenty of information that might appear to be drawn from the headlines, reflecting current anxieties, it is less focused on those anxieties than on how they occasion new forms of thought or, just as much, preclude older forms of thought. The narration is not stream of consciousness, but rather, like Ellmann's novel, explores how consciousness might operate when there is too much pressing in on it; Lizzie encounters myriad people, each with their own anxieties and concerns, and is unable to focus on any one issue. As Rebecca Tamás writes in her own series of fragmentary essays, published not long after *Weather*: 'With the death of different spaces, different environments, different histories and different bodily forms of moving through them, forms of thought die too.'[163] The traditional realist novel may not be fit to chart the endless disasters of contemporary life; rather than exploring the connections between people and themes, it can only juxtapose them. *Weather* bears close similarity not only to other fragmentary works focused on environmental issues, such as Megan Hunter's apocalyptic *The End We Start From*, but a range of other experimental texts from Jennifer Egan to Renee Gladman, each of which explores the possibility of new formal mechanisms in light of a potential failure of older forms of literary methods.[164]

In this light, the emphasis on formal fragmentation in Offill's novel can be seen less as a response to a particular issue, such as climate change, and more clearly in relation to a longer tradition of literary fragmentation. Wojciech Drąg's analysis of Offill's previous novel, *Dept. of Speculation*, draws attention to the same formal mechanisms that underlie *Weather* to argue that what these 'fragmented structures need in order not to collapse is the reader's ability and readiness to fuse the building blocks and supply the missing bricks'.[165] If the protagonist cannot make connections, the reader must. Drąg cites in particular Wolfgang Iser's argument that

> modern texts [...] are often so fragmentary that one's attention is almost exclusively occupied with the search for connections between the fragments; the object of this is not to complicate the 'spectrum' of connections, so much as to make us aware of the nature of our own capacity for providing links.[166]

Given that Iser's article was published in 1972, it might be difficult to say what is new about Offill's approach. Indeed, Brian Richardson traces ideas of 'narrative fragmentation and unexpected reconstruction' back to Laurence Sterne, and uses examples ranging from Virginia Woolf to Clarice Lispector to chart the frequency with which fragmentation emerges as an aesthetic in fiction from a variety of cultural and historical contexts.[167]

At the same time, like many of the texts discussed here, *Weather* could be considered in light of what Kristian Shaw and Sara Upstone call the transglossic, their proposed term for our current literary age. The characteristics of 'deep simultaneity' – or the fluid movement between different positions – 'planetary consciousness', 'intersectional transversality', 'artistic responsibility', 'productive authenticity' and 'trans-formalism' that Shaw and Upstone point to as demarcating contemporary literary production are all, to greater or lesser degrees, in evidence here.[168] For Shaw and Upstone, transglossic fiction may be, like postmodern fiction, 'stylistically fragmented, non-linear, and anarchic', but is more likely to emphasize 'explicit political intent'.[169] Contemporary fiction, in this perspective, may use many of the same forms and approaches as modernist and postmodern fiction, but is distinguished by a sense of authorial, ethical responsibility. This positioning of the author is central to many considerations of both Offill's and Ellmann's work, as well as Ali Smith's fiction, as discussed in the Conclusion.

While Offill's work is undoubtedly part of this lineage, what differentiates it is her focus on optimism. Late in the novel, in one of a series of fragments marked out in a box with dashed lines, containing a question and answer, Offill writes:

Q: How do you maintain your optimism?
A: If you are not getting enough iron, put a few iron nails in a bowl of lemon
   juice and leave it overnight. In the morning, make lemonade out of it.[170]

The fragment seems, perhaps, to be a joke, combining the cliché that one should make lemonade when handed lemons with a domestic tip that could apply, unappetisingly, either to improving one's diet or removing rust. Although this seems, in isolation, like bleak humour at best, it also echoes a number of other passages. On the facing page, various fragments concern both the apocalypse and the way to prepare for it, just as the longest fragment in the novel concerns the sort of practical skills one might need in a dystopian future. While the novel is focused on a quotidian present, the sense of a disastrous future looms throughout, such that the reader might not be surprised if the text took a more dystopian turn. Even in its ending, it raises both the spectre of disaster and the tension between macrocosmic and microcosmic scales: 'I wake to the sound of gunshots. Walnuts on the roof, Ben says. The core delusion is that I am here and you are there.'[171] While familiar domesticity is reinstated, the possibility of collapse remains. The ambiguous final line can be read as a call to collectivity, and the importance of common experience, and yet the reader is left with a sense of imminent, if only imagined, threat. Yet the novel takes the question of optimism seriously: it ends with the address of a website, www.obligatorynoteofhope. com, which contains links to Extinction Rebellion and other groups focusing on environmental crisis.[172] Collective change may not be occasioned within the novel, but the reader themselves might be inspired to do more; they might wish to move past fragmentation and reflection to direct action. The links between optimism and fragmentation, however, are arguably more complex.

As discussed in Chapter 1, Lauren Berlant's conception of 'cruel optimism' concerns relations where the object that is desired is an obstacle to the flourishing of the one who desires it. Political activity can be cruel in this way, for instance when, despite an awareness of the failures of the political sphere, 'members of the body politic return periodically to its recommitment ceremonies and scenes', such as voting, 'collective caring, listening, and scanning the airwaves': the very attachments that underpin Offill's novel.[173] Such activities, argues Berlant, not only ensure individual attachment to the political system, but legitimize it. That is, participation in a system which one believes to already be broken can lead to depression and negative affect. Yet if, as Berlant writes, there is no form of political attachment, including withdrawal, that 'will solve the problem of shaping the impasse of the historical present', one must ask what alternatives remain.[174] For Berlant, the solution is almost precisely the same as that found in *Weather*: a turn to the fragmentary and incomplete, the everyday and the encountered. Berlant writes:

> To recast the ordinary this way is to hazard the value of conventional, archaic political emotions and their objects/scenes. But this is what it means to take the measure of the impasse of the present: to see what is halting, stuttering, and aching about being in the middle of detaching from a waning fantasy of the good life; and to produce some better ways of mediating the sense of a historical moment that is affectively felt but undefined in the social world that is supposed to provide some comforts of belonging, so that it would be possible to imagine a potentialized present that does not reproduce all of the conventional collateral damage.[175]

This sense of approaching the present moment from within its centre, recognizing how the component elements may each speak to some form of brokenness and yet in their juxtaposition create a path for something new, if yet unenunciated, suggests the form of optimism that Offill's fragmentation allows. One can understand the present only by offering the possibility of new relations between different elements, and accepting that the effects of political change, or climate crisis, or family crisis, may be felt at the level of the individual, they are also known collectively.

Offill's use of fragmentary form thus appears very different from the approaches found in the first two sections of this chapter. While Luiselli, Missaghi and Kapil each use fragmentation, in different ways, to point to loss, Offill uses a similar aesthetic approach to foreground presence. Where they overlap, however, is in their focus on touch and care, and the function of writer, protagonist and reader as gleaner. For Sehgal, *Weather* can be read as an example of the 'transform[ation of] the novel of consciousness into a record of climate grief'.[176] If, as Tamás argues, for 'most Westerners [...] "climate grief" is a kind of a luxury, suffering without losing our means of survival, yet', Offill's work might be seen as recording a similar sense of luxury.[177] Although the news reports and podcasts Lizzie hears are frightful, there is little sense of the direct material effects of climate change on the individual. Yet, because this information is given its own emphasis in fragments, both protagonist and reader must find ways to connect it to other concerns. By not writing 'cli-fi' as such, but instead integrating climate change into a multi-faceted story, Offill illustrates that there is no world, no story, that can avoid taking account of this present and future loss. The various fragments are not simply juxtaposed, but touch each other, creating new forms of relation. Each fragment is known in itself and in constellation with all the other fragments that make up the work. Lizzie undoubtedly occupies a privileged position compared to the narrators above. Her task of sifting through official records and first-person testimonies, however, is remarkably similar in some senses. The fragmentary form allows her to make new forms of connection, as well as to discard information that may not be relevant. In this way, Offill anticipates Mars-Jones's criticism above: the fragmentary form is the apt one for making these connections between self and world precisely because it refuses conventional narrative forms in order to make way for a potentialized present, in Berlant's term.

Offill's fragmentary present is easily marked in the spaces between fragments, the use of italicization and section breaks, and other formal features. *Ducks, Newburyport,* on the contrary, is rarely described in terms of fragments, but instead is seen as an example of stream of consciousness and maximalism. The majority of the novel consists of clauses beginning 'the fact that', separated by commas and mostly without conjunctions. The sentence begins, as Offill's novel ends, with a natural and domestic incident – in this case raccoons banging empty yogurt cartons in the driveway – being mistaken for gunshots; it ends with the declaration that none of the tens of thousands of facts just listed 'bear thinking about'.[178] The primary concerns of the novel are, in many ways, the same as *Weather*, and like Offill's text it is inarguable that it privileges presence over absence: indeed, all the world is seemingly present in these pages. Yet there are three reasons to think of the novel in terms of fragmentation and gleaning, and to consider it here. Firstly, despite the vast majority of views focusing on the text as a single sentence, implying linearity and progression, the 'facts' are as much a list of distinct component parts: the relation between them is as arbitrary, in many senses, as in Offill's novel. The individual elements do not cohere so much as they touch each other. Secondly, as explored at greater length below, the main sentence, as connected with the unnamed protagonist, is not the only narrative strand: the text is interspersed with a number of episodes, told in more conventional prose, about the journey of a mountain lion. These fragments of non-human experience, set against a torrent of human concerns, are used to address not only ideas of environmental entanglement, but questions of care. Finally, the text's greatest relevance to my argument is the sheer impossibility of summary or accurate account. If the reader of the texts described above must sift through scattered fragments, here the task is doubled: if most of these works can be compared to gleaning the storm-tossed detritus found on a shore, reading Ellmann is like diving into the sea. The reader is implicated in this partiality: there can be no definitive account of the text, only one that is gleaned, reconstructed, imperfect and partial.

To select excerpts from the text is almost inherently misleading: to single out a single element reveals the reader's own predetermined interests. As a reader, for instance, I am interested in the juxtaposition of clauses such as 'the fact that they keep shooting all the grizzlies in Yellowstone, the fact that they've been taken off the Endangered list, the fact that we won't be content until we've killed absolutely *everything*, including ourselves, but I shouldn't think that way, dear me, the fact that it's not good to be negative' with the discussion of a film starring Rosalind Russell and Ralph Bellamy on the following page, where Russell is about to 'marry an insurance guy from Poughkeepsie or someplace'.[179] Reading these lines, which are separated with the phrase 'ducks, Newburyport', which the reader believes must be important because it is the title of the novel, but is here uncontextualized, I am able as to see how the novel might fit with a project on climate change, or on human and non-human relations; like the narrator I too have seen *His Girl Friday*, which is not explicitly named here, although my attention is drawn specifically because I lived in Poughkeepsie for several years and the name resonates with me. Reading the novel I seize on the allusions that I already know, particularly to films, and the locations and experiences that echo my own life. This process of selection and emphasis is inherent in any reading of the text: the elements that each reader gleans will be highly individualistic, based less on trying to ascertain the novel's meaning as such than on isolating particular echoes from the reader's own life.

This rhetorical function is central to the novel: like the texts discussed in Chapter 2, it invites the readers to consider their own entanglement in both text and world.[180] One of the epigraphs, from Thornton Wilder, highlights the multispecies vibrancy of any given location, while a lengthy digression – in a novel that may consist of nothing other than such digressions – on sea urchins gives rise to questions of coexistence:

> the fact that sea urchins come in all colors, the fact that maybe they're a kind of *cross* between a plant and an animal but nobody ever says so, the fact that some man somewhere or other started growing bark right out of his legs and arms, so maybe animal and vegetable elements can coexist more than we think, vegetal, the fact that I hate it when music sounds like my kitchen timer, the fact that it's very distracting, the fact that 'friendly' wolf eels eat sea urchins, friendly wolf eels, the fact that a wolf eel can crunch through a crab, a clam, or a sea urchin, no problemo.[181]

The discussion of sea urchins and wolf eels continues for at least another page. As the excerpted passage indicates, thinking of human-animal relations is not an intellectual exercise performed in a vacuum, but takes place in a real world filled with interruptions from a kitchen timer, and the narrator's own thoughts on seemingly everything else, in this passage from college students to the film *Fargo*. Ellmann's discussion of marine life parallels Eva Hayward's work on cup corals (or *B. elegans*). Hayward takes as her starting point Haraway's assertion that '[n]ever purely themselves, things are compound; they are made up of combinations of other things coordinated to magnify power, to make something happen, to engage the world, to risk fleshly acts of interpretation'.[182] Hayward argues that intertidal zones in particular are sites where 'species meet not just as different critters, but also as objects and subjects of different sight, sense, sensibility, and sensuality'.[183] Engagements between humans and other species provide new ways to think about agency and knowledge production, and about the role and types of sensory perception; Hayward writes that 'species are impressions, thresholds of emergence'.[184] These ideas of impression and encounter are similarly central to *Ducks, Newburyport*; if the narrator does not encounter sea urchins themselves, the fragmentary thought-as-encounter that fills the novel provides a way to avoid anthropocentric pronouncement in favour of what Hayward calls 'the in-between of encounter, a space of movement, of potential'.[185] Species, objects, intertextual allusions and abstract ideas all fill the same plane of existence: each is encountered simultaneously as itself and in relation to myriad other forms. As such, as in Offill's text, the reader and narrator must both seek to forge connections, or recognize when those connections fail.

Near the close of *Meeting the Universe Halfway*, Karen Barad likewise considers a cousin of the sea urchin, brittlestars, whose skeleton can be seen as a giant eye. If cup corals perceive the world through touch, brittlestars perceive it through sight: each is interesting, however, because they force us to reconsider what sight or touch might mean. As previously quoted in Chapter 2, Barad argues that:

> [brittlestars] challenge our Cartesian habits of mind, breaking down the usual visual metaphors for knowing along with its optics of mediated sight. Knowledge making is *not* a mediated activity, despite the common refrain to the contrary. Knowing is a direct material engagement, a practice of intra-acting with the world as part of the world in its dynamic material configuring, its ongoing articulation. The entangled practices of knowing and being are material practices.

I return to this quotation not only because the focus on marine life provides a way of connecting Ellmann's work with Burnett's, but because this idea of knowledge as unmediated material engagement might be the best way to articulate how *Ducks, Newburyport* functions. Although, as noted above, the text is not a stream of consciousness, it forces the reader to consider how consciousness might consist of encounters and impressions that are not only unmediated, but do not in themselves form a system of knowledge. Instead, the reader receives these impressions and interacts with them. This effect is heightened by the material presence of the book: the time spent not simply reading the novel, but carrying it around, is immense. I read the novel on a summer holiday, sitting in cars and on porches, reading in bed and in the middle of family conversations. A large portion of it was read on a transatlantic flight, where my seatmate objected to my using the reading light, and so I read by the dull glare of the seatback screen, the slow map of our plane's progress over the ocean lighting the pages. The text is approached not simply as assemblage, but as matter. The sheer heft of the book is daunting, and reconfigures the reader's response: my own awareness of the incompleteness of my engagement in the text undermined my own anthropocentric assumptions, as I discovered my own knowledge was not enough. At the same time, because the reader must necessarily leave off any stretch of reading midway through the sentence, the rhythms of the text transform into the rhythms of the reader's own inner monologue, making the relation between text and reader particularly porous.

In this sense, *Ducks, Newburyport* may not be a record of archival research, but is itself an archive, a trove of material through which the reader must sort, catching themselves in presence and absence, privileging accident over absolute knowledge. The novel could be seen as a recent example of what Frederick R. Karl terms the 'Mega-Novel': not simply a long novel, but a particular American form, usually associated with postmodernism, where America is presented as 'an indeterminate, problematic, unfixed place' while the 'seeming randomness of scenes not only subverts inevitability; it threatens order itself'.[186] Such works, David Letzler argues, highlight the selectivity of attention: Letzler uses the word 'cruft' to describe the long passages in such novels that contain apparently irrelevant material, claiming that the presence of apparently extraneous, confusing or boring text is used as a way to focus the reader's attention. Cruft is material that might seem incoherent or pointless, and which could be replaced with any other and as such 'draws attention to the importance of the distinctions we must make in processing their enormous and often wasteful texts'.[187] *Ducks, Newburyport* might, in an uncharitable reading, be considered nothing but cruft: there is no single 'fact' that could not be replaced with another. Although there is, especially in the novel's second half, a plot, it is of secondary importance in relation to the litany of facts and impressions. Reading the text is reminiscent of Nathalie Léger's account of archival work in *Suite for Barbara Loden*, itself one of Luiselli's explicit intertexts:

> What will you find there? Boxes, scraps, fakery, piles of things sweating excess and incompleteness and, in spite of brief triumphs, defeat. You must enter this place as though it means nothing to you, don't exaggerate but hide your excitement. You go in backwards, groping your way.[188]

Ducks, Newburyport is a record of excess and incompleteness: even a twenty-six page of list of certainties, ranging from the fact that 'the sun will rise and set every day' to 'Darcy will love Elizabeth Bennet / girls will get crushes on Colin Firth' to 'Californians will have water consumption problems / redwoods will fall over / the oceans will fill with / things made of plastic', does not suffice as explanation.[189] There is simply too much here.

If the immensity of Ellmann's works calls attention to the reader as a gleaner, however, it also can be read in relation not only to the works discussed in this chapter, but those in the previous ones. The novel does not only record the noise of contemporary life, but draws attention to the voices of those who cannot be heard, in particular to the world of non-human animals. The novel opens with the first of its sections depicting the life of a lioness in the same town as the narrator, who over the novel is depicted raising her cubs, losing them, being imprisoned and finally reunited, although still caged. The first sentence of the novel is not one of the 'facts', but a direct address to the reader: 'When you are all sinew, struggle and solitude, your young – being soft, plump, and vulnerable – may remind you of prey.'[190] The paragraphs are short, the sentences clear, the tone familiar: the passages discussing the lioness require a completely different reading strategy than the rest of the novel. These narratives, in Elisa Aaltola's words, are a form of 'simulative empathy, an imaginative gluing together of the non-human standpoint from various pieces of information'.[191] While at times they might appear sentimental or anthropomorphic, this is gradually used as a form of connection. The initial sections seem wholly unrelated to the rest of the novel, although the narrator is aware of reports that a mountain lion has been seen. Midway through, however, Ellmann describes the dreams of the lioness and her cubs: the 'mother's dreams were concrete and practical', while the 'kittens' dreams ranged more freely'.[192] This section transitions immediately into an account of the narrator's dreams: if we reject the earlier descriptions, we would also have to reject the latter, since animal and human protagonists are equally fictional constructs. Ellmann begins to suggest that we take mountain lions seriously: because the sections are presented in traditional prose, they are often not only easier to approach, but also more universally recognizable than the human-centred sections.

The mountain lion sections are used specifically as a declaration of entanglement and community formation. Ellmann writes:

> All mountain lions are one. You are just one example of a lion. Mountain-lionhood is strong and immense, and goes beyond the individual. Each lion is part of a continuum, and privy to everything good and bad that happens to other mountain lions. You tough things out on your own, but you're linked to the pleasures, pains, and drama, the leap and recoil and lonely deaths of others. All living things are.[193]

This is, I think, the moral of the novel, if the idea of a moral is not too old-fashioned. The individual can only be seen in community, and that community is not restricted to human life. If as readers we can accept this form of connection as intrinsic to animal life, we must also be able to accept it as intrinsic to human life. The act of gleaning in the novel, then, is central to its aims. In seeing how the narrator is like and unlike ourselves, in selecting particular elements, we construct a set of links to other creatures, and to the world. The lioness's care for her cubs is a clear point of identification for the narrator. The lioness's desire to 'love them and save them and feed them and teach them and never let them go' parallels the narrator's own desire to care for her children, and is the clearest example of care in the novel.[194] The lions' imprisonment, however, is just as much a point of identification for the narrator's daughter: the novel ends with the family planning a trip to the zoo, and it is 'the fact that Stacy seems to feel some kind of rapport with that woebegone creature, the fact that whether this is because she feels fierce or free, or caged and cowed' that finally 'doesn't bear thinking about'.[195] What matters is not the direction of empathy, but its existence. The lion is not an allegory for human struggles: rather, the integration of the lion into the larger narrative indicates the impossibility of telling one story exclusively. The lion's voice is that of the lost, it is the voice of absence, and its incorporation into the novel indicates the continued importance of motion and touch, of incompletion and constellation.

Ducks, Newburyport is an appropriate text to end the main body of this book in part because it encapsulates each of the main approaches articulated thus far. It is, like the works in Chapter 1, a story of solitude and attention. Like the texts in Chapter 2, it can be seen as a work of assemblage and entanglement. Like the other texts in Chapter 3, it privileges the relation between care and loss. What I hope to suggest, most simply, is that while the texts discussed here are undeniably different in form, theme and affect, each of them uses the fragment in a particularly distinctive way. Fragmentation is not simply a sign of ruin or loss: it is an invitation to the reader to glean, to collect and to choose. The connections made between any two fragments are ultimately partial, and this is their great advantage. A linear narrative, a story, might always privilege ideas of completion. The fragment is a way to incorporate everything left behind: it is a way to gesture towards absence, towards irritation, towards failure. Yet the fragment is not a pessimistic form. Rather, it generates new syntheses. In particular, I want to emphasize that it provides a new way to think about environmental and multispecies entanglement, although it is certainly not limited to this, as is especially clear in the work of a writer like Missaghi. Rather, the fragment is a form that privileges multiplicity and difference. It is a way to avoid pronouncing on other species, on climate change, or violence done to other humans or the other itself. The fragment is a way of opening the world.

Notes

1   Serenella Iovino and Serpil Oppermann, 'Introduction: Stories Come to Matter', in *Material Ecocriticism*, ed. Serenella Iovino and Serpil Oppermann (Bloomington and Indianapolis: Indiana University Press, 2014), 6, 8. Original emphasis. See also Pheng Cheah's claim that '[i]n its interdefinability with text, matter exceeds and confounds' binary forms of knowledge. Pheng Cheah, 'Non-Dialectical Materialism', in *New Materialisms: Ontology, Agency, and Politics*, ed. Diana Coole and Samantha Frost (Durham and London: Duke University Press, 2010), 74.

2   Jeffrey Jerome Cohen, 'Introduction: Ecostitial', in *Inhuman Nature*, ed. Jeffrey Jerome Cohen (Washington, DC: Oliphaunt Books, 2014), ii.

3   A. Kendra Greene, *The Museum of Whales You Will Never See: Travels among the Collectors of Iceland* (London: Granta, 2020), 59; Carolyn Forché, *In the Lateness of the World* (Hexham: Bloodaxe, 2020), 15.

4   Jean Sprackland, *Strands: A Year of Discoveries on the Beach* (London: Vintage, 2013), 236–7. In her account of mudlarking on the Thames, Lara Maiklem distinguishes between 'gatherers' like herself who 'generally enjoy the searching as much as the finding' and 'hunters' who are 'driven by the find', and tend to use metal detectors. In Maiklem's experience the former are more likely to be women, and the latter men. Lara Maiklem, *Mudlarking: Lost and Found on the River Thames* (London: Bloomsbury, 2020), 26.

5   Lisa Woollett, *Rag and Bone: A Family History of What We've Thrown Away* (London: John Murray, 2020), 9.

6   Woollett, *Rag and Bone*, 132, 205.

7   Woollett, *Rag and Bone*, 203.

8   Rebecca Solnit, *The Faraway Nearby* (London: Granta, 2013), 191.

9   Solnit, *Faraway*, 26, 79.

10 Solnit, *Faraway*, 107, 194.

11 Donna J. Haraway, *Staying with the Trouble: Making Kin in the Chthulucene* (Durham and London: Duke University Press, 2016), 31.

12 Haraway, *Staying*, 39. Original emphasis.

13 Judith Schalansky, *An Inventory of Losses*, trans. Jackie Smith (London: Maclehose Press, 2020), 44.

14 Solnit, *Faraway*, 22–5.

15 Solnit, *Faraway*, 106, 253.

16 Caroline Levine, *Forms: Whole, Rhythm, Hierarchy, Network* (Princeton and Oxford: Princeton University Press, 2015), 3.

17 Jenn Ashworth, *Notes Made while Falling* (London: Goldsmiths Press, 2019), 89.

18 Ashworth, *Notes*, 162.

19 Sarah Manguso, *Ongoingness: The End of a Diary* (Minneapolis: Graywolf, 2015), 93, 95.

20 Jean Sprackland, *These Silent Mansions: A Life in Graveyards* (London: Jonathan Cape, 2020), 194.

21 Sprackland, *These Silent*, 4.

22 This quotation, and the surrounding account of the book, is drawn from a conversation Ashworth had with the University of Aberdeen's Centre for the Novel, over Microsoft Teams, on 12 May 2020. The conversation largely focused on Ashworth's novel *Fell* but, like many online meetings and book groups that I participated in over the loneliness of the pandemic period, ventured much further afield.

23 Schalansky, *Inventory*, 12.

24 Schalansky, *Inventory*, 126.

25 Kate Zambreno, *Appendix Project: Talks and Essays* (South Pasadena: Semiotext(e), 2019), 69.

26 Jennifer Mae Hamilton and Astrida Neimanis, 'Composting Feminisms and Environmental Humanities', *Environmental Humanities* 10.2 (2018): 524. Original emphasis. Hamilton and Neimanis are particularly interested in the way that many thinkers at the forefront of feminist environmental humanities downplay the feminist lineage central to their thought.

27 Haraway, *Staying*, 57.

28 Haraway, *Staying*, 55. Haraway most simply defines the Chthulucene as 'a kind of timeplace for learning to stay with the trouble of living and dying in response-ability on a damaged earth' (2). Rather than recognizing the anthropocentric approach of terms such as Anthropocene or Capitalocene, the Chthulucene recognizes multi-species agency and kinship.

29 Haraway, *Staying*, 136.

30 Carolyn Steedman, *Dust* (Manchester: Manchester University Press, 2001), 166.

31 Sonja Boon, 'Speculation, Magic Realism, and Minding the Gaps', *History Workshop* (2 September 2020): historyworkshop.org.uk/speculation-magic-realism-and-minding-the-gaps/ [Accessed 11 October 2020].

32 Sonja Boon, *What the Oceans Remember: Searching for Belonging and Home* (Waterloo: Wilfrid Laurier University Press, 2019), 27.

33 Boon, *What the Oceans*, 42, 257.

34 Kate Zambreno, *To Write as If Already Dead* (New York: Columbia University Press, 2021), 77.

35 Dionne Brand, *A Map to the Door of No Return: Notes to Belonging* (Toronto: Vintage Canada, 2011), 19.

36 Christina Sharpe, *In the Wake: On Blackness and Being* (Durham and London: Duke University Press, 2016), 22. One of the clearest examples of the use of fragmentation to re/imagine the world is Tracy K. Smith's collection *Wade in the Water*, which in its central sections uses fragments, erasure and archival material to look at both the legacy of slavery and the effect of environmental devastation

on marginalized populations, in a context where so many voices are 'soon and unexpectedly cut off / Many, many, very many times'. Tracy K. Smith, *Wade in the Water* (London: Penguin, 2018), 20.

37   Brand, *Map to the Door*, 199.

38   Deborah Bird Rose and Thom van Dooren, 'Introduction', *Unloved Others: Death of the Disregarded in the Time of Extinction*, *Australian Humanities Review* 50 (2011): 4.

39   Each of these five authors lives, or has lived, in the United States: Luiselli emigrated from Mexico and Missaghi from Iran while Kapil, born in the UK to Indian parents, lived in the United States during the writing of several of the works discussed here before returning to the UK. Ellmann emigrated from the United States to Scotland, while Offill is still based in the United States. The chapter is not focused on American literature as such, however, but rather looks at each of these authors simultaneously in a more local and more planetary context.

40   María Puig De La Bellacasa, *Matters of Care: Speculative Ethics in More Than Human Worlds* (Minneapolis and London: University of Minnesota Press, 2017), 28.

41   Joan C. Tronto, *Moral Boundaries: A Political Argument for an Ethic of Care* (New York and London: Routledge, 1993), 104.

42   Puig de la Bellacasa, *Matters*, 161.

43   Eva Haifa Giraud, *What Comes after Entanglement?: Activism, Anthropocentrism, and an Ethics of Exclusion* (Durham and London: Duke University Press, 2019), 100.

44   Giraud, *What Comes*, 136. Original emphasis.

45   Puig de la Bellacasa, *Matters*, 213.

46   Boon, *What the Oceans*, 180–1.

47   Valeria Luiselli, *Lost Children Archive* (London: Fourth Estate, 2019), 7.

48   Luiselli, *Lost*, 381.

49   Luiselli, *Lost*, 139.

50   At the novel's end Luiselli provides a list of lines and words in *Elegies for Lost Children* taken from other sources, primarily the work of Joseph Conrad, T.S. Eliot, Ezra Pound, Marcel Schwob, Augusto Monterroso, Galway Kinnell, Juan Rulfo, Rainer Maria Rilke and Jerzy Andrzejewski; she also mentions that the structure of intersecting first-person narratives in *Lost Children Archive* is an allusion to Virginia Woolf's *Mrs Dalloway*.

51   Mary Wang, 'Valeria Luiselli: "There are always fingerprints of the archive in my books"', *Guernica* (12 February 2019): guernicamag.com/miscellaneous-files-interview-valeria-luiselli/ [Accessed 20 October 2020]. Luiselli's discussion of the shelf of books she keeps next to her while writing, 'where the only criteria is a book's relationship to what I'm writing', closely resembles the practice of Zambreno and Carson discussed above.

52   *Lost Children Archive* is equally in dialogue with Luiselli's first novel, *Faces in the Crowd*, a story of a very similar family that shares both a focus on fragments

and echoes, not least in discussion of Ezra Pound. At the start of the earlier book Luiselli frames the fragment in terms of family life, arguing that while '[n]ovels need a sustained breath', this text can only be written when the narrator is not taking care of her children: 'I know I need to generate a structure full of holes so that I can always find a place for myself on the page'. Valeria Luiselli, *Faces in the Crowd*, trans. Christina MacSweeney (London: Granta, 2012), 4, 10.

53 Luiselli, *Lost*, 99.

54 Valeria Luiselli, *Tell Me How It Ends: An Essay in Forty Questions* (London: Fourth Estate, 2017), 7. To add a layer of complexity, this volume is based on a shorter version written in English, which appeared in *Freeman's* in 2016, then translated into Spanish and expanded by Luiselli, and published as *Los niños perdidos* (*Un esayo en cuarenta preguntas*), again in 2016; the English volume combines Luiselli's original text with translations of the Spanish version back into English by Lizzie Davis. Luiselli explains in an interview that she began writing the novel first, then 'had to stop writing the novel because I was trying to dump in it all my political frustration and confusion and sadness and rage', and turned her attention to the essay instead. Scott Simon, 'Valeria Luiselli on the "Lost Children Archive"', *NPR Weekend Edition Saturday* (9 March 2019): npr.org/2019/03/09/701838156/valeria-luiselli-on-the-lost-children-archive [Accessed 22 October 2020].

55 Luiselli, *Lost*, 30.

56 Luiselli, *Tell Me*, 42.

57 Elizabeth Grosz, *Volatile Bodies: Toward a Corporeal Feminism* (Bloomington and Indianapolis: Indiana University Press, 1994), 167.

58 Alexandra Kingston-Reese, 'The Individual Reader', *Critique: Studies in Contemporary Fiction* (2020). https://doi.org/10.1080/00111619.2020.1810612 [Accessed 19 October 2020].

59 Luiselli, *Lost*, 172.

60 See, for instance, the controversy in early 2020 surrounding the publication of Jeanine Cummins's novel *American Dirt*, which was divisive precisely because its account of Mexican immigrants did not reflect the author's own experiences, and was received as 'pity porn'. André Wheeler, 'American Dirt: Why Critics Are Calling Oprah's Book Club Pick Exploitative and Divisive', *The Guardian* (22 January 2020): theguardian.com/books/2020/jan/21/american-dirt-controversy-trauma-jeanine-cummins [Accessed 19 October 2020].

61 Luiselli, *Lost*, 25–6.

62 Aimé Césaire, *Discourse on Colonialism*, trans. Joan Pinkham (New York: Monthly Review Press, 2000), 42.

63 Kathryn Yusoff, *A Billion Black Anthropocenes or None* (Minneapolis: University of Minnesota Press, 2018), 32.

64 Luiselli, *Tell Me*, 51.

65 Simon, 'Valeria Luiselli', n.p.

66 Luiselli, *Lost*, 38.

67 Luiselli, *Lost*, 215.

68 Luiselli, *Lost*, 103.

69 Lauret Savoy, *Trace: Memory, History, Race, and the American Landscape* (Berkeley, CA: Counterpoint, 2015), 28.

70 Savoy, *Trace*, 120, 158, 186.

71 Luiselli, *Lost*, 43.

72 Luiselli, *Lost*, 79.

73 Luiselli, *Tell Me*, 90.

74 Luiselli, *Lost*, 185.

75 Luiselli, *Lost*, 328.

76 Luiselli, *Lost*, 342–3.

77 Elizabeth Grosz, *Chaos, Territory, Art: Deleuze and the Framing of the Earth* (New York: Columbia University Press, 2020), 54.

78 Luiselli, *Lost*, 39.

79 Luiselli, *Lost*, 293.

80 Puig de la Bellacasa, *Matters of Care*, 51.

81 Marianne Hirsch, *The Generation of Postmemory: Writing and Visual Culture after the Holocaust* (New York: Columbia University Press, 2012), 15–16.

82 Hirsch, *Generation*, 16.

83 Jan Assmann, *Religion and Cultural Memory*, trans. Rodney Livingstone (Stanford: Stanford University Press, 2006), 6.

84 Luiselli, *Lost*, 142.

85 Luiselli, *Lost*, 142.

86 Luiselli, *Lost*, 201.

87 Sherilyn MacGregor, *Beyond Mothering Earth: Ecological Citizenship and the Politics of Care* (Vancouver and Toronto: UBC Press, 2006), 59. Original emphasis.

88 MacGregor, *Beyond*, 27.

89 See Timothy C. Baker, *Writing Animals: Language, Suffering, and Animality in Twenty-First Century Fiction* (Cham: Palgrave Macmillan, 2019), 160–3. Wright's focus on non-linear temporalities and Indigenous storytelling has been extensively discussed, particularly in relation to her earlier novel *Carpenteria*; for a recent overview see Lucy Rowland, 'Indigenous Temporality and Climate Change in Alexis Wright's *Carpenteria* (2006)', *Journal of Postcolonial Writing* 55.4 (2019): 541–54. While *Carpenteria* falls outside of the temporal scope of this project, and *The Swan Book* can arguably be considered an example of the dystopian fiction this monograph avoids, Wright's work often parallels some of the approaches discussed in this chapter, and deserves further attention.

90 Luiselli, *Lost*, 146.

91 Luiselli, *Lost*, 247. Here, as with the other archives, the pages are unnumbered, and resist linear temporality.

92   Puig de la Bellacasa, *Matters*, 77.

93   Claire Colebrook, 'Archivolithic: The Anthropocene and the Hetero-Archive',
     Derrida Today 7.1 (2014): 39.

94   Claire Colebrook, *Death of the Posthuman: Essays on Extinction, Vol. 1* (Ann
     Arbor: Open Humanities Press, 2014), 23. Original emphasis.

95   Luiselli, *Lost*, 349.

96   Ella Mudie, 'Beyond Mourning: On Photography and Extinction', *Afterimage* 44.3
     (2016): 22.

97   Mudie, 'Beyond Mourning', 27.

98   Barbara A. Misztal, *Theories of Social Remembering* (Maidenhead: Open
     University Press, 2003), 13.

99   Paul Connerton, *The Spirit of Mourning: History, Memory and the Body*
     (Cambridge: Cambridge University Press, 2011), 1.

100 Connerton, *Spirit of Mourning*, 29.

101 Han Kang, *The White Book*, trans. Deborah Smith (London: Portobello Books,
     2016), 6.

102 Poupeh Missaghi, *trans(re)lating house one* (Minneapolis: Coffee House Press,
     2020), 67. At the novel's opening Missaghi points to its origins in Roberto Bolaño's
     2666, one of the intertexts for Luiselli's novel as well.

103 Boon, *What the Oceans*, 200.

104 Verne Harris, 'The Archival Sliver: Power, Memory, and Archives in South Africa',
     Archival Science 2 (2002): 65.

105 Missaghi, *trans(re)lating*, 35. Missaghi is well-known for her translations both
     from Spanish and English into Persian, and from Persian into English.

106 Missaghi, *trans(re)lating*, 245.

107 Maria Eliades, '"I'm telling these stories for an audience, but I also want to digest
     this experience for myself": An Interview with Poupeh Missaghi', *Ploughshares*
     (6 February 2020): blog.plshares.org/index.php/im-telling-these-stories-for-an-
     audience-but-i-also-want-to-digest-this-experience-for-myself-an-interview-with-
     poupeh-missaghi [Accessed 24 October 2020].

108 Yanara Friedland, 'Mapping Tehran: A Conversation with Poupeh Missaghi', *World
     Literature Today* (6 February 2020): wordliteraturetoday.org/blog/interviews/
     mapping-tehran-conversation-poupeh-missaghi-yanara-friedland [Accessed
     24 October 2020].

109 Missaghi, *trans(re)lating*, 39.

110 Missaghi, *trans(re)lating*, 246–52. The overwhelming legacy of the dead is reflected
     in a very different way in Boon's memoir where, when reading accounting
     archives, Boon comes across the names of hundreds of enslaved people. The list
     of names, presented both in the body of the text and in two photographs of the
     archival record, is appalling and transformative. As Boon writes: 'This family
     history of enslavement was real. The pain of knowing was acute. [...] [T]here

was a rhythm to the names, and typing them out, one after another, became a meditation. Letters into sounds into words into names into communities.' Boon, *What the Oceans*, 85. Both authors, in these opposed ways, insist that knowing one story is insufficient: each named individual must stand for many more, yet each individual life must be seen as distinct and meaningful on its own.

111 Missaghi, *trans(re)lating*, 173.

112 Missaghi, *trans(re)lating*, 72.

113 Missaghi, *trans(re)lating*, 78; Lyn Hejinian, 'The Rejection of Closure', *Poetry Foundation* (13 October 2009): poetryfoundation.org/articles/69401/the-rejection-of-closure [Accessed 26 October 2020]. Although *The Newly Born Woman* is not one of the Cixous texts Missaghi cites, Cixous's notion of the woman's body 'articulat[ing] the proliferation of meaning that runs through it in every direction' implicitly underpins this line of thinking. Hélène Cixous and Catherine Clément, *The Newly Born Woman*, trans. Betsy Wing (Minneapolis: University of Minnesota Press, 1986), 95.

114 Hejinian, 'Rejection', n.p.

115 For a good overview of debates in archival studies, including the gendered and classed aspects that construct 'archival labor as a feminine service industry', see M.L. Caswell, '"The Archive" Is Not an Archives: Acknowledging the Intellectual Contributions of Archival Studies', *Reconstruction* 16.1 (2016). https://escholarship.org/uc/item/7bn4v1fk [Accessed 28 October 2020].

116 Page duBois, *Sappho Is Burning* (Chicago and London: University of Chicago Press, 1995), 39.

117 Maryanne Dever, Sally Newman and Ann Vickery, *The Intimate Archive: Journeys through Private Papers* (Canberra: National Library of Australia, 2009), 6.

118 Harris, 'Archival Sliver', 84–5.

119 Ernst van Alphen, *Staging the Archive: Art and Photography in the Age of New Media* (London: Reaktion, 2015), 14.

120 Grosz, *Volatile Bodies*, 141.

121 Grosz, *Volatile Bodies*, 119, 117.

122 Missaghi, *trans(re)lating*, 273.

123 Bhanu Kapil, *Ban en Banlieue* (New York: Nightboat Books, 2015), 14.

124 Kapil, *Ban en Banlieue*, 30–1.

125 Kapil, *Ban en Banlieue*, 90, 20.

126 Kapil, *Ban en Banlieue*, 30. For a video that illustrates Kapil's combined approach to reading and performance, see Harvard University, 'The Poet's Voice: Bhanu Kapil & Fred Moten / Woodberry Poetry Room', youtube.com/watch?v=yjsB3-7Oyw&t=1943s [Accessed 29 October 2020].

127 Kapil, *Ban en Banlieue*, 15.

128 Kapil, *Ban en Banlieue*, 100.

129   Kapil, *Ban en Banlieue*, 99.

130   Kapil, *Ban en Banlieue*, 103.

131   Bhanu Kapil, *Schizophrene* (Callicoon, NY: Nightboat Books, 2011), 71.

132   Elizabeth Grosz, *The Incorporeal: Ontology, Ethics, and the Limits of Materialism* (New York: Columbia University Press, 2018), 260–1.

133   Elizabeth Grosz, *Becoming Undone: Darwinian Reflections on Life, Politics, and Art* (Durham and London: Duke University Press, 2011), 1.

134   Grosz, *Becoming Undone*, 51. For a similar approach, again in relation to Deleuzian ideas of vibration, see Erin Manning's claim that '[d]espite appearances, movement is not of a body. It cuts across, co-composing with different velocities of movement-moving. It bodies.' Erin Manning, *Always More than One: Individuation's Dance* (Durham and London: Duke University Press, 2013), 14.

135   Kapil, *Ban en Banlieue*, 74.

136   Kapil, *Ban en Banlieue*, 84.

137   Bhanu Kapil, 'Profiles in Poetics and Linguistics: Bhanu Kapil', *Women's Quarterly Conversation: Aesthetic Diversity of Women Writers in the 21st Century* (13 November 2015): womensquarterlyconversation.com/2015/11/13/profiles-in-poetics-linguistics-bhanu-kapil/ [Accessed 9 July 2021].

138   Kapil, 'Profiles', n.p.

139   Rosi Braidotti, *Nomadic Subjects: Embodiment and Sexual Difference in Contemporary Feminist Theory*, 2nd ed. (New York: Columbia University Press, 2011), 117.

140   Rosi Braidotti, *Nomadic Theory: The Portable Rosi Braidotti* (New York: Columbia University Press, 2011), 332–3.

141   Giorgio Agamben, *Homo Sacer: Sovereign Power and Bare Life*, trans. Daniel Heller-Roazen (Stanford: Stanford University Press, 1998), 1; Braidotti, *Nomadic Theory*, 333.

142   Kapil, *Ban en Banlieue*, 41.

143   Kapil, *Ban en Banlieue*, 109.

144   Zambreno, *Appendix Project*, 80.

145   Zambreno, *Appendix Project*, 80.

146   Kapil, *Schizophrene*, i. Original emphasis.

147   Kapil, *Schizophrene*, 58.

148   Kapil, *Schizophrene*, 63–4.

149   Kapil, *Ban en Banlieue*, 53. See also Bhanu Kapil, 'Seven Poems for Seven Flowers & Love in All Its Forms', *Mal* 3 (2019): 17–24. In this fragmentary sequence Kapil combines images of flowers with discussions of loss to ask '[w]hat are the maximum and minimum forms a memory can take?' (18).

150   Bhanu Kapil, *Humanimal: A Project for Future Children* (Berkeley, CA: Kelsey Street Press, 2009), 62–3.

151 Kapil, *Humanimal*, 17.

152 Kapil, *Humanimal*, 41–2.

153 In an earlier work, however, Kapil begins by detailing two images of the cyborg, in implicit reference to Haraway: 'an immigrant from Mexico crossing into the U.S. beneath a floodlit court' and 'a Punjabi-British hitchhiker on a J1 visa'. Bhanu Kapil, *Incubation: A Space for Monsters* (Providence, RI: Leon Works, 2006), 3.

154 Grosz, *Incorporeal*, 12.

155 Adam Mars-Jones, 'obligatorynoteofhope.com', *London Review of Books* 42.13 (2 July 2020): 24.

156 Mars-Jones, 'obligatorynoteofhope.com', 25–6.

157 Parul Sehgal, 'How to Write Fiction When the Planet Is Falling Apart', *New York Times* (5 February 2020): nytimes.com/2020/02/05/magazine/jenny-offill-weather-book.html [Accessed 21 May 2020]. Sehgal introduces Offill as 'a rangy, obsessional reader, a rover of archives and libraries'.

158 Sehgal, 'How to Write Fiction', n.p.

159 Katy Waldman, 'Can One Sentence Capture All of Life?', *The New Yorker* (6 September 2019). https://www.newyorker.com/books/page-turner-can-one-sentence-campture-all-of-life [Accessed 31 October 2020].

160 Jenny Offill, *Weather* (London: Granta, 2020), 58.

161 Offill, *Weather*, 10.

162 Offill, *Weather*, 108.

163 Rebecca Tamás, *Strangers: Essays on the Human and Nonhuman* (London: Makina Books, 2020), 46.

164 The narrator of Lauren Oyler's novel *Fake Accounts* at one point, hilariously, attempts to write in fragments so as to better understand women, noting that '[w]hat's amazing about this structure is that you can just dump any material you have in here and leave it up to the reader to connect it to the rest of the work' before lamenting that she 'is not very good at this structure. I keep going on too long.' Lauren Oyler, *Fake Accounts* (London: Fourth Estate, 2021), 180, 189. Patricia Lockwood's *No One Is Talking about This*, published at the same time as Oyler's novel, is probably the most popular example of the use of fragmentary form that Oyler disparages.

165 Wojciech Drąg, 'Jenny Offill's *Dept. of Speculation* and the Revival of Fragmentary Writing', *Miscelánea: A Journal of English and American Studies* 56 (2017): 69.

166 Wolfgang Iser, 'The Reading Process: A Phenomenological Approach', *New Literary History* 3.2 (1972): 285.

167 Brian Richardson, *Unnatural Voices: Extreme Narration in Modern and Contemporary Fiction* (Columbus: Ohio State University Press, 2006), 2.

168 Kristian Shaw and Sara Upstone, 'The Transglossic: Contemporary Fiction and the Limitations of the Modern', *English Studies* (2021): 8. https://doi.org/10.1080/0013838X.2021.1943894 [Accessed 10 July 2021].

169 Shaw and Upstone, 'Transglossic', 3. The particular discussion here surrounds Ali Smith's *Autumn*.

170 Offill, *Weather*, 186.

171 Offill, *Weather*, 201.

172 That said, when I selected Offill's work for an online climate change reading group in July 2020, the other members were baffled that I had titled the section 'Optimism', and in general found the text alarming.

173 Lauren Berlant, *Cruel Optimism* (Durham and London: Duke University Press, 2011), 227. The opening epigraph of Offill's novel is drawn from the notes of a town meeting in Milford, Connecticut in 1640, where the townspeople vote that the earth is the Lord's, that it is given to the saints and that they are the saints; at the very least, this suggests the degree to which voting is not ultimately a solution.

174 Berlant, *Cruel Optimism*, 259.

175 Berlant, *Cruel Optimism*, 263.

176 Sehgal, 'How to Write Fiction', n.p.

177 Tamás, *Strangers*, 83.

178 Lucy Ellmann, *Ducks, Newburyport* (Norwich: Galley Beggar Press, 2019), 998.

179 Ellmann, *Ducks*, 278–9.

180 This invitation is repeated, in different ways, in Ellmann's subsequent collection of essays, largely focused on the patriarchy, which was published in July 2021 and opens with the claim that '[a]ll of life is pandemonium. With plague in our midst, everything feels like an emergency.' To read Ellmann's work, like Offill's, is to be invited to think of how a text matters in the exact time that it is published. Lucy Ellmann, *Things Are against Us* (Norwich: Galley Beggar, 2021), 11.

181 Ellmann, *Ducks*, 294.

182 Donna J. Haraway, *When Species Meet* (Minneapolis and London: University of Minnesota Press, 2008), 250.

183 Eva Hayward, 'Fingeryeyes: Impressions of Cup Corals', *Cultural Anthropology* 25.4 (2010): 580.

184 Hayward, 'Fingeryeyes', 580.

185 Hayward, 'Fingeryeyes', 581.

186 Frederick R. Karl, 'American Fictions: The Mega-Novel' *Conjunctions* 7 (1985): 248–60, 249, 251.

187 David Letzler, *The Cruft of Fiction: Mega-Novels and the Science of Paying Attention* (Lincoln and London: University of Nebraska Press, 2017), 18.

188 Nathalie Léger, *Suite for Barbara Loden*, trans. Natasha Lehrer and Cécile Menon (London: Les Fugitives, 2015), 55.

189 Ellmann, *Ducks*, 645, 653, 655.

190 Ellmann, *Ducks*, 11.

191 Elisa Aaltola, *Varieties of Empathy: Moral Psychology and Animal Ethics* (London and New York: Rowman & Littlefield, 2018), 37.

192 Ellmann, *Ducks*, 374.
193 Ellmann, *Ducks*, 407.
194 Ellmann, *Ducks*, 959.
195 Ellmann, *Ducks*, 998.

Conclusion: 'Particle Sings to Particle' – Gleaning the present

In a series of brief fragments explaining her own fragmentary writing, Sinéad Gleeson argues that '[s]ometimes the world steers you towards the broken apart, the work that refuses to be glued together, that basks in its un-ness'.[1] Gleeson's essay was published on 24 March 2020, just a handful of days after Britain went into lockdown, and the world as a whole seemed both radically transformed and known in its un-ness: conversations focused – and still do, eight months later, as I write this – on what has been lost, on what no longer fits into a narrative. Gleeson differentiates between the material fragment, which 'only exists as a component of another object', and the written fragment, which is 'its own atomic being. A just-born republic, gleefully declaring its independence'.[2] As I have tried to show, however, and as Gleeson herself argues, these fragments cannot ultimately be seen as independent entities, but must always be known in constellation. Each fragment, and each fragmentary text, is complete in itself, but understood in relation. Fragments are not only a sign of brokenness, but suggest new ideas of connection and community. Fragmentary narratives give us new ways to think about attention, entanglement and loss, as the three chapters of this book have shown. Attending to the world is a way of seeing yourself entangled in it, and of recognizing all that has been left behind.

Attention is also, as Sarah Manguso makes clear in the series of aphorisms that close her fragmentary illness memoir *Two Kinds of Decay*, a form of love: 'to pay attention is to love everything. // To see the future as *brightness*.'[3] While some chapters have treated this idea more explicitly than others, I have tried to argue throughout this book that, despite its association with ruins and absence, the fragment is also a form that focuses on both the present and the future. Fragmentary narratives offer a way of thinking that does not rely on conventional rhythms of storytelling and the need to move inexorably to a conclusion; they offer a form of resistance to the official language of the archive and the catalogue. The fragment, seen in constellation, is a way of being in the world. As such, it is perhaps the form best suited to writing of our own time, a time when seismic change seems imminent, or already here, and in which our language and our literary conventions often fail to meet the challenges we face. The fragment does not provide an answer to larger paradigms of climate change or the Anthropocene: the narratives discussed here reflect the same anxieties and concerns found in much recent dystopian fiction. Yet the value of the fragment is that it does not show planetary change as something that is happening to us, as if imposed by an outside force. Rather, it suggests that our understanding of the world, partial as it is, comes from our attention to our immediate environment. Attending to the world permits new forms of relation, or constellation, and new ways of seeing our own entanglement with other forms of life. This leads, as I argue in Chapter 3, to a new emphasis on ideas of care, coupled with a recognition of all those whose stories are not told. This care, or love, is not sentimental or easy, but requires the active participation of each individual.

Throughout this book, I have used the idea of gleaning to encompass a variety of responses to fragmentation. Gleaning, even more than assemblage, highlights principles of selection or curation as fundamentally active, and based on individual choice. Gleaning leaves space for all of the material that cannot be included: it is a way to recognize the limitations of individual vision. Jen Hadfield summarizes this approach well in a short essay about Shetland, where she cautions against 'turning real places into imaginary ones': gleaning, or foraging, is a way to understand the 'reality' of the physical environment.[4] Hadfield describes the thrill of leaving her house to forage for welks: 'the journey from desk-writer to gatherer is like the journey from solitariness to mating: a total absorption in the now. The forage is a place where I'm lost to myself.'[5] Gleaning, in this sense, is not merely a process of selecting and relinquishing material objects but relinquishing the self: it is a form of communion with the environment that, while not eradicating the boundary between self and others, makes the self more porous. Gleaning, for Hadfield, is a primal need, a process of immersion in the world.

Gleaning can also be a way of situating the self in relation to the world. In the same collection as Hadfield's essay, Kathleen Jamie's *Antlers of Water*, Linda Cracknell, much like Jamie herself, describes her desk: 'a scatter of books, maps, letters, pebbles' and most importantly a child's bicycle pedal, encrusted with barnacles.[6] Cracknell describes finding the pedal in 2017, on a beach at low tide, during a residency on the Rosneath peninsula. Cracknell writes that while her gleaning was largely accidental – as all gleaning must be – it began to reveal the 'entanglements of the natural world with the manufactured'.[7] If gleaning for Cracknell is not as immersive as it is for Hadfield, it is nevertheless a way of understanding the world at a human, microcosmic scale. Neither author writes extensively of planetary change, whether environmental or political; rather each, in their texts on knowing one particular place in Scotland, suggests that the act of gleaning is a form of knowing that privileges the imminent, the partial, the contingent and the fragmentary.

These concerns are certainly shared with many of the writers discussed in this book. At the end of *The Mushroom at the End of the World*, Anna Lowenhaupt Tsing positions gleaning as a necessary form of engaging with the present:

> Without stories of progress, the world has become a terrifying place. The ruin glares at us with the horror of its abandonment. It's not easy to know how to make a life, much less avert planetary destruction. Luckily there is still company, human and not human. We can still explore the overgrown verges of our blasted landscapes – the edges of capitalist discipline, scalability, and abandoned resource plantations. We can still catch the scent of the latent commons – and the elusive autumn aroma.[8]

If, as I argued in the Introduction, stories of climate change or planetary destruction as such often either revel in apocalyptic nihilism or propose a vision of progress that seems untethered to reality, storytelling as gleaning, as a way of looking at the peripheral and the fragmentary, provides a path to recognizing our entanglement with the world, and creating company. Donna Haraway makes a similar point at the end of *Staying with the Trouble*, turning both to the work of Tanya Tagaq, as discussed in Chapter 2, and to the image of compost, as discussed in Chapter 3. Tagaq is presented as the inspiration for Haraway's future 'Speakers for the Dead', a group of future voices, emerging from three hundred years of 'Communities of Compost', who 'teach practices of remembering and mourning' as part of the 'layered, curious practice of becoming-with others for a habitable, flourishing world'.[9] Haraway's science-fictional scenario is in many ways entirely unlike Tsing's focus on quotidian activity, but addresses the same set of problems. For both, looking at the present destruction of the earth, and of all the creatures who inhabit it, makes storytelling itself seem both impossible and increasingly necessary. There must, both writers suggest, be a way of moving from our own time into the future, but that way can only be partial and contingent, predicated on loss as much as on regeneration.

This desire to imagine a more plural, multispecies, entangled future that is predicated on attention to the present and incorporates stories of loss and devastation without giving way to despair has underpinned this book. The book traces several kinds of movement: from solitude to community, from attention to care and from anthropocentric concerns to visions of humans as participants in a more-than-human environment. As I will show below, this same progression appears in Ali Smith's *Summer*, with which I close. But it is also important to pause here and reflect on these questions not simply as matters for academic contemplation, but as part of an academic process. This book has, unexpectedly, been written in a time of global change; the first draft was completed during a series of lockdowns in 2020 in response to Covid-19. Writing a book at this time has been, in part, a process of escape, and reflects a growing sense of my own enmeshment in the world. I have had no access to archives, even those as familiar as university libraries or my own office shelves, but have written this work on the basis of the hundreds of volumes piled on my living room floor. This has been a work of seclusion and isolation. But every moment of writing has been preceded by walks and runs in Aberdeen, where I live: I have watched the otters and the starlings, seen dolphins and seals and countless dogs, tracked the changing of the light and the movement of the leaves. This is a work compiled from texts, but it has been written in an awareness of a world in which texts are only a small part.

The constraints of writing mean that the echoes of other versions of this book are more present in my mind as I write than usual. All criticism, as I have argued, is an act of gleaning. As much as monographs are positioned as a definitive statement on a particular idea, or set of texts, they often reflect both serendipitous discoveries and careless omissions. The omissions in this work haunt me. I meant to write much more about Korean fiction and Aboriginal fiction. I meant to write much more about memoirs. I spent an entire week rereading Annie Dillard, which was not fruitful for this project but was an excellent way to spend a week. If length and time were limitless I would have written about Esther Kinsky and Alexis Wright, Michelle Tea and Alicia Kopf, Yara Rodrigues Fowler and Sheila Heti, Leanne Betasamosake Simpson and Patricia Lockwood, and so many more. It seems inconceivable to me that I have reached the end of this book and not spoken at length about luminaries such as Anne Carson, Cole Swensen and Annie Ernaux, who have done much to bring fragmentary forms to prominence, or Zadie Smith, whose work was one of my initial inspirations for pursuing this path. And there have been structural changes as well, not just missing chapters but whole approaches. At one point this book was designed to comprise eighty thousand-word fragments, each on a different text, without contextual explanation. At another it was meant to have been organized around the University of Aberdeen's zoology museum, and include a greater focus on non-human animals. Writing on gleaning has taught me, however, the importance of relinquishing: this book is not comprehensive because, perhaps, no book can be comprehensive. Instead, the texts I have gleaned are those that mostly clearly worked in constellation and enabled me to trace a particular line of thought.

As literary critics we too often insist on our own objectivity. In writing this book, I have been consistently afraid not simply of mansplaining, but also of undoing the work of fragmentation by constructing a linear argument. If this text is not definitive in any firm sense, it nevertheless pronounces on a set of texts that themselves attempt to avoid pronouncement. This tension is, perhaps, unavoidable, and I am heartened to find it echoed in Smith's *Summer*. Smith's novel is the final one I consider here not simply because it was both released in and set during the time when this book was written, nor simply because Smith studied at the same university where I teach and I like to believe that gives us a connection, but because the novel, to my surprise, follows the same pattern that I have articulated in the chapters above, moving from attention to gleaning to love and constellation. As the final novel of a quartet published in as close to real time as possible, and which reflects many concerns of our own time, including Brexit and refugees, climate change and loss of political agency, and isolation and loss of community, *Summer* has the unenviable task of having to conclude a set of ruminations that themselves resist conclusive interpretation.[10] Readers of Smith's work are necessarily gleaners, finding their own paths through the texts, whether concentrating on specific thematic elements, focusing on intertextual allusions to Dickens and Shakespeare, or discussions of a series of twentieth-century women artists. While the novels, particularly the first volume *Autumn*, have been convincingly read in terms of contemporary politics, particularly Brexit and immigration, they can just as easily be read in relation to intergenerational friendship, familial bonds, the relation between England and Scotland, and many more themes.[11] In telling the story of our time, Smith insists that any one story is insufficient; rather, stories must be told in conjunction.

While Smith's writing does not appear as fragmentary on the page as some of the works discussed above, then, it exemplifies what I term the maximalist fragment, as can also be seen in relation to Ellmann's *Ducks, Newburyport*. As I define the term, the maximalist fragment privileges assemblage over linearity, mixes temporal and spatial spheres, offers repetition as a central organizing principle and emphasizes reader agency. Each of these elements is key to Ellmann's and Smith's work, but could as easily be applied to work by writers such as Kinsky and Wright. While it is a particularly useful term for thinking of long texts in terms of fragmentation, these features also clearly apply to many of the texts discussed in Chapter 3, especially those by Luiselli and Kapil. These works point, as Alex Calder argues in a discussion of Smith's work, to 'the connective possibilities of storytelling as a challenge to ubiquitous disengagement from local and global issues such as ecological decline and refugee crises'.[12] This emphasis on forms of storytelling and fragmentation as a way to privilege polyvocal narratives, allowing a multiplicity of perspectives, is similar to the work by Tagaq and Polwart discussed in Chapter 2. Smith describes her own approach as 'collage', in a conversation in *Autumn* that plays on the relation between 'college' and 'collage': 'Collage is an institute of education where all the rules can be thrown into the air, and size and space and time and foreground and background all become relative.'[13] Smith's multifocal approach simultaneously requires the reader to create connections between the often disjointed themes and characters in the work, but also to choose their own areas of interest.

To that extent, to read Smith's Seasonal Quartet as a commentary on climate change is equally true and misleading. Certainly environmental devastation is ever-present in the novels, growing in importance over the four volumes. *Autumn* begins with an epigraph on soil erosion, while global warming is explicitly mentioned in the opening of *Winter*. *Winter*, like many of the texts discussed in the Introduction, includes discussions of plastic carrier bags as a marker of the Anthropocene, while the fact that 'there is now *80% more plastic in the earth's seas and on its shores than estimated*' is presented as one of a series of television headlines later in the novel.[14] While '*nature is dead*', however, the natural world is also used as a symbol of resilience: immediately following the alarming headlines Smith reflects on a buddleia growing in the wall: 'After the Second World War, when so many of the cities were in ruins, buddleia was one of the most common plants to take hold in the wreckage. The ruins filled with it here and all over Europe.'[15] By *Spring*, the third volume, the tone is more pugnacious: while the 'plants that push up through the junk and the plastic, earlier, later, [are] coming, regardless', the conclusion to be drawn is '[m]ess up my climate, I'll fuck with your lives'.[16] While it would be easy to read the first three volumes, especially, as contrasting the continuity of nature with temporary, if destructive, human concerns, Smith's depiction of environmental change is arguably more nuanced. Even as the most effusive and poetic passages in most of the quartet are given to the seasons themselves, the natural environment is not observed at a distance.

As Daniel Gluck, the closest the quartet has to a main character, argues at *Autumn's* beginning:

Language is like poppies. It just takes something to churn the earth round them up, and when it does up come the sleeping words, bright red, fresh, blowing about. Then the seedheads rattle, the seeds fall out. Then there's even more language waiting to come up.[17]

If this is a bit fanciful, Smith is sincere in drawing a connection between language and plants, and other more-than-human creatures. Both are known in their generative possibilities, and in their failure to be fixed. They highlight what a character in *Winter* calls 'natural unity in seeming disunity', where 'unity can be revealed against the odds by the random grace of snow's relationship with wind direction'.[18] Both language and nature can be seen in terms of Braidotti's ideas of zoe, as discussed above, and in the larger discourse of fragmentation that has occupied this volume. Neither plants nor words are sufficient in themselves; both must be seen in constellation and enmeshment. As the voice of silence says, at the end of a lengthy list of seemingly everything in the world:

I'm everything that makes everything. I'm everything that unmakes everything. I'm fire. I'm flood. I'm pestilence. I'm the ink, the paper, the grass, the tree, the leaves, the leaf, the greenness in the leaf. I'm the vein in the leaf. I'm the voice that tells no story.[19]

Texts do not comment on the world, but are the world, no more or less enmeshed than a single leaf, or all the leaves together. This is one of the great advantages, as I have been arguing, of the fragment: in not explaining, in not contextualizing, the world itself comes ever more to the fore. This intertwining of attention and language, of text and thing, parallels the relationships formed in Baume's texts, as well as Kapil's. While the scale of Smith's writing is in sharp distinction to those works, all three showcase the possibilities that arrive from a problematization of an anthropocentric perspective.

While the idea of attention to both language and world is paramount to Smith's work, and throughout the quartet largely framed in terms of hope, Smith's maximalist style also raises the question of what is, or is not, included, much like Ellmann's and Offill's works. As Alice Bennett asks, '[i]f we take seriously the relationship between attention and care, how an we also account for the positive regard that Smith's fiction shows for distraction?'[20] Smith's work resists, in Bennett's terms, a 'hierarchy of attentions' that privileges only certain themes.[21] Instead, as Justyna Kostkowska argues, Smith's work highlights the relation between text and world. Kostkowska draws on the work of Timothy Morton to frame Smith's work as ecomimetic in the dual sense of featuring explicit responses to environmental crises, often framed through 'environmentally conscious narrators', and by being 'environmental in form' by breaking 'the illusion of fictional safety' in order to remind readers that they inhabit a real world.[22] Rather than framing fiction as escapist, Smith suggests that reading is a form of engagement with the world, and that this engagement requires its own forms of gleaning and care.

Smith is particularly clear about the ethical parameters of her work in an online interview for the Edinburgh International Book Festival as part of the promotion tour for *Summer*.[23] Smith speaks, like virtually all writers interviewed in the summer of 2020, about the role of literature in shaping the present moment: she twice calls Covid-19 'the tiniest biggest disruption ever' at the same time that she argues for the importance of relinquishment: 'I don't know what's special about the present moment except "then it's gone"'. It is impossible not to focus on the world as immediate and known; it is impossible not to see it as already past. Throughout her interview she emphasizes the importance of texts as dialogue: reading is 'an individual act that peoples us', such that books can be seen as fundamentally communal, allowing for a meeting of minds, or of reality and imagination. Like over a thousand other viewers, I watched Smith's interview live, discussing it on Twitter in real time. I was also hampered by the repeated buffering of the live stream, every so often having to refresh just when Smith seemed about to say something important. The event thus, even if accidentally, illustrated many of Smith's concerns in *Summer* itself: there was a real community, formed in relation to a text, but it was precarious and fleeting. This sense of a community that is responsive to the world, but cannot be sustained, underpins much of the novel: as much as it is figured as a tale of hope, it is equally occupied with a prevailing sense of loss.

Midway through *Summer* Smith encapsulates the entire argument not only of her book, but also of mine:

> But when the words that once meant a person meet a living breathing shape, it's like when a lone bird sings in a tree like that one above her just did, and then a bird many gardens away sings the same song back to it. Particle sings to particle, crumb of grime to crumb of grime, fragment-hank to fragment. Something connects. A smatter of dust meets the thought of water, and then the thought of oxygen, carbon, nitrogen, hydrogen, calcium, phosphorus, mercury, potassium, magnesium, ion, so on, molecular alphabet.[24]

In this passage, which functions as a synecdoche for the novel as a whole, the self is known through attention to the world, through an assemblage of fragments and finally through an enmeshment in physical reality. The voices of the past appear to us as echoes – indeed, 'Echo' is used as a name for the Alexa household device – and may instantly vanish. Late in the novel one character returns to a graveyard where she once had a meaningful encounter with another person, and takes a picture of an old gravestone to commemorate her experience, only to find 'that though it was a beautiful picture you couldn't see any of the words on the stone to read them, and all she'd actually got a record of was a blur of twigs, a surface of old stone, some bright lichen'.[25] Art and words are how we remember the past, and yet they are ultimately ephemeral. Art, as one character says, is important because it exists, and 'then because we encounter it, we remember we exist too. And that one day we won't'.[26] This statement is just as true of the natural environment: the attentive encounter, as in Baume's writing, is a form of connection that highlights the precarity and vulnerability of the self. Learning to pay attention is important not because it provides explanations of the world, but because it reveals the contingency and fleetingness of every encounter.

More than the first three novels in the quartet, *Summer* is filled with scenes of environmental devastation. There are accounts of fires in Australia and discussions of the relationship between climate change and the imagination. A school lockdown in May is juxtaposed with the return of the swifts, and the juxtaposition of a disrupted present with the continuity of nature is seen as significant. As a character later describes the nesting of pigeons: 'It *is* meaningful. It is. It's hopeful, and natural'.[27] Throughout the novel, characters repeatedly insist that the promise of summer, and perhaps the promise of *Summer*, is that attending to nature provides a way of thinking past immediate concerns. Nature is framed as what endures, even as the natural world is marked by loss and violence. Summer is only 'an imagined end', a promise that 'one day soon we'll be treated well by the world. Like there really is a kinder finale and it's not just possible but assured'.[28] Smith's insistence on hope, written from a period in which hope seems a thing of fancy, or somehow distant, is immensely moving. I cannot begin to imagine how *Summer* will appear to readers a decade hence, or what changes will have befallen the planet in the meantime: the novel might appear prophetic or naïve. Smith insists, however, far more than in her earlier novels, that this hope for a better future is the function of art. Art not only gives us a prism on nature: it reveals how humans are entangled in nature, and cannot see their own lives in isolation. Hope is communal.

As Smith writes in an unusual first-person fragment, the etymology of 'summer' comes from a word 'meaning both *one* and *together*'.[29] Yet this sentence is immediately followed with a gleaned fragment closer to the work of Zambreno or Missaghi than anything else in Smith's writing. She explains 'I can't remember where this next quote you're about to read is from. [...] But I copied it into a notebook some years ago and now I can't find its source'.[30] The quotation itself argues for the power of art to address societal problems. Art, again, is a form of communion. Yet the passage is marked for its emphasis on Smith's, or the narrator's, own gleaning process: the text is divorced from its original context, and seen only as fragment. As such, art's power to reshape the world, or to create community, is derived in part from its own partiality. Meaning is not found by adhering to a preordained philosophy, but by telling stories about individual encounters, and making connections between them. Smith's idea of storytelling as a form of connection that does not ignore the violence of the world has much in common with Luiselli's approach. For both authors, despite their clear differences, the presentation of multiple narrative strands that give voice to those left out of current political discourse – in particular, in Smith's work, refugees and immigrants – is fundamentally hopeful. Both authors use fragmentary forms to indicate that while the reader is not getting a unified account of the world, their own ability to shape these disparate pieces into a story is itself a form of care.

Summer begins with a call to attention: 'The level of attention I'm talking about is necessary for *everything*.'[31] Like the texts discussed in Chapter 1, attention is a way out of solipsism: paying attention to the world changes what is seen as significant, and leads to a sense of enmeshment. It ends, like the texts in Chapter 3, and like Tokarczuk's work discussed in the Introduction, with a call for constellation. One character, a boy named Robert, has been making screenprints at school that map 'facial recognition technique faceprints like stars across a night sky', so that 'his constellations were all faces'.[32] In making the faces of his family constellations, he simultaneously shows them as enmeshed in the physical world, and highlights the myriad possibilities of the self. A self, a book, is not one thing, but always known in relation. In the final scene of the novel, save for a brief postscript, Robert's family gathers to look at the night sky: 'they all looked up together to point out which constellations they knew the names for and to guess at the ones they didn't'.[33] The scene is simple and familiar. As a finale to a lengthy project, however, it carries the same weight as the final act of relinquishment at the conclusion of *Ducks, Newburyport*. Attending to the world includes attending to what you do not know, as well as what you do. The family is constellated as much as the stars: they are known in their conjunction.

Smith's work, like virtually all of the texts discussed above, indicates that fragmentation is a productive way to consider our relation not only to our environment, but also to each other. Precisely because of its apparent individuation or atomism, the fragment insists on connection. These texts indicate, again and again, that there is no final truth, no overarching story and no easy resolution. The changes to the earth are real, but they are not new: literature is always responsive to and often complicit in overarching narratives of violence and devastation. The fragment is a way to make space for what is lost, for the voices that have not been heard. It is a way to emphasize contingency and accident, and to be responsive to the present, rather than focused on a future that has already been framed to appear as a past. The fragment is a way to highlight individual responsibility and responsiveness. The works I have discussed here follow in a long line of women's environmental writing, in particular, but are notably attuned to the present. In finding new formal possibilities for literature, they show the importance of individual encounter with both world and text. This is a new world, and requires new forms, however fleeting and incomplete. Framing gleaning both as artistic and critical practice provides a way to think of texts in terms of multiplicity and individual encounter. This thinking, I want to suggest, opens up how we think not only of literary works, but our own encounter with a multiple, complex, more-than-human world, in which we are always known in constellation. As for me, I'm going to go look at some birds.

Notes

1   Sinéad Gleeson, 'Fragmented Narratives Are Broken, Independent, and Honest', *Literary Hub* (24 March 2020): lithub.com/fragmented-narratives-are-broken-independent-and-honest/ [Accessed 14 November 2020].

2   Gleeson, 'Fragmented Narratives', n.p.

3   Sarah Manguso, *Two Kinds of Decay* (London: Granta, 2011), 183. Original emphasis.

4   Jen Hadfield, 'I Da Welk Ebb', in *Antlers of Water: Writing on the Nature and Environment of Scotland*, ed. Kathleen Jamie (Edinburgh: Canongate, 2020), 136.

5   Hadfield, 'I Da Welk Ebb', 137.

6   Linda Cracknell, 'Lunar Cycling', in *Antlers of Water: Writing on the Nature and Environment of Scotland*, ed. Kathleen Jamie (Edinburgh: Canongate, 2020), 83.

7   Cracknell, 'Lunar Cycle', 88.

8   Anna Lowenhaupt Tsing, *The Mushroom at the End of the World: On the Possibility of Life in Capitalist Ruins* (Princeton and Oxford: Princeton University Press, 2015), 282.

9   Donna J. Haraway, *Staying with the Trouble: Making Kin in the Chthulucene* (Durham and London: Duke University Press 2016), 164, 168.

10   Smith has discussed her writing process for the quartet in a vast number of interviews; see, for example, Claire Armistead, 'Ali Smith: 'This young generation is showing us that we need to change and we can change'', *The Guardian* (23 March 2019): theguardian.com/books/2019/mar/23/ali-smith-spring-young-generation-brexit-future [Accessed 15 November 2020]. At the time of writing a further volume, *Companion Piece*, has been advertised but not yet published.

11   For a reading of Smith's work in relation to Brexit, see Petra Rau, '*Autumn* after the Referendum', in *Brexit and Literature: Critical and Cultural Responses*, ed. Robert Eaglestone (London and New York: Routledge, 2018), 31–43. For a focus on immigration, see Peter Ely, 'Limits and Transgressions: National Community in Ali Smith's *Quartet*', in *Community in Contemporary British Fiction: From Blair to Brexit*, ed. Sara Upstone and Peter Ely (London: Bloomsbury, 2022), (Forthcoming).

12   Alex Calder, '"The Great Connective": Contemporaneous Storytelling and Emergent Seriality in Ali Smith Seasonal', *Alluvium* (16 December 2019): alluvium-journal.org/2019/12/16/contemporaneous-storytelling-and-emergent-storytelling-in-ali-smiths-seasonal/ [Accessed 15 November 2020].

13   Ali Smith, *Autumn* (London: Hamish Hamilton, 2016), 71–2. For a queer reading of this approach, see Anni Kangas et al., 'Smashing Containers, Queering the International through Collaging', *International Feminist Journal of Politics* 21.3 (2019): 355–82.

14   Ali Smith, *Winter* (London: Hamish Hamilton, 2017), 219. Original emphasis.

15   Smith, *Winter*, 220.

16   Ali Smith, *Spring* (London: Hamish Hamilton, 2019), 7–8.

17   Smith, *Autumn*, 69.

18   Smith, *Winter*, 53. This idea is mocked by the other character in the scene.

19   Smith, *Autumn*, 192. This litany echoes the repetition of leaf/leave/live in Smith's earlier *Hotel World*.

20   Alice Bennett, *Contemporary Fictions of Attention: Reading and Distraction in the Twenty-First Century* (London: Bloomsbury, 2018), 80.

21   Bennett, *Contemporary Fictions*, 80.

22   Justyna Kostkowska, *Ecocriticism and Women Writers: Environmentalist Poetics of Virginia Woolf, Jeanette Winterson, and Ali Smith* (Basingstoke: Palgrave Macmillan, 2013), 159.

23 Ali Smith, 'Ali Smith & Sarah Wood: Festival – A Film', *Edinburgh International Book Festival* (28 August 2020): edbookfest.co.uk/the-festival/whats-on/ali-smith-sarah-wood-festival-a-film/player [Accessed 28 August 2020].

24 Ali Smith, *Summer* (London: Hamish Hamilton, 2020), 201–2.

25 Smith, *Summer*, 317.

26 Smith, *Summer,* 330.

27 Smith, *Summer,* 327. Original emphasis.

28 Smith, *Summer,* 289.

29 Smith, *Summer,* 263.

30 Smith, *Summer,* 263.

31 Smith, *Summer,* 12.

32 Smith, *Summer,* 366.

33 Smith, *Summer,* 375.

Bibliography

Aaltola, Elise. *Varieties of Empathy: Moral Psychology and Animal Ethics*. London and New York: Rowman and Littlefield, 2018.

Agamben, Giorgio. *Homo Sacer: Sovereign Power and Bare Life*, translated by Daniel Heller-Roazen. Stanford: Stanford University Press, 1998.

Ahmed, Sara. *The Cultural Politics of Emotion*, 2nd ed. Edinburgh: Edinburgh University Press, 2014.

Ahmed, Sara. *Queer Phenomenology: Orientations, Objects, Others*. Durham and London: Duke University Press, 2006.

Alaimo, Stacy. *Bodily Natures: Science, Environment, and the Material Self*. Bloomington and Indianapolis: Indiana University Press, 2010.

Alaimo, Stacy. 'Oceanic Origins, Plastic Activism, and New Materialism at Sea'. In *Material Ecocriticism*, edited by Serenella Iovino and Serpil Oppermann, 186–203. Bloomington and Indianapolis: Indiana University Press, 2014.

Alaimo, Stacy. *Undomesticated Ground: Recasting Nature as Feminist Space*. Ithaca and London: Cornell University Press, 2000.

Anderson, Elizabeth. *Material Spirituality in Modernist Women's Writing*. London: Bloomsbury, 2020.

Anderson, Elizabeth. 'Reading the World's Liveliness: Animist Ecologies in Indigenous Knowledges, New Materialism and Women's Writing', *Feminist Modernist Studies* 3.2 (2020): 205–16.

Andrews, Abi. 'Q+A with Abi Andrews about *The Word for Woman Is Wilderness*', *Two Dollar Radio* (2018): twodollarradio.com/blogs/radiowaves/q-a-with-abi-andrews-about-the-word-for-woman-is-wilderness.

Andrews, Abi. *The Word for Woman Is Wilderness*. London: Serpent's Tail, 2018.

Anohni. *Helplessness*. London: Rough Trade, 2015.

Appadurai, Arjun. 'The Thing Itself', *Public Culture* 18.1 (2006): 15–21.

Apple, Fiona. *Fetch the Bolt Cutters*. New York: Epic Records, 2020.

Arigo, Christopher. 'Notes toward an Ecopoetics: Revising the Postmodern Sublime and Juliana Spahr's *This Connection of Everyone with Lungs*', *How2* 3.2 (2008): asu.edu/pipercwcenter/how2journal/vol_3_no_2/ecopetics/essays/arigo.html.

Armistead, Claire. 'Ali Smith: "This Young Generation Is Showing Us That We Need to Change and We Can Change"', *The Guardian* (23 March 2019): theguardian.com/books/2019/mar/23/ali-smith-spring-young-generation-brexit-future.

Arnold, Annika. *Climate Change and Storytelling: Narratives and Cultural Meaning in Environmental Communication* (Cham: Palgrave Macmillan, 2018).

Arvin, Maile, Eve Tuck and Angie Morrill. 'Decolonizing Feminism: Challenging Connections between Settler Colonialsm and Heteropatriarchy', *Feminist Formations* 25.1 (2013): 8–34.

Ashworth, Jenn. *Notes Made while Falling*. London: Goldsmiths Press, 2019.

Assmann, Jan. *Religion and Cultural Memory*, translated by Rodney Livingstone. Stanford: Stanford University Press, 2006.

Bachelard, Gaston. *The Poetics of Space*, translated by Maria Jolas. London: Beacon, 1994.

Baker, Timothy C. 'The Gender Politics of Trees'. In *Nonhuman Agencies in the Twenty-First-Century Anglophone Novel*, edited by Yvonne Liebermann, Judith Rahn, and Bettina Burger, 169–86. Cham: Palgrave, 2021.

Baker, Timothy C. 'Harmonic Monads: Reading Contemporary Scottish Fiction through the Enlightenment', *Scottish Literary Review* 9.1 (2017): 95–113.

Baker, Timothy C. *Writing Animals: Language, Suffering, and Animality in Twenty-First-Century Fiction*. Cham: Palgrave Macmillan, 2019.

Barad, Karen. *Meeting the Universe Halfway: Quantum Physics and the Entanglement of Matter and Meaning*. Durham and London: Duke University Press, 2007.

Barnes, Kateryna. 'Soundtrack to Settler-Colonialism: Tanya Tagaq's Music as Creative Nonfiction Horror', *Gothic Nature* 2 (2021): 62–83. https://gothicnaturejournal.com/.

Battistini, Emiliano. '"Sealfie", "Phoque you" and "Animism": The Canadian Inuit Answer to the United States Anti-sealing Activism', *International Journal for the Semiotics of Law* 31 (2008): 561–94.

Baudelaire, Charles. *The Painter of Modern Life and Other Essays*, translated and edited by Jonathan Mayne. New York: Da Capo, 1986.

Baume, Sara. *Handiwork*. Dublin: Tramp Press, 2020.

Baume, Sara. *A Line Made by Walking*. London: Heinemann, 2017.

Baume, Sara. *Spill Simmer Falter Wither*. Dublin: Tramp Press, 2015.

Bell, Julia. *Radical Attention*. London: Peninsula, 2020.

Bell, Lucy. 'Recycling Materials, Recycling Lives: Cardboard Publishers in Latin America'. In *Literature and Sustainability: Concept, Text and Culture*, edited by Adeline Johns-Putra, John Parham and Louise Squire, 76–96. Manchester: Manchester University Press, 2017.

Benjamin, Walter. *The Arcades Project*, translated by Howard Eiland and Kevin McLaughlin. Cambridge, MA, and London: Belknap/Harvard University Press, 2002.

Benjamin, Walter. *Illuminations*, translated by Harry Zohn, edited by Hannah Arendt. New York: Schocken, 1969.

Bennett, Alice. *Contemporary Fictions of Attention: Reading and Distraction in the Twenty-First Century*. London and New York: Bloomsbury Academic, 2018.

Bennett, Claire-Louise. *Pond*. Dublin: Stinging Fly, 2015.

Bennett, Jane. *The Enchantment of Modern Life: Attachments, Crossings, and Ethics*. Princeton and Oxford: Princeton University Press, 2001.

Bennett, Jane. *Vibrant Matter: A Political Ecology of Things*. Durham and London: Duke University Press, 2010.

Berlant, Lauren. *Cruel Optimism*. Durham and London: Duke University Press, 2011.

Berlant, Lauren. 'Structures of Unfeeling: *Mysterious Skin*', *International Journal of Politics, Culture, and Society* 28 (2015): 191–213.

Berlant, Lauren and Kathleen Stewart. *The Hundreds*. Durham and London: Duke University Press, 2019.

Berlin, Isaiah. *The Hedgehog and the Fox: An Essay on Tolstoy's View of History*, edited by Henry Hard, 2nd ed. Princeton: Princeton University Press, 2013.

Bernstein, Sarah. *The Coming Bad Days*. London: Daunt Books, 2021.

Blythe, Andrea. 'Poet Spotlight: Melissa Eleftherion on Survival and How Language Reshapes Our Perception of the World', *Andrea Blythe: Speculative Poetry and Fiction* (8 October 2019): andreablythe.com/2019/10/08/poet-spotlight-melissa-eleftherion-on-survival-and-how-language-reshapes-our-perception-of-the-world/.

Boon, Sonja. 'Speculation, Magic Realism, and Minding the Gaps', *History Workshop* (2 September 2020): historyworkshop.org.uk/speculation-magic-realism-and-minding-the-gaps/.

Boon, Sonja. *What the Oceans Remember: Searching for Belonging and Home*. Waterloo: Wilfrid Laurier University Press, 2019.

Boon, Sonja, Lesley Butler and Daze Jeffries. *Autoethnography and Feminist Theory at the Water's Edge: Unsettled Islands*. Cham: Palgrave Macmillan, 2018.

Botha, Marc. 'Precarious Present, Fragile Futures: Literature and Uncertainty in the Early Twenty-First Century', *English Academy Review* 31.2 (2014): 1–19.

Bracke, Astrid. *Climate Crisis and the 21st-Century British Novel*. London: Bloomsbury, 2018.

Braidotti, Rosi. 'Four Theses on Posthuman Feminism'. In *Anthropocene Feminism*, edited by Richard Grusin, 21–48. Minneapolis and London: University of Minnesota Press, 2017.

Braidotti, Rosi. *Metamorphoses: Towards a Materialist Theory of Becoming*. Cambridge: Polity, 2002.

Braidotti, Rosi. *Nomadic Subjects: Embodiment and Sexual Difference in Contemporary Feminist Theory*, 2nd ed. New York: Columbia University Press, 2011.

Braidotti, Rosi. *Nomadic Theory: The Portable Rosi Braidotti*. New York: Columbia University Press, 2011.

Braidotti, Rosi. *Patterns of Dissonance: A Study of Women in Contemporary Philosophy*, translated by Elizabeth Guild. Cambridge: Polity, 1991.

Braidotti, Rosi. *Posthuman Knowledge*. Cambridge: Polity, 2019.

Braidotti, Rosi. 'A Theoretical Framework for the Critical Posthumanities', *Theory, Culture and Society* 36.6 (2019): 31–61.

Braidotti, Rosi. *Transpositions: On Nomadic Ethics*. Cambridge: Polity, 2006.

Brand, Dionne. *A Map to the Door of No Return: Notes to Belonging*. Toronto: Vintage Canada, 2011.

Bridgers, Phoebe. *Punisher*. Bloomington, IN: Dead Oceans, 2020.

Brown, Bill. *Other Things*. Chicago and London: University of Chicago Press, 2015.

Bruno, Giuliana. *Atlas of Emotion: Journeys in Art, Architecture, and Film*. New York: Verso, 2018.

Buell, Lawrence. *The Future of Environmental Criticism: Environmental Crisis and Literary Imagination*. Malden, MA, and Oxford: Blackwell, 2005.

Burnett, Elizabeth-Jane. *The Grassling*. London: Penguin, 2019.

Burnett, Elizabeth-Jane. 'Little Peach', *The Willowherb Review* 2 (2019): thewillowherbreview.com/little-peach-elizabeth-jane-burnett.

Burnett, Elizabeth-Jane. *Of Sea*. London: Penned in the Margins, 2021.

Burnett, Elizabeth-Jane. *A Social Biography of Contemporary Innovative Poetry Communities: The Gift, the Wager, and Poethics*. Cham: Palgrave Macmillan, 2017.

Burnett, Elizabeth-Jane. 'Sounding the Non-Human in John Clare and Maggie O'Sullivan', *John Clare Society Journal* 35 (2016): 31–52.

Burnett, Elizabeth-Jane. *Swims*. London: Penned in the Margins, 2019.

Burnett, Elizabeth-Jane. '"Swims": Body, Ritual, and Erasure', *Jacket 2* (5 February 2016): jacket2.org/article/swims.

Burnett, Elizabeth-Jane and Rebecca Thomas. 'The Folds of the Fields: A Performative Collaboration in the South of England', *Green Letters* 23.3 (2019): 257–67.

Burnett, Elizabeth-Jane and Tony Lopez. 'Sea Holly', *Poetry* (December 2016): 246–51. https://www.poetryfoundation.org/poetrymagazine/poems/91306/sea-holly-582211e1069f8.

Butler, Judith. *Bodies That Matter: On the Discursive Limits of 'Sex'*. London and New York: Routledge Classics, 2011.

Butler, Judith. *Precarious Life: The Powers of Mourning and Violence*. London and New York: Verso, 2006.

Calarco, Matthew. 'Claimed by Roadkill'. In *Feeling Animal Death: Being Host to Ghosts*, edited by Brianne Donaldson and Ashley King, 75–90. London and New York: Rowman and Littlefield, 2019.

Calder, Alex. '"The Great Connective": Contemporaneous Storytelling and Emergent Seriality in Ali Smith Seasonal', *Alluvium* (16 December 2019): alluvium-journal.org/2019/12/16/contemporaneous-storytelling-and-emergent-storytelling-in-ali-smiths-seasonal/.

Campbell, Alexandra. 'Atlantic Exchanges: The Poetics of Dispersal and Disposal in Scottish and Caribbean Seas', *Journal of Postcolonial Writing* 55.2 (2019): 196–208.

Caswell, M.L. '"The Archive" Is Not an Archives: Acknowledging the Intellectual Contributions of Archival Studies', *Reconstruction* 16.1 (2016). https://escholarship.org/uc/item/7bn4v1fk.

Césaire, Aimé. *Discourse on Colonialism*, translated by Joan Pinkham. New York: Monthly Review Press, 2000.

Chakrabarty, Dipesh. 'The Climate of History: Four Theses', *Critical Inquiry* 35.2 (2009): 197–222.

Chałczyk, Franciszek. 'Around the Anthropocene in Eighty Names – Considering the Urbanocene Proposition', *Sustainability* 12 (2020), article 4458: doi:10.3990/su12114458.

Cheah, Pheng. 'Non-Dialectical Materialism'. In *New Materialisms: Ontology, Agency, and Politics*, edited by Diana Coole and Samantha Frost, 70–91. Durham and London: Duke University Press, 2010.

Chowdhry, Maya. *Fossil*. Leeds: Peepal Tree, 2016.

Cixous, Hélène and Catherine Clément. *The Newly Born Woman*, translated by Betsy Wing. Minneapolis: University of Minnesota Press, 1986.

Clark, Timothy. *Ecocriticism on the Edge: The Anthropocene as a Threshold Concept*. London: Bloomsbury, 2015.

Clarke, Michael Tavel and David Wittenberg. 'Introduction'. In *Scale in Literature and Culture*, edited by Michael Tavel Clarke and David Wittenberg, 1–32. Cham: Palgrave Macmillan, 2017.

Clayton, Susan and Bryan T. Karazsia. 'Development and Validation of a Measure of Climate Change Anxiety', *Journal of Environmental Psychology* 69 (2020). https://www.sciencedirect.com/science/article/pii/S0272494419307145. doi.org./10.1016/j.envp.2020.101434.

Clover, Joshua and Juliana Spahr. 'Gender Abolition and the Ecotone War'. In *Anthropocene Feminism*, edited by Richard Grusin, 147–67. Minneapolis and London: University of Minnesota Press, 2017.

Cohen, Jeffrey Jerome. 'Introduction: Ecostitial'. In *Inhuman Nature*, edited by Jeffrey Jerome Cohen, i–x. Washington, DC: Oliphaunt Books, 2014.

Cole, Teju. *Blind Spot*. London: Faber, 2016.

Colebrook, Claire. 'Archivolithic: The Anthropocene and the Hetero-Archive', *Derrida Today* 7.1 (2014): 21–43.

Colebrook, Claire. *Death of the Posthuman: Essays on Extinction, Vol. 1*. Ann Arbor: Open Humanities Press, 2014.

Colebrook, Claire. 'The Future in the Anthropocene: Extinction and the Imagination'. In *Climate and Literature*, edited by Adeline Johns-Putra, 263–80. Cambridge: Cambridge University Press, 2019.

Colebrook, Claire. 'We Have Always Been Post-Anthropocene: The Anthropocene Counterfactual'. In *Anthropocene Feminism*, edited by Richard Grusin, 1–20. Minneapolis and London: University of Minnesota Press, 2017.

Collins, Sophie. *Who Is Mary Sue?* London: Faber, 2018.

Connerton, Paul. *The Spirit of Mourning: History, Memory and the Body*. Cambridge: Cambridge University Press, 2011.

Conradson, David. 'Freedom, Space and Perspective: Moving Encounters with Other Ecologies'. In *Emotional Geographies*, edited by Joyce Davidson, Liz Bondi and Mick Smith, 103–16. Aldershot and Burlington, VT: Ashgate, 2005.

Conway, Anne. *The Principles of the Most Ancient and Modern Philosophy*, translated and edited by Allison P. Coudert and Taylor Corse. Cambridge: Cambridge University Press, 1996.

Cracknell, Linda. 'Lunar Cycling'. In *Antlers of Water: Writing on the Nature and Environment of Scotland*, edited by Kathleen Jamie, 81–93. Edinburgh: Canongate, 2020.

Crist, Meehan. 'Is It OK to Have a Child?' *London Review of Books* 42.5 (5 March 2020): 9–14.

Cusk, Rachel. *Coventry*. London: Faber, 2019.

Cusk, Rachel. *Kudos*. London: Faber, 2018.

Davey, Moyra. *Index Cards*, edited by Nicolas Linnert. London: Fitzcarraldo, 2020.

Davis, Heather and Zoe Todd. 'On the Importance of a Date, or Decolonizing the Anthropocene', *ACME: An International Journal for Critical Geographies* 16.4 (2017): 761–80.

DeLanda, Manuel. *Assemblage Theory*. Edinburgh: Edinburgh University Press, 2016.

Deleuze, Gilles and Claire Parnet, *Dialogues II*, translated by Hugh Tomlinson and Barbara Habberjam. London and New York: Continuum, 2006.

Deleuze, Gilles and Félix Guattari. *A Thousand Plateaus*, translated by Brian Massumi. London: Bloomsbury, 2013.

Derrida, Jacques. *Archive Fever: A Freudian Impression*, translated by Eric Prenowitz. Chicago and London: University of Chicago Press, 1996.

Desmond, Jane. 'Requiem for Roadkill: Death and Denial on America's Roads'. In *Environmental Anthropology: Future Directions*, edited by Helen Kopnina and Eleanor Shoreman-Ouimet, 46–58. New York and London: Routledge, 2013.

Dever, Maryanne, Sally Newman, and Ann Vickery. *The Intimate Archive: Journeys through Private Papers*. Canberra: National Library of Australia, 2009.

Diamond, Beverley. 'The Power of Stories: Canadian Music Scholarship's Narratives and Counter-Narratives', *Intersections* 33.2 (2013): 155–65.

Drąg, Wojciech. 'Jenny Offill's *Dept. of Speculation* and the Revival of Fragmentary Writing', *Miscelánea: A Journal of English and American Studies* 56 (2017): 57–72.

duBois, Page. *Sappho Is Burning*. Chicago and London: University of Chicago Press, 1995.

Duschinsky, Robbie and Emma Wilson. 'Flat Affect, Joyful Politics and Enthralled Attachments: Engaging with the Work of Lauren Berlant', *International Journal of Politics, Culture, and Society* 28 (2015): 179–90.

Egan, Michael. 'Culture and Collapse: Theses on Catastrophic History for the Twenty-First Century'. In *The Discourses of Environmental Collapse: Imagining the End*, edited by Alison E. Vogelaar, Brack W. Hale, and Alexandra Peat, 15–31. London and New York: Routledge, 2018.

Eleftherion, Melissa. *field guide to autobiography*. Brooklyn, NY: The Operating System, 2018.

Eleftherion, Melissa. *little ditch*. Ottawa: Above/Ground Press, 2018.

Eliades, Maria. "'I'm telling these stories for an audience, but I also want to digest this experience for myself'": An Interview with Poupeh Missaghi', *Ploughshares* (6 February 2020): blog.plshares.org/index.php/im-telling-these-stories-for-an-audience-but-i-also-want-to-digest-this-experience-for-myself-an-interview-with-poupeh-missaghi.

Elias, Camelia. *The Fragment: Towards a History and Poetics of a Performative Genre.* Bern: Peter Lang, 2004.

Ely, Peter. 'Limits and Transgressions: National Community in Ali Smith's *Quartet*'. In *Community in Contemporary British Fiction: From Blair to Brexit*, edited by Sara Upstone and Peter Ely. London: Bloomsbury, 2022 (Forthcoming).

Ellmann, Lucy. *Ducks, Newburyport.* Norwich: Galley Beggar, 2019.

Ellmann, Lucy. *Things Are against Us.* Norwich: Galley Beggar, 2021.

Emmett, Robert S. and David E. Nye. *The Environmental Humanities: A Critical Introduction.* Cambridge, MA: MIT Press, 2017.

Ensor, Sarah. 'The Ecopoetics of Contact: Touching, Cruising, Gleaning', *ISLE: Interdisciplinary Studies in Literature and Environment* 25.1 (2018): 150–68.

Ergin, Meliz. *The Ecopoetics of Entanglement in Contemporary Turkish and American Literatures.* Cham: Palgrave Macmillan, 2017.

Falconer, Rachel. 'Midlife Music: *The Overhaul* and *Frissure*'. In *Kathleen Jamie: Essays and Poems on Her Work*, edited by Rachel Falconer, 156–67. Edinburgh: Edinburgh University Press, 2015.

Farrier, David. *Anthropocene Poetics: Deep Time, Sacrifice Zones, and Extinction.* Minneapolis: University of Minnesota Press, 2019.

Felman, Shoshana. 'Education and Crisis, or the Vicissitudes of Teaching'. In *Testimony: Crises of Witnessing in Literature, Psychoanalysis and History*, edited by Shoshana Felman and Dori Laub, 1–56. New York and Abingdon: Routledge, 1992.

Ferns, Chris. *Narrating Utopia: Ideology, Gender, Form in Utopian Literature.* Liverpool: Liverpool University Press, 1999.

Fisk, Anna. *Sex, Sin, and Our Selves: Encounters in Feminist Theology and Contemporary Women's Literature.* Eugene, OR: Pickwick Publications, 2014.

Forché, Carolyn. *In the Lateness of the World.* Hexham: Bloodaxe, 2020.

Fraiman, Susan. *Extreme Domesticity: A View from the Margins.* New York: Columbia University Press, 2017.

Friedland, Yanara. 'Mapping Tehran: A Conversation with Poupeh Missaghi', *World Literature Today* (6 February 2020): wordliteraturetoday.org/blog/interviews/mapping-tehran-conversation-poupeh-missaghi-yanara-friedland.

Friedman, Susan Stanford. 'Scaling Planetarity: *Spacetime* in the New Modernist Studies – Virginia Woolf, H.D., Hilma af Klint, Alicja Kwade, Kathy Jetñil- Kijiner', *Feminist Modernist Studies* 3.2 (2020): 118–47.

Gaard, Greta. 'Toward New EcoMasculinities, EcoGenders, and EcoSexualities'. In *Ecofeminism: Feminist Intersections with Other Animals and the Earth*, edited by Carol J. Adams and Lori Gruen, 225–39. New York and London: Bloomsbury, 2014.

Gairn, Louisa. '"Connective Leaps": *Sightlines* and *the Overhaul*'. In *Kathleen Jamie: Essays and Poems on Her Work*, edited by Rachel Falconer, 134–45. Edinburgh: Edinburgh University Press, 2015.

Galloway, Kate. 'The Aurality of Pipeline Politics and Listening for Nacreous Clouds: Voicing Indigenous Ecological Knowledge in Tanya Tagaq's *Animism* and *Retribution*', *Popular Music* 39.1 (2020): 121–44.

Garrard, Greg et al. *Climate Change Scepticism: A Transnational Ecocritical Analysis* (London: Bloomsbury, 2019).

Ghosh, Amitav. *The Great Derangement: Climate Change and the Unthinkable*. Chicago and London: University of Chicago Press, 2016.

Gilbert, Suzanne. 'Orality and the Ballad Tradition'. In *The Edinburgh Companion to Scottish Women's Writing*, edited by Glenda Norquay, 35–42. Edinburgh: Edinburgh University Press, 2012.

Giraud, Eva Haifa. *What Comes after Entanglement?: Activism, Anthropocentrism, and an Ethics of Exclusion*. Durham and London: Duke University Press, 2019.

Gleeson, Sinéad. *Constellations: Reflections from Life*. London: Picador, 2019.

Gleeson, Sinéad. 'Fragmented Narratives Are Broken, Independent, and Honest', *Literary Hub* (24 March 2020): lithub.com/fragmented-narratives-are-broken-independent-and-honest/.

Glissant, Édouard. *Poetics of Relation*, translated by Betsy Wing. Ann Arbor: University of Michigan Press, 1997.

Goodbody, Axel and Adeline Johns-Putra. 'The Rise of the Climate Change Novel'. In *Climate and Literature*, edited by Adeline Johns-Putra, 229–45. Cambridge: Cambridge University Press, 2019.

Gordon, Andrew. 'The Renaissance Footprint: The Material Trace in Print Culture from Dürer to Spenser', *Renaissance Quarterly* 71 (2018): 478–529.

Green, Louise. *Fragments from the History of Loss: The Nature Industry and the Postcolony*. University Park, PA: Pennsylvania State University Press, 2020.

Greene, A. Kendra. *The Museum of Whales You Will Never See: Travels among the Collectors of Iceland*. London: Granta, 2020.

Griffin, Susan. *Woman and Nature: The Roaring Inside Her*. London: The Women's Press, 1978.

Griffiths, Alison. *Wondrous Difference: Cinema, Anthropology, and Turn-of-the-Century Visual Culture*. New York: Columbia University Press, 2002.

Griffiths, Matthew. *The New Poetics of Climate Change*. London: Bloomsbury, 2017.

Grosz, Elizabeth. *Becoming Undone: Darwinian Reflections on Life, Politics, and Art*. Durham and London: Duke University Press, 2011.

Grosz, Elizabeth. *Chaos, Territory, Art: Deleuze and the Framing of the Earth*. New York: Columbia University Press, 2020.

Grosz, Elizabeth. *The Incorporeal: Ontology, Ethics, and the Limits of Materialism*. New York: Columbia University Press, 2018.

Grosz, Elizabeth. *Volatile Bodies: Toward a Corporeal Feminism*. Bloomington and Indianapolis: Indiana University Press, 1994.

Hacking, Ian. *Mad Travellers: Reflections on the Reality of Transient Mental Illness*. London: Free Association Books, 1999.

Hadfield, Jen. *Byssus*. London: Picador, 2014.

Hadfield, Jen. 'I Da Welk Ebb'. In *Antlers of Water: Writing on the Nature and Environment of Scotland*, edited by Kathleen Jamie, 133–42. Edinburgh: Canongate, 2020.

Hallstein, D.Lynn O'Brien. 'Where Standpoint Stands Now: An Introduction and Commentary', *Women's Studies in Communication* 23.1 (2000): 1–15.

Hamilton, Jennifer Mae and Astrida Neimanis. 'Composting Feminisms and Environmental Humanities', *Environmental Humanities* 10.2 (2018): 501–27.

Han Kang. *The White Book*, translated by Deborah Smith. London: Portobello Books, 2016.

Haraway, Donna J. *The Companion Species Manifesto: Dogs, People, and Significant Otherness*. Chicago: Prickly Paradigm Press, 2003.

Haraway, Donna J. *Simians, Cyborgs, and Women: The Reinvention of Nature*. New York and Abingdon: Routledge, 1991.

Haraway, Donna J. *Staying with the Trouble: Making Kin in the Chthulucene*. Durham and London: Duke University Press 2016.

Haraway, Donna J. *When Species Meet*. Minneapolis and London: University of Minnesota Press, 2008.

Harding, Sandra. 'Rethinking Standpoint Epistemology: What Is "Strong Objectivity?"'. In *Feminist Epistemologies*, edited by Linda Alcoff and Elizabeth Potter, 49–82. New York and London: Routledge, 1993.

Harris, Melanie L. *Ecowomanism: African American Women and Earth-Honoring Faiths*. Maryknoll, NY: Orbis Books, 2017.

Harris, Verne. 'The Archival Sliver: Power, Memory, and Archives in South Africa', *Archival Science* 2 (2002): 63–86.

Harvard University. 'The Poet's Voice: Bhanu Kapil & Fred Moten/Woodberry Poetry Room': youtube.com/watch?v=yjsB3-7Oyw&t=1943s.

Haushofer, Marlen. *The Wall*, translated by Shaun Whiteside. San Francisco: Cleis Press, 1990.

Hawitt, Rowan Bayliss. '"It's a Part of Me and I'm a Part of It": Ecological Thinking in Contemporary Scottish Folk Music', *Ethnomusicology Forum* 29.3 (2020): 333–55. https://doi.org.10.1080/17411912.2021.1897950.

Hawkins, Gay. 'Plastic Materialities'. In *Political Matter: Technoscience, Democracy, and Public Life*, edited by Bruce Braun and Sarah J. Whatmore, 199–138. Minneapolis: University of Minnesota Press, 2010.

Hayward, Eva. 'Fingeryeyes: Impressions of Cup Corals', *Cultural Anthropology* 25.4 (2010): 577–99.

Head, Lesley and Jennifer Atchison. 'Cultural Ecology: Emerging Human-Plant Geographies', *Progress in Human Geography* 33.2 (2009): 236–45.

Heddon, Deirdre. 'Confounding Ecospectations: Disappointment and Hope in the Forest', *Green Letters* 20.3 (2016): 324–39.

Hejinian, Lyn. 'The Rejection of Closure', *Poetry Foundation* (13 October 2009): poetryfoundation.org/articles/69401/the-rejection-of-closure.

Helford, Elyce Rae. 'Going "Native": Le Guin, Misha, and the Politics of Speculative Literature', *Foundation* 71 (1997): 77–88.

Hildyard, Daisy. *Hunters in the Snow*. London: Vintage, 2014.

Hildyard, Daisy. *The Second Body*. London: Fitzcarraldo, 2017.

Hirsch, Marianne. *The Generation of Postmemory: Writing and Visual Culture after the Holocaust*. New York: Columbia University Press, 2012.

Hoffman, Krzystof. 'Always towards, Not From-to: Experiment, Travel, and Deconstruction in *Flights* by Olga Tokarczuk', translated by Dorota Mackenzie, *Czas Kultury* 3 (2019): 113–20.

hooks, bell. *Belonging: A Culture of Place*. New York and London: Routledge, 2009.

Horton, Zach. 'Composing a Cosmic View: Three Alternatives for Thinking Scale in the Anthropocene'. In *Scale in Literature and Culture*, edited by Michael Tavel Clarke and David Wittenberg, 35–60. Cham: Palgrave Macmillan, 2017.

Houser, Heather. *Ecosickness in Contemporary U.S. Fiction: Environment and Affect*. New York: Columbia University Press, 2014.

Ingold, Tim. *The Perception of the Environment: Essays on Livelihood, Dwelling and Skill*. London and New York: Routledge, 2000.

Iovino, Serenella and Serpil Oppermann. 'Introduction: Stories Come to Matter'. In *Material Ecocriticism*, edited by Serenella Iovino and Serpil Oppermann, 1–17. Bloomington and Indianapolis: Indiana University Press, 2014.

Iser, Wolfgang. 'The Reading Process: A Phenomenological Approach', *New Literary History* 3.2 (1972): 279–99.

Jamie, Kathleen. *The Bonniest Company*. London: Picador, 2015.

Jamie, Kathleen. *Findings*. London: Sort Of, 2005.

Jamie, Kathleen. *Jizzen*. London: Picador, 1999.

Jamie, Kathleen. *The Overhaul*. London: Picador, 2012.

Jamie, Kathleen. *Surfacing*. London: Sort Of, 2019.

Jenks, Chris. *Visual Culture*. London: Routledge, 1995.

Jetñil-Kijiner, Kathy. 'Dome Poem Part III: "Anointed" Final Poem and Video': kathyjetnilkijiner.com/dome/poem-iii-anointed-final-poem-and-video/.

Jetñil-Kijiner, Kathy. *Iep Jāltok: Poems from a Marshallese Daughter*. Tucson: University of Arizona Press, 2017.

Johns-Putra, Adeline. *Climate Change and the Contemporary Novel*. Cambridge: Cambridge University Press, 2019.

Kainulainen, Maggie. 'Saying Climate Change: Ethics of the Sublime and the Problem of Representation', *Symplokē* 21.1–2 (2013): 109–23.

Kangas, Anni et al. 'Smashing Containers, Queering the International through Collaging', *International Feminist Journal of Politics* 21.3 (2019): 355–82.

Kapil, Bhanu. *Ban en Banlieue*. New York: Nightboat Books, 2015.

Kapil, Bhanu. *Humanimal: A Project for Future Children*. Berkeley, CA: Kelsey Street Press, 2009.

Kapil, Bhanu. *Incubation: A Space for Monsters*. Providence, RI: Leon Works, 2006.

Kapil, Bhanu. 'Profiles in Poetics and Linguistics: Bhanu Kapil', *Women's Quarterly Conversation: Aesthetic Diversity of Women Writers in the 21st Century* (13 November 2015): womensquarterlyconversation.com/2015/11/13/profiles-in-poetics-linguistics-bhanu-kapil/.

Kapil, Bhanu. *Schizophrene*. Callicoon, NY: Nightboat Books, 2011.

Kapil, Bhanu. 'Seven Poems for Seven Flowers & Love in All Its Forms', *Mal* 3 (2019): 17–24.

Karl, Frederick R. 'American Fictions: The Mega-Novel', *Conjunctions* 7 (1985): 248–60.

Kay, Lisa. 'Research as Bricolage: Navigating in/between the Creative Arts Disciplines', *Music Therapy Perspectives* 34.1 (2016): 26–32.

Keller, Catherine. *Cloud of the Impossible: Negative Theology and Planetary Entanglement*. New York: Columbia University Press, 2015.

Kenneally, Rhona Richman. '"I am Off-White Walls": Exploring and Theorizing Domestic Space'. In *The Vibrant House: Irish Writing and Domestic Space*, edited by Rhona Richman Kenneally and Lucy McDiarmid, 13–35. Dublin: Four Courts, 2017.

Keown, Michelle. 'Children of Israel: US Military Imperialism and Marshallese Migration in the Poetry of Kathy Jetnil-Kijiner', *Interventions: A Journal of Postcolonial Studies* 19.7 (2016): 930–47.

Kerrigan, Catherine. 'Introduction'. In *An Anthology of Scottish Women Poets*, edited by Catherine Kerrigan, 1–11. Edinburgh: Edinburgh University Press, 1991.

Kimmerer, Robin Wall. *Braiding Sweetgrass: Indigenous Wisdom Scientific Knowledge, and the Teachings of Plants*. Minneapolis: Milkweed Editions, 2013.

Kimmerer, Robin Wall. *Gathering Moss: A Natural and Cultural History of Mosses*. Corvallis, OR: Oregon State University Press, 2003.

Kingston-Reese, Alexandra. 'The Individual Reader', *Critique: Studies in Contemporary Fiction* (2020). https://doi.org/10.1080/00111619.2020.1810612.

Knox-Russell, Allyse. 'Futurity without Optimism: Detaching from Anthropocentrism and Grieving Our Fathers in *Beasts of the Southern Wild*'. In *Affective Ecocriticism: Emotion, Embodiment, Environment*, edited by Kyle Bladlow and Jennifer Ladino, 213–32. Lincoln and London: University of Nebraska Press, 2018.

Kostkowska, Justyna. *Ecocriticism and Women Writers: Environmentalist Poetics of Virginia Woolf, Jeanette Winterson, and Ali Smith*. Basingstoke: Palgrave Macmillan, 2013.

Krzywoszynska, Anna. 'Caring for Soil Life in the Anthropocene: The Role of Attentiveness in More-than-Human Ethics', *Transactions of the Institute of British Geographers* 44 (2019): 661–75.

Lacoue-Labarthe, Philippe and Jean-Luc Nancy. *The Literary Absolute: The Theory of Literature in German Romanticism*, translated by Philip Banard and Cheryl Lester. Albany: State University of New York Press, 1988.

Lahiri, Jhumpa. *Whereabouts*. London: Bloomsbury, 2021.

Laing, Olivia. *The Lonely City: Adventures in the Art of Being Alone*. Edinburgh: Canongate, 2016.

Latour, Bruno. *An Inquiry into the Modes of Existence: An Anthropology of the Moderns*. Cambridge, MA: Harvard University Press, 2013.

Law, John and Marianne Lien, 'Denaturalizing Nature'. In *A World of Many Worlds*, edited by Marisol de la Cadena and Mario Blaser, 131–71. Durham and London: Duke University Press, 2018.

Law, John and Michael Lynch. 'Lists, Field Guides, and the Descriptive Organization of Seeing: Birdwatching as an Exemplary Observational Activity', *Human Studies* 11.2–3 (1988): 271–303.

Leder, Drew. *The Absent Body*. Chicago: University of Chicago Press, 1990.

Léger, Nathalie. *Suite for Barbara Loden*, translated by Natasha Lehrer and Cécile Menon. London: Les Fugitives, 2015.

Le Guin, Ursula K. *Always Coming Home: Author's Expanded Edition*, edited by Brian Attebery. New York: Library of America, 2019.

Le Guin, Ursula K. *Dancing at the Edge of the World: Thoughts on Words, Women, Places*. New York: Harper & Row, 1990.

Le Guin, Ursula K. 'Deep in Admiration'. In *Arts of Living on a Damaged Planet*, edited by Anna Tsing, et al., M15–M21. Minneapolis and London: University of Minnesota Press, 2017.

Leibniz, Gottfried Wilhelm. *Discourse on Metaphysics and Other Essays*, translated and edited by Daniel Garber and Roger Ariew. Indianapolis and Cambridge: Hackett Publishing, 1991.

Letzler, David. *The Cruft of Fiction: Mega-Novels and the Science of Paying Attention*. Lincoln and London: University of Nebraska Press, 2017.

Levinas, Emmanuel. *Totality and Infinity*, translated by Alphonso Lingis. Pittsburgh, PA: Duquesne University Press, 1969.

Levine, Caroline. *Forms: Whole, Rhythm, Hierarchy, Network*. Princeton and Oxford: Princeton University Press, 2015.

Lilley, Deborah. 'Kathleen Jamie: Rethinking the Externality and Idealisation of Nature', *Green Letters* 17.1 (2013): 16–26.

Luiselli, Valeria. *Faces in the Crowd*, translated by Christina MacSweeney. London: Granta, 2012.

Luiselli, Valeria. *Lost Children Archive*. London: Fourth Estate, 2019.

Luiselli, Valeria. *Tell Me How It Ends: An Essay in Forty Questions*. London: Fourth Estate, 2017.

Lynch, Michael and John Law. 'Pictures, Texts, and Objects: The Literary Language Game of Bird-watching'. In *The Science Studies Reader*, edited by Mario Biagioli, 317–41. New York and London: Routledge, 1999.

Mabey, Richard. *Nature Cure*. London: Pimlico, 2006.

MacGillivray, William. *A Hebridean Naturalist's Journal 1817–1818*, edited by Robert Ralph. Stornoway: Acair, 2017.

MacGillivray, William. *A Walk to London*, edited by Robert Ralph. Stornoway: Acair, 1998.

MacGregor, Sherilyn. *Beyond Mothering Earth: Ecological Citizenship and the Politics of Care*. Vancouver and Toronto: UBC Press, 2006.

MacNeice, Louis. *Collected Poems*. London: Faber, 1979.

Macpherson, Alan. 'Art, Trees, and the Enchantment of the Anthropocene: Caroline Wendling's *White Wood*', *Environmental Humanities* 10.1 (2018): 241–56.

Maiklem, Lara. *Mudlarking: Lost and Found on the River Thames*. London: Bloomsbury, 2020.

Manfredi, Camille. *Nature and Space in Contemporary Scottish Writing and Art*. Cham: Palgrave Macmillan, 2019.

Manguso, Sarah. *Ongoingness: The End of a Diary*. Minneapolis: Graywolf, 2015.

Manguso, Sarah. *Two Kinds of Decay*. London: Granta, 2011.

Manning, Erin. *Always More than One: Individuation's Dance*. Durham and London: Duke University Press, 2013.

Marland, Pippa. 'The Gannet's Skull versus the Plastic Doll's Head: Material "Value" in Kathleen Jamie's "Findings"', *Green Letters* 19.2 (2015): 121–31.

Mars-Jones, Adam. 'obligatorynoteofhope.com', *London Review of Books* 42.13 (2 July 2020): 24–6.

Marshall, Kate. 'What Are the Novels of the Anthropocene? American Fiction in Geological Time', *American Literary History* 27.3 (2015): 523–38.

Martin, Keavy. *Stories in a New Skin: Approaches to Inuit Literature*. Winnipeg: University of Manitoba Press, 2012.

Mathews, Freya. *The Ecological Self*. London: Routledge, 1991.

McBride, Eimear. *A Girl Is a Half-Formed Thing*. Norwich: Galley Beggar, 2013.

McBride, Eimear. *Strange Hotel*. London: Faber, 2020.

McClory, Helen. *Bitterhall*. Edinburgh: Polygon, 2021.

McClory, Helen. *Flesh of the Peach*. Glasgow: Freight Books, 2017.

Mehnert, Antonia. *Climate Change Fictions: Representations of Global Warming in American Culture*. Cham: Palgrave Macmillan, 2016.

Merchant, Carolyn. *The Anthropocene and the Humanities: From Climate Change to a New Age of Sustainability*. New Haven and London: Yale University Press, 2020.

Merchant, Carolyn. *The Death of Nature: Women, Ecology, and the Scientific Revolution*. New York: HarperOne, 1990.

Merchant, Carolyn. *Science and Nature: Past, Present, and Future*. New York and London: Routledge, 2018.

Merola, Nicole M. '"*What Do We Do but Keep Breathing as Best We Can This /Minute Atmosphere*": Juliana Spahr and Anthropocene Anxiety'. In *Affective Ecocriticism: Emotion, Embodiment, Environment*, edited by Kyle Bladow and Jennifer Ladino, 25–49. Lincoln and London: University of Nebraska Press, 2018.

Missaghi, Poupeh. *trans(re)lating house one*. Minneapolis: Coffee House Press, 2020.

Misztal, Barbara A. *Theories of Social Remembering*. Maidenhead: Open University Press, 2003.

Monicat, Bénédicte. 'Autobiography and Women's Travel Writings in Nineteenth-Century France: Journeys through Self-Representation', *Gender, Place and Culture* 1.1 (1994): 61–70.

Morton, Timothy. *Ecology without Nature: Rethinking Environmental Aesthetics.* Cambridge, MA, and London: Harvard University Press, 2007.

Moshfegh, Ottessa. *My Year of Rest and Relaxation.* London: Jonathan Cape, 2018.

Mudie, Ella. 'Beyond Mourning: On Photography and Extinction', *Afterimage* 44.3 (2016): 22–7.

Murphy, Patrick D. *Ecocritical Explorations in Literary and Cultural Studies: Fences, Boundaries, and Fields.* Lanham, MD and Plymouth: Rowman and Littlefield, 2010.

Murphy, Patrick D. *Literature, Nature, and Other: Ecofeminist Critiques.* Albany: State University of New York Press, 1995.

Murray, Donald S. *The Dark Stuff: Stories from the Peatlands.* London: Bloomsbury, 2018.

Neimanis, Astrida. *Bodies of Water: Posthuman Feminist Phenomenology.* London: Bloomsbury Academic, 2019.

Ngai, Sianne. *Ugly Feelings.* Cambridge, MA, and London: Harvard University Press, 2007.

Nixon, Lindsay. *nîtisânak.* Montreal: Metonymy Press, 2019.

Northern Flyway. *Northern Flyway.* Sheffield: Hudson Records, 2018.

NPR Music. 'Karine Polwart Trio: NPR Music Tiny Desk Concert', *NPR Music* (18 April 2019): youtube.com/watch?v=qoyc83-56EY.

O'Connor, Brian. 'Introduction'. In *The Adorno Reader*, edited by Brian O'Connor, 4–19. Oxford and Malden, MA: Blackwell, 2000.

Offill, Jenny. *Weather.* London: Granta, 2020.

Ogura, Hikaru. 'On New Travel Literature and Central Europe as a Blank Space: Notes on Olga Tokarczuk's Novel *Bieguni* and Her Lecture Series in Japan'. In *Perspectives on Contemporary East European Literature: Beyond National and Regional Frames*, edited by Kenichi Abe, Slavic Eurasian Studies 30, 9–15. Sapporo: Slavic-Eurasian Research Center, 2016.

Olufemi, Lola. *Feminism, Interrupted: Disrupting Power.* London: Pluto Press, 2020.

The Online Scots Dictionary. https://www.scotsonline.org/dictionary/scots_english.php.

Oswald, Alice. *Dart.* London: Faber, 2003.

Oyler, Lauren. *Fake Accounts.* London: Fourth Estate, 2021.

Pareles, Jon, Jon Caramanica, Wesley Morris and Lindsay Zoladz. 'Fiona Apple Is Back and Unbound: Let's Discuss', *The New York Times* (17 April 2020): nytimes.com/2020/04/17/arts/music/fiona-apple-fetch-the-bolt-cutters.html.

Plumwood, Val. 'The Concept of a Cultural Landscape: Nature, Culture and Agency of the Land', *Ethics and the Environment* 11.2 (2006): 115–50.

Plumwood, Val. *Feminism and the Mastery of Nature.* London and New York: Routledge, 1993.

Polwart, Karine. 'I Burn but I Am Not Consumed', *BBC iPlayer* (20 January 2017): bbc. co.uk/programmes/p04q5cmf.

Polwart, Karine. *Wind Resistance*. London: Faber, 2017.

Polwart, Karine and Pippa Murphy. *A Pocket of Wind Resistance*. Sheffield: Hudson Records, 2017.

Pratt, Mary Louise. 'Coda: Concept and Chronotope'. In *Arts of Living on a Damaged Planet*, edited by Anna Tsing et al., G167–74. Minneapolis and London: University of Minnesota Press, 2017.

Puig de la Bellacasa, María. *Matters of Care: Speculative Ethics in More than Human Worlds*. Minneapolis and London: University of Minnesota Press, 2017.

Ralph, Robert. *William MacGillivray: Creatures of Air, Land and Sea*. London: Merrell Holberton and The Natural History Museum, 1999.

Rau, Petra. 'Autumn after the Referendum'. In *Brexit and Literature: Critical and Cultural Responses*, edited by Robert Eaglestone, 31–43. London and New York: Routledge, 2018.

Red Bull Music Academy. 'Tanya Tagaq Talks Björk, Throat Singing and the Polaris Prize', *YouTube* (7 October 2016): youtube.com/watch?v=YkD00mGqBxE.

Reddy, Jini. *Wanderland: A Search for Magic in the Landscape*. London: Bloomsbury, 2020.

Richardson, Brian. *Unnatural Voices: Extreme Narration in Modern and Contemporary Fiction*. Columbus: Ohio State University Press, 2006.

Rigby, Kate and Owain Jones, 'Roadkill: Multispecies Mobility and Everyday Ecocide'. In *Kin: Thinking with Deborah Bird Rose*, edited by Thom van Dooren and Matthew Chrulew, 112–34. Durham and London: Duke University Press, 2022.

Riley, Denise. '*Am I That Name?*': Feminism and the Category of 'Women' in History. Basingstoke: Macmillan, 1988.

Robertson, Kate. 'Tanya Tagaq Wins the Polaris Prize 2014', *Now Toronto* (22 September 2014): nowtoronto.com/tanya-tagaq-wins-the-polaris-prize-2014.

Robinson, Kim Stanley. *Green Earth*. New York: Del Rey, 2015.

Rojcewicz, Stephen. 'Olga Tokarczuk: The Right Time and Place', *Delos* 35.1 (2020): 101–15.

Rose, Deborah Bird. 'Dialogue with Place: Toward an Ecological Body', *Journal of Narrative Theory* 32.3 (2002): 311–25.

Rose, Deborah Bird. 'Multispecies Knots of Ethical Time', *Environmental Philosophy* 9.1 (2012): 127–40.

Rose, Deborah Bird. 'What If the Angel of History Were a Dog?' *Cultural Studies Review* 12.1 (2006): 67–78.

Rose, Deborah Bird and Thom van Dooren. 'Introduction', *Unloved Others: Death of the Disregarded in the Time of Extinction, Australian Humanities Review* 50 (2011): 1–4.

Rose, Jacqueline. *On Violence and On Violence against Women*. London: Faber, 2021.

Rowland, Lucy. 'Indigenous Temporality and Climate Change in Alexis Wright's *Carpentaria* (2006)', *Journal of Postcolonial Writing* 55.4 (2019): 541–54.

Sandilands, Catriona. *The Good-Natured Feminist: Ecofeminism and the Quest for Democracy*. Minneapolis and London: University of Minnesota Press, 1999.

Savoy, Lauret. *Trace: Memory, History, Race, and the American Landscape*. Berkeley, CA: Counterpoint, 2015.

Schalansky, Judith. *An Inventory of Losses*, translated by Jackie Smith. London: Maclehose Press, 2020.

Schoene, Berthold. *The Cosmopolitan Novel*. Edinburgh: Edinburgh University Press, 2010.

Scranton, Roy. *Learning to Die in the Anthropocene: Reflections on the End of a Civilization*. San Francisco: City Lights, 2015.

Sehgal, Parul. 'How to Write Fiction When the Planet Is Falling Apart', *New York Times* (5 February 2020): nytimes.com/2020/02/05/magazine/jenny-offill-weather-book.html.

Seigworth, Gregory J. and Melissa Gregg. 'An Inventory of Shimmers'. In *The Affect Theory Reader*, edited by Melissa Gregg and Gregory J. Seigworth, 1–25. Durham and London: Duke University Press, 2010.

Seymour, Nicole. *Bad Environmentalism: Irony and Irreverence in the Ecological Age*. Minneapolis and London: University of Minnesota Press, 2018.

Shapton, Leanne. *Guestbook: Ghost Stories*. London: Particular Books, 2019.

Sharpe, Christina. *In the Wake: On Blackness and Being*. Durham and London: Duke University Press, 2016.

Shaw, Kristian and Sara Upstone. 'The Transglossic: Contemporary Fiction and the Limitations of the Modern', *English Studies* (2021): 1–28. https://doi.org/10.1080/0013838X.2021.1943894.

Shotwell, Alexis. *Against Purity: Living Ethically in Compromised Times*. Minneapolis and London: University of Minnesota Press, 2016.

Simon, Scott. 'Valeria Luiselli on the "Lost Children Archive"', *NPR Weekend Edition Saturday* (9 March 2019): npr.org/2019/03/09/701838156/valeria-luiselli-on-the-lost-children-archive.

Simpson, Leanne Betasamosake. *As We Have Always Done: Indigenous Freedom through Radical Resistance*. Minneapolis and London: University of Minnesota Press, 2017.

Simpson, Leanne Betasamosake. *Dancing on Our Turtle's Back: Stories of Nishnaabeg Re-Creation, Resurgence and a New Emergence*. Winnipeg: ARP Books, 2011.

Simpson, Leanne Betasamosake. *Noopiming: The Cure for White Ladies*. Minneapolis and London: University of Minnesota Press, 2021.

Six Shooter Records. 'Tanya Tagaq Talks Animism (EPK)', *Six Shooter Records* (2 September 2014): youtube.com/watch?v=pFHL341OpHU.

Smith, Ali. 'Ali Smith & Sarah Wood: Festival – A Film', *Edinburgh International Book Festival* (28 August 2020): edbookfest.co.uk/the-festival/whats-on/ali-smith-sarah-wood-festival-a-film/player.

Smith, Ali. *Autumn*. London: Hamish Hamilton, 2016.

Smith, Ali. *Spring*. London: Hamish Hamilton, 2019.

Smith, Ali. *Summer*. London: Hamish Hamilton, 2020.

Smith, Ali. *Winter*. London: Hamish Hamilton, 2017.

Smith, Tracy K. *Wade in the Water*. London: Penguin, 2018.

Solnit, Rebecca. *The Faraway Nearby*. London: Granta, 2013.

Spahr, Juliana. *That Winter the Wolf Came*. Oakland, CA: Commune Editions, 2015.

Spahr, Juliana. *The Transformation*. Berkeley: Atelos, 2007.

Sprackland, Jean. *Strands: A Year of Discoveries on the Beach*. London: Vintage, 2013.

Sprackland, Jean. *These Silent Mansions: A Life in Graveyards*. London: Jonathan Cape, 2020.

Steedman, Carolyn. *Dust*. Manchester: Manchester University Press, 2001.

Steffen, Will, Paul J. Crutzen and John R. McNeill. 'The Anthropocene: Are Humans Now Overwhelming the Great Forces of Nature', *Ambio: A Journal of the Human Environment* 40 (2007): 614–21.

Stengers, Isabelle. *In Catastrophic Times: Resisting the Coming Barbarism*, translated by Andrew Goffey. Lüneberg: Open Humanities Press/Meson Press, 2015.

Stepanova, Maria. *In Memory of Memory: A Romance*, translated by Sasha Dugdale. London: Fitzcarraldo, 2021.

Stévance, Sophie. 'Analysis of the Inuit Katajjaq in Popular Culture: The Canadian Throat-Singer Superstar Tanya Tagaq', *Itamar. Revista de Investigación Musical: Territorios Para El Arte* 3 (2010): 82–9.

Stevens, Wallace. *The Palm at the End of the Mind: Selected Poems and a Play*, edited by Holly Stevens. New York: Vintage, 1990.

Stewart, Kathleen. 'Pockets', *Communication and Critical/Cultural Studies* 9.4 (2012): 365–8.

Stewart, Susan. *On Longing: Narratives of the Miniature, the Gigantic, the Souvenir, the Collection*. Durham and London: Duke University Press, 1993.

Summary of Letter to Alexander Macdonald of Kepplestone from Leon Durand, 20 October 1871, Papers of Alexander Macdonald of Kepplestone and his trustees, c. 1852–1903. DD391/13/10/1. https://www.aberdeencity.gov.uk/sites/default/files/Alexander_Macdonald_of_Kepplestone_o.pdf.

Swart, Sandra. 'Reviving Roadkill?: Animals in the New Mobilities Studies', *Transfers* 5.2 (2015): 81–101.

Swensen, Cole. *Art in Time*. New York: Nightboat, 2021.

Tabak, Eline D. 'Science in Fiction: A Brief Look at Communicating Climate Change through the Novel', *RCC Perspectives* 4 (2019): 97–104.

Tagaq, Tanya. *Animism*. Toronto: Six Shooter Records, 2014.

Tagaq, Tanya. *Retribution*. Toronto: Six Shooter Records, 2016.

Tagaq, Tanya. *Split Tooth*. Toronto: Viking, 2018.

Tagaq, Tanya. '"Uja" and "Umingmak" (live)', *Polaris Music Prize* (2014): polarismusicprize.ca/videos/tanya-tagaq-uja-and-umingmak-live/.

Tamás, Rebecca. *Strangers: Essays on the Human and Nonhuman*. London: Makina Books, 2020.

'Tanya Tagaq's Animism Wins the 2014 Polaris Music Prize', *Manitoba Music* (22 September 2014): manitobamusic.com/news/read.article/6177/Tanya-tagaq-s-animism-wins-the-2014-polaris-music-prize.

Taylor, Jesse Oak. 'Atmosphere as Setting, or, "Wuthering" the Anthropocene'. In *Climate and Literature*, edited by Adeline Johns-Putra, 31–44. Cambridge: Cambridge University Press, 2019.

Todd, Zoe. 'Indigenizing the Anthropocene'. In *Art in the Anthropocene: Encounters among Aesthetics, Politics, Environments and Epistemologies*, edited by Heather Davis and Etienne Turpin, 241–54. London: Open Humanities Press, 2015.

Todd, Zoe. 'An Indigenous Feminist's Take on the Ontological Turn: "Ontology" Is Just Another Word for Colonialism', *Journal of Historical Sociology* 29.1 (2016): 4–22.

Tokarczuk, Olga. *Flights*, translated by Jennifer Croft. London: Fitzcarraldo, 2017.

Torlasco, Domietta. 'Digital Impressions: Writing Memory after Agnès Varda', *Discourse* 33.3 (2011): 390–408.

Trexler, Adam. *Anthropocene Fictions: The Novel in a Time of Climate Change*. Charlottesville: University of Virginia Press, 2015.

Tronto, Joan C. *Moral Boundaries: A Political Argument for an Ethic of Care*. New York and London: Routledge, 1993.

Tsing, Anna Lowenhaupt. *Friction: An Ethnography of Global Connection*. Princeton and Oxford: Princeton University Press, 2005.

Tsing, Anna Lowenhaupt. *The Mushroom at the End of the World: On the Possibility of Life in Capitalist Ruins*. Princeton and Oxford: Princeton University Press, 2015.

Tsing, Anna Lowenhaupt. *In the Realm of the Diamond Queen: Marginality in an Out-of-the-Way Place*. Princeton: Princeton University Press, 1993.

Tym, Linda. 'Perilous Boundaries: Affective Experience in Three Scottish Women Writers' Short Fiction', *Journal of the Short Story in English* 61 (2013): 1–14.

van Alphen, Ernst. *Staging the Archive: Art and Photography in the Age of New Media*. London: Reaktion, 2015.

van Dooren, Thom, Eben Kirksey and Ursula Münster. 'Multispecies Studies: Cultivating Arts of Attentiveness', *Environmental Humanities* 8.1 (2016): 1–23.

Varda, Agnès. 'Director's Note', *The Gleaners and I*, press release. https://zeitgeistfilms.com/media/films/44/presskit.pdf.

Varda, Agnès. *The Gleaners and I*. Ciné-tamaris, 2000. In *The Agnès Varda Collection Volume 1*. Artificial Eye, 2009.

Varda, Agnès. *The Gleaners and I: Two Years Later*. C.N.D.P, Canal+, Centre National du Cinéma et de l'Image Animée and Ciné-tamaris, 2002. In *The Agnès Varda Collection Volume 1*. Artificial Eye, 2009.

Varley-Winters, Rebecca. *Reading Fragments and Fragmentation in Modernist Literature*. Eastbourne: Sussex Academic Press, 2019.

Vermeulen, Pieter. *Literature and the Anthropocene*. London and New York: Routledge, 2020.

Verran, Helen. 'On Assemblage: Indigenous Knowledge and Digital Media (2003–2006), and *HMS Investigator* (1800–1805)', *Journal of Cultural Economy* 2.1–2 (2009): 169–82.

Waldman, Katy. 'Can One Sentence Capture All of Life?', *The New Yorker* (6 September 2019). https://www.newyorker.com/books/page-turner-can-one-sentence-capture-all-of-life.

Walkowitz, Rebecca L. *Cosmopolitan Style: Modernism beyond the Nation*. New York: Columbia University Press, 2006.

Walton, Samantha. 'Feminism's Critique of the Anthropocene'. In *The New Feminist Literary Studies*, edited by Jennifer Cooke, 113–28. Cambridge: Cambridge University Press, 2020.

Walton, Samantha. *The Living World: Nan Shepherd and Environmental Thought*. London: Bloomsbury, 2020.

Wang, Mary. 'Valeria Luiselli: "There Are Always Fingerprints of the Archive in My Books"', *Guernica* (12 February 2019): guernicamag.com/miscellaneous-files-interview-valeria-luiselli/.

Warwick, Hugh. *A Prickly Affair: The Charm of the Hedgehog*. London: Penguin, 2010.

Watercutter, Angela. 'Taylor Swift and the Risks and Rewards of the Pandemic Album', *Wired* (7 July 2020): wired.com/story/taylor-swift-folklore-album-date-release-pandemic/.

Waterton, Claire. 'From Field to Fantasy: Classifying Nature, Construction Europe', *Social Studies of Science* 32.2 (2002): 177–204.

Waterton, Claire. 'Performing the Classification of Nature', *The Sociological Review* 51.2 (2003): 111–29.

Weik von Mossner, Alexa. *Affective Ecologies: Empathy, Emotion, and Environmental Narrative*. Columbus: Ohio State University Press, 2017.

Weik von Mossner, Alexa. 'Science Fiction and the Risks of the Anthropocene: Anticipated Transformations in Dale Pendell's *The Great Bay*', *Environmental Humanities* 5 (2014): 203–16.

Weil, Simone. *Gravity and Grace*, translated by Emma Crawford and Mario von der Ruhr. London and New York: Routledge Classics, 2002.

Weintrobe, Sally. 'The Difficult Problem of Anxiety in Thinking about Climate Change'. In *Engaging with Climate Change: Psychoanalytic and Interdisciplinary Perspectives*, edited by Sally Weintrobe, 33–47. London and New York: Routledge, 2013.

Weston, Daniel. *Contemporary Literary Landscapes: The Poetics of Experience*. London and New York: Routledge, 2016.

Wheeler, André, 'American Dirt: Why Critics Are Calling Oprah's Book Club Pick Exploitative and Divisive', *The Guardian* (22 January 2020): theguardian.com/books/2020/jan/21/american-dirt-controversy-trauma-jeanine-cummins.

Whitehead, Anne. *Trauma Fiction*. Edinburgh: Edinburgh University Press, 2004.

Williams, Terry Tempest. *Erosion: Essays of Undoing*. New York: Farrar, Straus and Giroux, 2019.

Willows, Elin. *Inlands*, translated by Duncan J. Lewis. Whitstable: Nordisk Books, 2020.

Woloshyn, Alexa. "'Welcome to the Tundra": Tanya Tagaq's Creative and Communicative Agency as Political Strategy', *Journal of Popular Music Studies* 29.4 (2017): 1–14. https://doi.org/10.1111/jpms.12254.

Wood, Mikael. 'Fiona Apple's Stunningly Intimate New Album Makes a Bold Show of Unprettiness', *Los Angeles Times* (16 April 2020): latimes.com/entertainment-arts/music/story/2020-04-16/fiona-apple-fetch-the-bolt-cutters-review.

Woolf, Virginia. *The Diary of Virginia Woolf, Volume III: 1925–30*, edited by Anne Olivier Bell. Harmondsworth: Penguin, 1982.

Woollett, Lisa. *Rag and Bone: A Family History of What We've Thrown Away*. London: John Murray, 2020.

Wright, Tama, Peter Hughes, and Alison Ainley. 'The Paradox of Morality: An Interview with Emmanuel Levinas'. In *The Provocation of Levinas: Rethinking the Other*, edited by Robert Bernasconi and David Wood, 168–80. London and New York: Routledge, 1988.

Yusoff, Kathryn. *A Billion Black Anthropocenes or None*. Minneapolis: University of Minnesota Press, 2018.

Zambreno, Kate. *Appendix Project: Talks and Essays*. South Pasadena, CA: Semiotext(e), 2019.

Zambreno, Kate. *To Write as if Already Dead*. New York: Columbia University Press, 2021.

Zolf, Rachel. 'Rachel Zolf on Juliana Spahr: The Transformation Thinks Wit(h)ness', *Lemon Hound*: lemonhound.com/2014/11/14/rachel-zolf-on-juliana-spahr-the-transformation-thinks-withness/.

Index

Lightning Source UK Ltd.
Milton Keynes UK
UKHW021828310722
406641UK00003B/223